WHERE IS MOSES WHEN WE NEED HIM?

WHERE IS MOSES WHEN WE NEED HIM?

TEACHING YOUR KIDS THE TEN VALUES THAT MATTER MOST

BROADMAN
& HOLMAN
PUBLISHERS

Nashville, Tennessee

4261-81
0-8054-6181-7

Dewey Decimal Classification: 649
Subject Heading: Parenting \ Christian Ethics \ Ten
Commandments
Library of Congress Card Catalog Number: 95-3390

Unless otherwise noted, all Scripture quotations are taken from the
Holy Bible, New International Version, copyright © 1973, 1978, 1984
by International Bible Society. Other versions used are NASB, the
New American Standard Bible, © the Lockman Foundation, 1960,
1962, 1963, 1968, 1971, 1972, 1973, 1975, 1977; used by permission;
and TLB, The Living Bible, copyright © Tyndale House Publishers,
Wheaton, Illinois, 1971, used by permission.

Library of Congress Cataloging-in-Publication Data
Peel, William Carr.
  Where is Moses when we need him? : teaching your kids the ten values
that matter most / Bill and Kathy Peel.
      p.   cm.
  ISBN 0-8054-6181-7
  1. Ten commandments—Study and teaching. 2. Christian education
of children. 3. Christian education of young people. 4. Christian education
—Home training.
  I. Peel, Kathy, 1951– . II. Title.
  BV4655.P42   1995
  248.8'45—dc20   95-3390
                                                                CIP

Contents

For Morris Eugene Weeks,
father and father-in-law,
a man of consistent character
for all seasons.

Introduction

HOW TO WIN AT DOUBLE JEOPARDY

IN THE YEARS WHEN I WAS A PROFESSIONAL stay-at-home mom, I had several things in common with my colleagues, that is, other stay-at-home moms. We all tried to maintain some semblance of order in our homes. We hosted parties for friends who sold plasticware that burped. We discovered 101 things to do with tuna. We ran miles of errands, washed mounds of clothes, watched our toddlers eat dirt on the playground—all before four o'clock. Then we all took some time off. We sent the children outside to play while we did something for ourselves. We all looked forward to things like reading a book other than Dr. Suess, relaxing in a warm bubble bath, or taking a short nap. One woman spent her thirty minutes of downtime in a different way from the rest of us: she watched the television game show *Jeopardy.*

Now she really didn't like to admit that she watched a game show. So why did she do it? When she confessed her feelings, they mirrored what most of us were feeling. She admitted that she wanted to know if her brain was still operational. When the most intellectually challenging part of her day had been measuring fabric softener, there was something stimulating about hearing answers to a wide variety of questions and trying to ask the right questions before the contestants did.

Frankly I thought this wasn't such a bad way to spend thirty minutes. And this part of her day wasn't all that different from the rest of an average day for most of us. As parents we spent countless hours

1

trying to figure out what were the important questions in life, not to mention the answers. She was just getting a little extra practice. Questions are important.

For instance, a friend told me that one day her little girl came home from kindergarten with a pressing question. "Mommy, where did I come from?"

The mother, of course, had been dreading this day. But she was prepared. She launched into a lengthy explanation about how God created men and women, mommies and daddies, and how He made a way for them to become parents. Luckily, before she started the Anatomy 101 portion of her answer, she paused to catch her breath and gain her composure.

At that point, her daughter interjected, "Mommy, my friend Lisa came from Minneapolis. I just want to know where I came from!"

This simple little story tells us a lot. It tells us about listening with sharp ears to hear just what our kids are really asking us. It also says quite a bit about answering kids' questions on the level they're asked. But I think the crucial thing it teaches us, whether we're five or forty-five, is that the questions we ask make a difference. As parents, every single one of us owes it to our children, ourselves, and our God to keep looking for the right questions and the right answers as we make our way through life.

Our Questions

A few weeks ago I was in California for a speaking engagement. I turned on the television in my hotel room to try to catch some news. What I saw instead was an advertisement for a local news program. It went like this: "You have questions? We have answers." A woman's voice blared this slogan repeatedly over shots of the day's disasters and fiascoes. It was really annoying. Then she gave us snippets of that day's headlines without, of course, sharing any real news or giving any answers. The station did, however, promise that all our questions would be answered at 11:00 P.M.

How nice it would be, I thought, if life were this simple, if we could just tune into a some heavenly hot line and get all our questions answered. I don't know about you, but I'd use that line several times a day.

Maybe my son James wants to know why he has to do his homework before he can go over to his friend's house. I could snap back,

"Because I said so, and because the Bible says 'honor your mother.'" Or I could tune into what's really going on here, get in touch with my heavenly hot line, so to speak, and take the opportunity to explain about responsibilities, teach him the value of hard work, the value of following his mother's wishes, and the disciplines of learning.

I could surely have used the heavenly hot line when Joel overheard me say that I loved a birthday present a friend had sent me, but he also saw me scrunch up my face. It wouldn't have been so bad if he hadn't heard me two minutes before exclaim to Bill, "What on earth am I going to do with this?"

What do I do now, I thought to myself? I took a deep breath and explained that I should not have said that I loved something I didn't like at all. I should have thanked my friend for thinking of me and left it at that. That gave me the opportunity to admit that parents make mistakes—something important for kids to hear. And it gave me the opportunity to reinforce what the commandment about telling the truth is really all about. But more about that later.

In truth, we all have questions about how to conduct ourselves in the way God intended and how best to raise our children so they'll do the same. Our local news station might not have answers, but God does. Not only does God have answers, He is not stingy with the truth. When we ask, He gives answers. What's more, God teaches us the right questions to ask to get the answers we need.

God's Answers

This book is about right living and how to raise ourselves and our children to live lives that please God. Unfortunately, we live in an age in which the idea that there are moral absolutes is up for grabs. The essence of the Christian faith is primarily a relationship, not a moral code. But that relationship implies a certain lifestyle—a code of ethics that comes to us as part of God's family. God gave us a specific set of guidelines for living our lives according to His plan and for teaching our children to do the same. The Bible is full of these moral absolutes for people of all ages, but nowhere is His desire for us more succinctly stated than in the Ten Commandments.

For centuries people who wanted to set their sights high, to please God, have paid close attention to the moral implications of the Ten Commandments. They are not entry requirements for God's family (it's a good thing, because none of us would qualify), but they are God's "house rules." They are not ten suggestions for smart living, not ten hints for successful relationships, nor ten options for good behavior. But they are ten standards of righteousness that should be striven for, ten virtuous rules that should be followed, ten moral laws that should be obeyed by grateful children. Together they are the most complete description of absolute good mankind has ever been given. Through them we learn that we must bend our lives to conform to that goodness, not redefine good to fit our crookedness. When individuals and cultures thumb their nose at God's moral laws, disaster always ensues.

Parents First

None of us wants this for our family, so the first people who need to bend are mom and dad. We believe that we can't teach our children values unless we live them out ourselves, so this is more than a get-the-kids-in-shape book. It's a let's-all-get-our-act-together book. If we want our children's lives to reflect godly virtues, we need to live them and talk about them—at home, in the car, at church, everywhere.

But don't think we are just talking about conformity to a set of rules. God doesn't want us to obey because He's bigger than we are—kind of a cosmic bully who always gets His way. He wants us to obey because we love Him, because we want to grow in relationship with Him. But not only does He want us to love Him, He wants us to love our neighbors on this planet, including ourselves and our children. And we want to teach our children to obey God's rules because we love them and Him. We don't need to take anyone else's word for it. We have Jesus' word about what the most important commandments are:

> "The most important one," answered Jesus, "is this: 'Hear, O Israel, the Lord our God, the Lord is one. Love the Lord your God with all your heart and with all your soul and with all your mind and with all your strength. The second is this: 'Love your neighbor as yourself.' There is no commandment greater than these."
>
> MARK 12:29–31

So if the Ten Commandments are really this helpful, why don't people use them more often? Unfortunately, most Americans, while suggesting their importance, can't repeat the Ten Commandments without consulting their Bibles. And those who can recite them, maybe even word for word, often have no clue about how to apply them in today's world. Maybe that's because they learned them as a set of rules designed to prevent them from doing things, rather than as rules to help them live out God's plan. Maybe, even though they can recite them, they're so busy judging how others are applying them that they're failing to look into their soul's own mirror. Maybe they only haul them out and dust them off after their lives have gone out of kilter.

Double Jeopardy

The Ten Commandments are important to us, and they're important to our children. This is a double jeopardy, double payoff proposition. When we ignore God's rules, we not only hurt ourselves, we teach our children, by our example, to ignore them as well. When we live by God's rules, not only are our lives more in line with His intended purpose, but we have a perfect set of guidelines for teaching our children right and wrong in a day of confusing moral signals. We don't have to guess. In this sea of gray we know what is black and what is white and can spell it out for those who follow us.

That's what this book is all about. When we become more familiar with the Ten Commandments, we understand the implications for us personally, for our children, and for our culture. As parents, we have a responsibility toward our children. Children need to be taught spiritual truth—told what and what not to do—over and over again, presented according to their age level and their own personalities. We call this *indoctrination*. Our children need more than good information, however. They need to be *immersed* in a spiritual value system. They need to see, experience, hear, and apply spiritual truth in the midst of everyday living. They need the opportunity of daily prayer, helping others, and learning how to have a relationship with God. This is called *initiation*. And finally, children don't need just to hear their parents talking in high-falluting religious words about spiritual vales. They need to see their parents in action—dealing honestly in business, visiting the sick, forgiving one another, and putting God first. They need to see truth *incarnated* in their parents' lives.

Kathy and I have worked on this book together, just as we work on parenting together. Some of the stories and ideas originated with her. Some of them originated with me. Most of the time you'll be able to tell who's talking just by the context. But who wrote what isn't all that important because Kathy and I and our children—and you and your children—are all in this together, trying to live out God's plan for our lives in a world that has cut itself away from the mooring dock of God's moral law.

If you come away after reading this book only with a passion to teach your children what not to do, then we have failed. Many children, especially those growing up in Christian homes, have a basic understanding of right and wrong. Unfortunately, many appear moral on the outside, but it's a different story on the inside. They have learned plenty about the don'ts of life—do not steal, do not lie, do not covet—but don't know much about the dos of life—do be giving, do be patient, do be thankful. As we strive to inculcate the principles of the Ten Commandments into our children's lives, it's important that we don't become preoccupied with suppressing evil at the expense of encouraging good. If Kathy and I only teach ten-year-old James to control his angry outbursts and neglect to teach him the importance of being sensitive to other people's feelings, then we've missed the boat. Or if we tell seventeen-year-old Joel, who drives a nine-year-old car with 140,000 miles on it, that he should not covet his friend's brand new convertible, but we fail to help him develop an attitude of thankfulness for the many other blessings of life, then we are not doing our job. Both are important, and we must strive for a balance.

At the end of each chapter, you'll find some ideas and strategies to aim for—not only for the don'ts, but also the dos. Not all of them will be right for your family. As you read through them, pick a few to try that feel right for where you are in your parenting pilgrimage and that seem harmonious with the personalities and learning styles of your children. As you seek to teach your children, don't ever doubt that you are the most potent force in your child's life. As discouraged as the world around us might make us feel, nothing can touch the influence you have as a parent.

Since this is a book about the Ten Commandments, it seems appropriate that we should be honest with you up front. We confess that we embarked upon this project believing that teaching children right from wrong is very important. And it is. After doing some research, we learned parents are feeling a little desperate about building values into kids in a practically valueless society, and they can use some encouragement and fresh ideas about how to do it. This too is good reason to write a book. But after writing twelve books between us, you would think we'd have learned that God won't let us rush out to do our part to change the world without reminding us that we need changing as well.

This has been a very personally convicting book to write. Both of us have seen new areas in our own lives that need work, even some that need a complete overhaul. And so we hope that as you read this book and discover areas where you feel deficient as a parent, you'll take heart like we did and turn to God for His help. He is always there with a never-ending supply of forgiveness, encouragement, and answers.

Warmly,
Bill and Kathy Peel
Nashville, Tennessee

The future is purchased by the present.
—SAMUEL JOHNSON

Chapter 1

PARENTHOOD: NO LICENSE REQUIRED

DATELINE: DALLAS, JULY 26, 1974.   Texas in July is an oven—on broil. The south wind blows through my hair like a giant hair dryer. My pantyhose cling to my body as I waddle down the front walk. Bill, carrying my suitcase, tenderly helps me situate my whalelike body in our compact car, then whisks me away to the hospital for the delivery of our first baby.

I leave our home spotless. Earlier that year Bill had predicted that the president would resign before I'd catch the nesting instinct and clean our house from stem to stern. "It will never happen," Bill said emphatically. He was wrong.

Actually, Bill had some basis for his prediction. Until recently, I had to hoe my floors before I could mop. Now we could eat off of them. I had dusted the furniture to a high gloss, not worrying about damaging the fossils I found. And the time-release explosives worked wonders on our bathroom. (Previously, my idea of fighting mildew was to caulk over it.)

We were ready for parenthood. We had bumper pads around the bathtub as well as the bassinet. We were college graduates in our early twenties, owned a car, and had almost completed our sterling silver pattern.

Now, thirty minutes away from my appointed time to arrive at the hospital for the doctor to induce labor, we were about to take on the biggest responsibility of our life—without much of a job description.

We Were Babes in the Woods

Every so often, Bill had suggested that I spend the day with a friend and her children, so I could watch her in action. But I had no curiosity about cleaning up baby diarrhea or dodging projectile vomit. I thought I could learn all this from books. I thought Bill could learn this way, too.

Some people might have thought Bill didn't need to learn anything, since he was just going to be the dad. I, the mom, would have to assume most of the responsibility for this new person about to enter our lives. But Bill and I didn't feel that way. We believed men were just as capable as women of recognizing when a diaper had reached its saturation point. And a man could walk the floor in the middle of the night just as well as a woman. We had resolved to begin on equal footing, doing something we called team-parenting. We're in this together, we reasoned, and if that means crossing some invisible territorial gender lines that say the woman takes care of the baby and the man earns the living, then so be it. We were, after all, the product of the sixties: civil rights, women's liberation, and equal footing for all.

We also believed (as we still do) that dad is more than somebody who signs the checks and doles out praise or punishment at the end of the day. Bill wanted to be as involved in our child's life as I did. We were naive, though. Neither of us had a clue just how much involvement a new baby requires, especially in the middle of the night. A few weeks into our new venture we reassessed equality. One of us had to get up for an eight o'clock Greek class. It didn't seem fair that he should take equal turns at sleepless nights.

Like everyone else in our generation, we bought the latest child-raising books by the so-called experts and made notes. We wrote down some parenting principles—what we would do and what we would never, repeat never do. One such no-no was to say words like "goo-goo" and "ga-ga." Another was not to revolve our life around our child's bowel movements. As you can plainly see, we didn't know much.

Truth to tell, we were bilingual—in English and Baby Babble—by the time our first child was a week old. And soon thereafter our entire schedule revolved around loose or solid stools.

Friends and family helped us furnish our nursery in early Storkland. They also gave us baby clothes for every hour of every day and every season of the year. I loved this part. I couldn't wait to dress up our little bundle of joy. Bill wondered aloud what we'd do with all those baby dresses if we had a boy.

"Honey, it's okay for baby boys to wear dresses," I said.

"My son will wear a dress over my dead body. That's disgusting," was his considered, typically male response. He was wrong. Again.

Still very much alive, and grinning ear to ear, Bill proudly held our firstborn son, dressed in a pale blue pima-cotton dress.

It was only a matter of time, however, before we became testy. Bill put down his fork one night and said, "Maybe it's something you're eating that's making John a little fussy after you nurse him."

"Well, if it's something I'm eating that's making him fussy," I snapped, "it stands to reason that it's something I'm cooking that's making him fussy. Are you saying he doesn't like my cooking?"

"I'm merely suggesting that you go a little lighter on the garlic, especially on the fruit salad," he replied.

Actually, John was sleeping quite well. It was his parents who were having trouble. He slept for six- to eight-hour stretches. We could have too if we hadn't felt compelled to stick a mirror under his nose every twenty minutes to see if he was still breathing. We called the pediatrician at all hours of the night to report hiccups. We hovered over this kid like he was a movie star. By the time he was two months old, we were comatose.

Eternal optimists that we are, we speculated that this was the hard part of child-raising. Give him a few years, and he could flush the toilet and tie own his shoes. Then we could kick back and relax.

That's what we thought.

There's something a lot more important. Most of us dream about what our child will become—an athlete breaking Olympic records, a Supreme Court justice making landmark decisions, a doctor discovering the cure for AIDS, a musician receiving a platinum record, a head of a multinational corporation, a senator debating in Congress, or maybe even the president of the United States addressing the nation.

Dreaming grand dreams for our children's future accomplishments is fine as long as we honor God's design in each child. But there is something more basic that parents need to dream for their child. That is who, not what, this child will be. It is our job as parents to shape the character of our children as they grow, to give them a sense of right and wrong, and to provide them with an inner compass that will guide them through life.

Anyone who thinks that the hardest part of parenting is providing food, clothing, and shelter is two eggs short of an omelet. Taking care of our children's physical needs is a stroll in the park compared to helping them develop strong character. Teaching them to eat green vegetables isn't nearly as important (or as hard) as teaching them what's right and wrong. Whether or not they grow up eating broccoli really doesn't matter; whether or not they grow up understanding the dignity of human life and treating others with respect does. In the grand scheme of life, becoming the most powerful person in the world is of little significance if they don't learn to have control over their own selfish appetites. Arguing a winning cause before the Supreme Court means nothing if a person cannot be counted on to tell the truth.

Although Bill and I are slow on the uptake about some things, our kids taught us early how important it would be to teach them right and wrong. By the time we had a toddler and a five-year-old, we knew we were in for a lifelong learning curve. It may have been when our two-year-old denied having a dirty diaper, while the aroma permeating the air around him told us otherwise. We could see that lying came quite naturally to him. Or maybe it was when our five-year-old ran to my car after kindergarten and said, "Hi Mom, what the h——'s going on?" (He was repeating a phrase he had heard on television.) We decided it was time we developed a strategy for teaching our kids the values we wanted them to embrace.

When our boys were young, our attempts at shaping their character left a lot to be desired—like a straitjacket for the kids and smart pills for us. Why we thought two overenergized preschoolers would sit still to listen to an in-depth Bible lesson is a mystery.

The painting at the bookstore made it look so easy. Father sat in a straight-backed chair in front of the fireplace and read aloud from the King James Bible. Mother, the dog, and the children gazed at him attentively, hanging on his every word. Needless to say, things looked different at our house. For one, we didn't have a fireplace. For two, the only way we could get our kids to sit still for a character-building lesson was by threatening to take away their favorite toys. Somehow we'd forgotten all that stuff about logical consequences and age-appropriate activities we'd read about in the child-rearing books. Not to worry, our kids kept reminding us.

We discovered quickly that no one in our family (including the parents) had the attention span, not to mention the time, for long, boring Bible studies. But we wanted to instill the values set forth in the Bible into our boys. We wanted them to truly understand that in spite of our human weaknesses, frailties, bad attitudes, and sinful behavior, God loves us extravagantly.

After some prayer and soul-searching, we decided the best place to begin was where God began—by asking us to be in a loving relationship with Him and by giving us guidelines to conduct our lives so that we continued to grow in that relationship. We got smart and decided to follow the advice from Deuteronomy.

> Hear, O Israel: The LORD our God, the LORD is one. Love the LORD your God with all your heart and with all your soul and with all your strength. These commandments that I give you today are to be upon your hearts. Impress them on your children. Talk about them when you sit at home and when you walk along the road, when you lie down and when you get up. Tie them as symbols on your hands and bind them on your foreheads. Write them on the doorframes of your houses and on your gates.
>
> DEUTERONOMY 6:4–9

In a way, you might say we were back to reading child-rearing manuals. The difference is that this manual carries the authority of the voice of God. It's a manual that provides us with, in the parlance of our time, unlimited on-line access. All we need to do is ask. And ask we did. Then, with God's help, we came up with a plan to put spiritual values into action in our lives and to teach them to our sons.

Today our boys are twenty, seventeen, and ten. When John went away to college two years ago, Bill and I stopped to assess our strategy once again. There was something about sending off our firstborn that made us want to evaluate. Did we teach him what he needs to know? Can he make wise decisions on his own? Is there anything we forgot to tell him? These questions and more flooded our thoughts.

Honestly, we must say we don't know if we taught John everything he needed to know. He'll make some wise decisions, and he'll make some not-so-wise ones. And we're sure there are many things we forgot to tell him. But although we know we made (and continue to make) some mistakes, and although we are not perfect parents and we do not have perfect children, if we had to start all over again, we'd use the same strategy.

We developed our strategy working from the old axiom, "If you aim at nothing, you'll hit it every time." Lots of people apply this philosophy when they're talking about getting a new job, achieving a sales goal, or earning "enough" money. We figured that our kids were the most important things in our life apart from God, so we spent time aiming at something—teaching them to be what God meant them to be. And we'd set our sights high.

At first we tried to schedule time at home to work together on a plan. Bad idea. In a week's time there were approximately four minutes, thirty-six seconds when the phone wasn't ringing, the dog wasn't barking, the washer wasn't dancing across the floor, the pasta wasn't boiling over, and the kid's weren't tugging at our shirttails.

Week two we tried a different approach. After dropping the kids off at preschool, we found a quiet booth at a coffee shop and worked on our strategy in peace and quiet. This worked so well that we set aside the next five Monday mornings to have breakfast meetings together. We not only experienced some great one-on-one time as a couple, we formulated our teaching-our-children-values strategy— what we'd aim at and what we'd use for ammunition.

Yes, this took time. And yes, we could have been accomplishing other things, like making money and mopping floors. And yes, it was worth the time and effort.

We decided we needed to spend time with our kids both individually and as a whole family. We resolved to spend time praying together. We asked God to help us be aware of opportunities to teach our children right from wrong. We resolved to tell our children what we believed about God. We asked Him for the strength to be examples of right living for our children. And we resolved to tell our children the stories of our faith in our own words, introducing them gradually and in age-appropriate ways to the Scripture that guides our lives.

When we met on those Monday mornings, we asked ourselves some bottom-line questions. We knew that we tried to follow the Bible in our own lives and that we wanted our children to do the same. But the Bible is a pretty big book. Where would we start?

After some talk, thought, and prayer, it came to us that the Ten Commandments were, as we said in the introduction, the best possible place.

Okay, we said. But what's it going to mean to teach the Ten Commandments to children? After more cups of coffee, more talking, more praying, we discovered three things. One, we couldn't teach our children to follow the Ten Commandments if we didn't follow them ourselves. Two, we couldn't teach the commandments to our children if we only had a superficial understanding of what they meant. Three, once we'd figured out how to live the commandments in our everyday lives, we trusted God would show us how to impart them to our kids. He has.

Four Principles to Teach the Ten Commandments

Now we felt that we were getting somewhere. Then we started to talk about what it meant to study, learn, and teach the Ten Commandments. We'd both memorized them many years ago. We could rattle them off at the drop of a hat. We even remembered to remember them sometimes in the course of our busy days. But what was it that would help us remember to teach them and live them? What would help our sons do the same?

That's when we came up with the following four principles. They're not fancy or complicated. They're about living in the real world, the way God wants us to. They're about looking at our lives and our children's lives with the help of God's eyes.

The Principle of Incarnation. As parents, we cannot just tell kids what to do or not do. If we want children to adopt biblical values, we must hold them ourselves and live them out consistently before them. Truth must be incarnate in our lives. Incarnate simply means "in the flesh." Truth must be fleshed out in our lives, our daily routines. Our kids need certain things, like seeing mom and dad spend time daily communing with God through Bible study and prayer. They need to hear mom and dad treat each other with respect, even when they get angry or differ in opinion. They need to watch a parent turn off a television program because it glamorizes sin. They need to see their parents reach out to help people in need.

On numerous occasions Kathy and I have spent time counseling with people in our home or on the phone trying to help them work out a problem. Although some of these sessions happen at inopportune times, and embarrassingly we wonder why people can't schedule their crises at times that don't interfere with something else we had hoped to do, we want our kids to know that it's important to help others.

Try as we may, we can't force our values upon our children any more than we can force them to sit still during family devotions. But we can influence their decisions by how we live day by day.

15

The Principle of Indoctrination. Kids need to know right from wrong, and we need to tell them. We would not let our children drive a car without indoctrinating them first, that is, teaching them how the car works, what the rules of the road are, and what new responsibilities are—everything from having a driver's license to filling up Mom's tank with gas before you return the car. When you think of it, there are hundreds of rules and bits of information kids need to know to drive. It takes time to teach and learn these things. How much more important is it that they learn to drive their lives in God's direction! They can pick up a lot from our lives, but if we never stop to explain the rules, we give our children a moral handicap.

We need to take time to teach our children the tenets of our shared faith formally. This means taking advantage of the opportunities available to us, like Sunday school, summer Bible camps, or maybe volunteering to help start or run a youth group.

It also means taking time at home for everything from "old-fashioned" memorization of Scripture verses and prayers to "new-fangled" discussions on how to apply those same verses to our everyday lives. You do not have to be a theologian or have a Ph.D. in childhood development to participate in your children's formal religious education. You've already got all the credentials you need, from God, who gave you these children to teach and love.

Plus each of us has the responsibility to keep learning more about our faith. And miracle of miracles, as we teach our children, we learn more ourselves.

The Principle of Initiation. Our kids need more than incarnation —truth modeled in our lives. They need more than indoctrination— formal teaching of spiritual truth. They need initiation, the opportunity to apply the truth themselves. To initiate someone is to introduce him to a new stage of life or a new responsibility. At each stage, our children need plenty of opportunity to apply what they have learned and to feel our encouragement as they move closer toward responsible adulthood.

Initiation also marks the passage from one stage of life to another. In our culture, we think of initiation in terms of admitting someone into a fraternity or club. Yet life is full of other examples of everyday initiation. It might be initiating a nine-year-old into the responsibility of planning family devotions once a month. Whatever practices are important to you spiritually need to be brought into your children's lives. And creating an occasion, having some sort of simple initiation ceremony, is one way to make sure children remember them.

When our boys became teenagers we had a special time of initiation. We took them to a nice restaurant of their choice and talked about the new privileges and responsibilities of being a teenager, about the temptations they would face and also about the wonderful opportunities they would have. Then we presented them a silver ring with a cross on it. We explained that this ring was a symbol to remind them that wherever they went and whatever they did, God would be present with them.

Initiation is not just an occasion, it is a process that lasts from birth until the time we launch our children into independent adulthood. During this process, it is important that we give them new responsibilities. One reason so many well-taught children from good homes falter when they leave home is that they have never tried out their own wings. They've never been given the responsibility to make their own choices and to learn the consequences of their choices. Childhood is a continuum from dependence to independence. Over the years, decision-making gradually shifts from mom and dad's shoulders to the child's. Before they are out on their own in the world, our kids need plenty of opportunities to try out the truths and values we are teaching them. As they go through the life-initiation process, they will grow more confident that what we have taught them works.

As we give children new responsibilities, more likely than not, they will fail at some. When they do, mom and dad will be there to pick them up, lovingly correct them, and point them in the right direction again. Lessons learned in the pain of failure are seldom forgotten. But if a child never has the opportunity to succeed or fail on his own, he will only know the truth in theory. A gradual initiation to responsibility prepares the child to make healthy choices on his own when mom and dad are absent.

The Principle of Immersion. Quite simply, our kids need to see, hear, and experience spiritual truth in a clear and consistent manner as much as possible. This is what Moses was reminding his people of in Deuteronomy 6:6–9, that spiritual truth needed to permeate their lives, all day, every day.

The word *immerse* means to dip. In the textile industry, it is used to describe the process of dying a piece of cloth. When a piece of cloth is immersed in a vat of dye, it takes on the color of the dye. We do our children a favor when the environment in our home is so characterized by godly values that their hearts are permeated by the truth from frequent exposure. Of course, we can't isolate our children from evil, but we can try to give them a godly environment as much as possible. Every day of our lives, both public and private, should consistently and constantly expose children to the truth, taking advantage of every opportunity to explain God's truth. We need to seize teachable moments in the course of everyday life to teach children God's truth. When we're late for an important meeting or the pot roast is turning to stone *is* the time to take a sobbing small child into our arms and say, "I love you." When siblings are hitting one another *is* the time to separate them and tell them that we don't believe in settling our quarrels by beating up on each other. There is no other time.

Immersing children in a spiritual value system is really what we're doing when we consistently practice the first three principles. We let them see, hear, and experience spiritual truth in the midst of everyday living. The power of the truth is not contained in just words, but words coupled with deeds. Kids need more than to hear the truth.

On the days when we feel less than qualified to raise our children and unfit to teach them values, we must not give up. We must not give into the destructive mind-set Madeleine L'Engle poignantly describes. "In our terror of becoming destructive mothers and fathers, we refuse to be parents at all. We abdicate parenthood and turn over our responsibilities to strangers." The federal government and schools cannot rear our children and teach them right from wrong. No one can do a better job of raising our children and teaching them values than their parents. If you are fearful, turn to God.

> For God did not give us a spirit of timidity; but a spirit of power, of love, and of self-discipline.
>
> 2 TIMOTHY 1:7

Don't fear your role of value teacher to your children. It is a divinely commissioned position you don't have to fulfill alone.

Over the past twenty years of parenting, we've spent much time thinking about what we wanted to teach our children, what values we wanted them to embrace, and what we wanted them to be like when they grew up. The older we get, though, the more we think about how much we need to learn ourselves, what values we need to embrace personally, and what kind of people we need to be, so when our kids grow up to be like us, we will like what they have become.

Time Out for Inventory

At times we all need to stop and take inventory of our own lives—evaluate where we're going, how we're growing, what we're teaching our children by the way we're living. We've found the categories in Luke 2:52 a good model to follow.

> And Jesus grew in wisdom and stature, and in favor with God and men.

This verse tells us that Jesus grew intellectually, physically, spiritually, socially, and emotionally. We would all do well to stop every now and then to evaluate these categories of our lives, and to ask ourselves the following questions.

Intellectual. Am I constantly learning something new? Can my kids look at my life and see that learning is important and it never stops?

Physical. Do I take care of my body by eating wisely and exercising regularly? Am I abusing my body in any way by taking drugs, for instance, or drinking alcohol excessively? Am I using my body in a way that honors God?

Spiritual. Do I take time each day to get to know God better by reading, studying, memorizing, and obeying His word? Is prayer a natural part of everything I do, or is it something I do only when an emergency rises? Am I developing my faith by acting upon what I say I know to be true?

Social. Do I make an effort to be a good friend to the friends I have? Do I practice hospitality and open our home to our friends and our kids' friends? Am I honest in my relationships?

Emotional. Do I feel good about who I am and how God made me? Am I angry about anything in my past or present, and is there anyone to whom I need to make amends? Am I willing to forgive those who have hurt me in the past?

Aiming High

We don't know where you are in your role as a parent. Maybe you've just begun and you're wondering how you'll ever be able to teach your kids what is right when there's so much wrong with the world. Maybe you've been shooting in the dark and you feel like you need to adjust your aim. Maybe you're an old hand at this parenting business but just feel like you need a few new ideas. Wherever you are, we'd like to suggest that you think about the following ideas—what they mean to you as a value-teacher and what they could mean to your children.

Choose the ones that fit you and your children and try them. Feel free to adapt them to your own needs.

∞

Remember this: what we leave in our children is far more important than what we leave to them.

∞

"The great thing in this world is not so much where we are, but in what direction we are moving"—Oliver Wendell Holmes. When you think of teaching your children values, in what direction are you moving? Talk with your spouse about your desires in this area for your family.

∞

Set aside some time to make a list of the values you want to pass on to your children. Share your list with your kids in words they can understand.

∞

"I am only one; but still I am one. I cannot do everything, but still I can do something; I will not refuse to do the something I can do"—Helen Keller. If you are the only person in your family committed to teaching your kids biblical values, don't give up. You don't know what good your efforts may do. Teach by your example.

∞

Seek out a wise, older mother or father to be your mentor. "A single conversation across the table with a wise man is worth a month's study of books"—Chinese proverb.

∞

Start a collection of good books about teaching values to children. Bookstore clerks, youth pastors, church librarians, and your friends are all good sources for book ideas. As you read, make notes of principles you want to remember and keep them in a journal.

∞

"God has not called me to be successful; he has called me to be faithful"—Mother Theresa. Strive to be the best parent you can be and do all you can to instill a strong sense of right and wrong in your children. But remember that you cannot control how your children turn out.

∞

Begin a prayer journal with each of your children. Using Luke 2:52 as a model, have them list specific ways they want to grow strong intellectually, physically, spiritually, socially, and emotionally. For example, they may want to pray for help in catching onto algebra, for the ability to work hard and make the basketball team, for the discipline to read one chapter of the Bible each day, for wisdom about who to invite to the homecoming dance, and for the ability to control their temper. Pray for your kids separately about developing strong values in every area of life.

∞

Teach your kids that they must stand for something or they'll fall for anything. Talk specifically about what they're willing to stand for.

∞

Keep a picture of your children on your desk at work or at home to remind yourself to pray for them during the day.

∞

Ask your children to pray for you—that God will help you be a good parent to them.

∞

Studies show that parents spend an average of twenty minutes a day communicating with their children, and nine of those minutes are spent in disciplinary situations. Try to disprove this by spending time having fun together and watching for natural opportunities to talk about what's right and wrong.

∞

Bring back family dinnertime. Eating together is an unparalleled opportunity for discussions of issues both large and small. Encourage conversation by not allowing television and phone calls during dinner.

∞

What new life passage will your child embark upon soon? Turn this into a special memory by doing something special to initiate him or her into this new era.

∞

Get involved in a share group with parents of like-minded values. We all need a support group of friends.

∞

"Victory is not won in miles but in inches. Win a little now, hold your ground, and later win a little more"—Louis L'Amour. Usually kids don't learn right from wrong overnight. Be patient.

∞

Talk with your older children about your hopes and dreams for them regarding living by strong values and how those might differ from what you experienced when you were their age. You can be honest about your own feelings without dragging out the "dirty laundry."

∞

Talk casually and consistently with your children. When you run an errand in your car, take a child with you. Sometimes staring through a windshield is a nonthreatening time to talk about a touchy issue.

∞

Children are like sponges. They absorb our values and perceptions. Don't forget that they are learning even when you're not aware of teaching.

"I have hidden your word in my heart that I might not sin against you" (Ps. 119:19). Set up a fun and creative reward system to help your child memorize Scripture.

∞

"One today is worth two tomorrows; never leave that till tomorrow which you can do today"—Benjamin Franklin. Don't wait until tomorrow to start teaching your children values. Today pray with your children, read them a Bible story, or sing a hymn together.

∞

As parents we should remember that one day our children will follow our example instead of our advice.

"Trust in the Lord with all your heart, and do not lean on your own understanding; in all your ways acknowledge him, and he will make your paths straight" (Prov. 3:5–6). When it's time to initiate your children into a new passage of freedom and responsibility in their life, remember this verse and share it with your child.

Our society finds Truth too strong a medicine to digest undiluted.
In its purest form Truth is not a polite tap on the shoulder;
it is a howling reproach.
What Moses brought down from Mount Sinai
were not the Ten Suggestions
. . . they are commandments.
Are, not were.

—TED KOPPEL

Chapter 2

HE WHO OWNS THE BALL RULES

In 1956, when I was a fresh-faced first-grade boy, every six-year-old had three chances to rise or fall in the pecking order: winning the picture of the week contest, lunchtime, and recess. If you happened to be a boy, you could forget about the teacher choosing your artwork to display. Girls—obnoxious, think-they-know-it-all-girls—always (at least in my memory, which may be faulty these many years later) had their pictures chosen. They did neater work, a major virtue in those days. Given a printed picture, they always colored inside the lines. And they drew boring stuff like pictures of their families or flowers, never interesting stuff like cars or rocket ships or monsters.

Boys had a somewhat more even chance to gain clout at lunchtime, unless you had a girl in your class like Mary Margaret, whose mother studied under Betty Crocker. Mary Margaret's lunches were the envy of our whole class. She didn't have boring carrot sticks. She had carrot curls. Most of us made do with peanut butter and jelly sandwiches on the bread that made you strong twelve ways. Mary Margaret probably ate peanut butter as much as the rest of us. But her sandwiches were always cut into stars or circles or moon shapes. Her mother would have rather walked across hot coals in her bare feet than send Mary Margaret to school with a store-bought cookie. How could you compete with a girl whose cupcake wrappers had cartoons printed on them?

I was an average first-grade boy with no remarkable features to propel me into a leadership position in my class. I knew I didn't have a prayer when it came to winning a drawing contest, and my lunches were, well, let's say average. My mother thought a well-balanced meal—sandwich, fruit, vegetable, milk—in a plain lunchpail was sufficient. I knew better than to ask if I could send away for the rocket-shaped thermos bottle advertised on the back of a cereal box. She would have pointed out that it was probably shoddy and would break in no time. (It would be many years before I appreciated my mother's wisdom in this and many other things.) Recess was my only hope.

For the most part our teacher allowed us to roam free on the playground, to do—within limits—what our little six-year-old hearts desired. The girls made clover chains and monopolized the swings. The boys often played team sports. I'll never forget the first day we tried to play football.

I proudly carried the football as we paraded single-file from the classroom to the playground. The other boys huddled around me, and I proceeded to tell them how we were going to play. I was prepared. The night before I had quizzed my dad about the basic rules. I'd just begun to divide the boys into teams when the big shot of the group stood in my face and told me we weren't going to play by my "stupid rules." With that a clamor ensued, and several others joined in the rebellion.

It was my first experience as a leader, and I had already lost control. I quickly discovered, however, that I had a major bargaining chip: I owned the football. We were going to play my way, or we weren't going to play at all. Reluctantly, the malcontents gave in, and the game began. That day I learned a very important principle: he who owns the ball rules.

For centuries, Western society has generally agreed that the ball belongs to God. As Creator of this celestial ball we call Earth, He knows the best way the game of life should be played. In fact, the most widely accepted rules of life ever written are ten laws God gave to Moses. We know them today as the Ten Commandments. They are the most widely accepted rules of life ever written.

Do the Ten Commandments have any meaning for us at the close of the twentieth century? Were they written exclusively for the Jews? Are they valid for Christians living in an age of grace? Is there any point in teaching them to our children? Do they still guide us through the moral quicksand of modern ethics, or are they still with us because no one has dared to question "the way we've always done it"? Some have certainly concluded the later.

We don't have to look hard to find theologians who agree with postmodern culture—that there are no absolute rights or wrongs. Today, according to prevalent practice, what is right or wrong has to be decided in each situation. When it comes to personal ethics, each person must decide in a given situation what love would command him to do rather than seek an outside moral standard. Far from being helpful, many consider the ancient life wisdom given by God to Moses as more of a hindrance.

Some people concluded that long ago a cosmic kill-joy must have leaned out of heaven and thought, "Those people are having too much fun. It's time to clamp down. I'm going to lay down the law and make them miserable." Thus the Ten Commandments and God's other rules for life are viewed as impositions—to make life dreary and dull.

Nothing could be further from the truth. God isn't trying to make our lives miserable. In reality, God saw men and women continually ruining their lives, enslaving themselves to sin and its consequences. So He summarized ten life-directing principles to bring order and harmony to life. They describe how free men and women live. He gave us a great gift, not a great burden.

Far from being arbitrary regulations, God's moral laws, the Bible's pronouncements of right and wrong, are based on God's character. Certain behaviors are black or white because they are what God would do or wouldn't do Himself. Ultimately, what makes anything right or wrong is whether it corresponds or contradicts God's character. The reason why it is wrong to lie and right to be honest, for example, is because God never lies.

> God is not a man, that he should lie,
> nor a son of man, that he should change his mind.
> Does he speak and then not act?
> Does he promise and not fulfill?
> NUMBERS 23:19

A Way of Life

The Ten Commandments sound so austere on the surface, but they are more than severe commandments written on cold stone. To understand the Ten Commandments this way will drastically alter the way we look at God's will and the reasons why we obey Him. The commandments are not icy justice. They come from a personal God who wants the best for His people: Since I am your God who delivered you from slavery, this is what I want you to do and not do. The authority of His commandments issues from God's person, His active love, and His character, rather than from isolated legal assertion.

God's desire expressed in the Ten Commandments is that men and women would enjoy a life of harmony with Him, conforming to His will from a heart of gratitude, love, and awe, not compulsion. His will was never meant to stand in isolation apart from the historic acts of love He performed on behalf of His children.

In other words, if we are going to live in God's household and enjoy His blessings, then we are going to have to live in a way that pleases Him and is consistent with His character. Parents often say to kids, "As long as you're living in my house, you'll follow my rules!" What we need to tell them is that we all follow rules—mom and dad as well as the kids—and we have house rules based on God's rules. When children are small, we begin to teach them the rules of living together in harmony as a family. We can use this concrete teaching that they can see—following family rules to enjoy family harmony—to teach them about following God's rules and living in harmony in His family.

God's wish is certainly our command. God wants men and women to obey His commands out of love, gratitude, desire for blessing, and because we are part of His family, but that does not mean that disobedience is without consequence. When we violate His will, we face His justice. In the New Testament, Paul makes this clear.

> Do not be deceived: God cannot be mocked. A man reaps what he sows. The one who sows to please his sinful nature, from that nature will reap destruction; the one who sows to please the Spirit, from the Spirit will reap eternal life. Let us not become weary in doing good, for at the proper time we will reap a harvest if we do not give up. Therefore, as we have opportunity, let us do good to all people, especially to those who belong to the family of believers.
>
> GALATIANS 6:7–10

God made this very clear to the Jews as they entered the land of Canaan. Conformity to His standards meant they could enjoy freedom in the land, the place of His prosperity and blessing. Violating these standards meant removal from the land and loss of freedom, loss of prosperity, and a return to slavery. Historically, this is exactly what happened. After repeated violations of His law and warnings from His prophets, the Jews lost their freedom and went into captivity again. When they later turned to God and renounced their destructive ways, He restored their freedom and returned them to their homeland (see Jer. 29:10–14).

The Ten Commandments: Light, Leash, and Level

Because morality is timeless, the Ten Commandments are important to every generation. Certain things are always right or always wrong because God's character never changes. What was morally right or wrong in the time of Moses was also right or wrong during the life of Christ and is still today because "Jesus Christ is the same yesterday and today and forever" (Heb. 13:8). Keeping the commandments is no longer a sign of the covenant, but it does show that we take God seriously.

The Ten Commandments serve several important purposes today. They light our way, rein us in when we're out of line, and keep us balanced as we grow in our relationship with a loving God. As part of our family life, they are our house rules for living and are important to pass on to our children.

The Ten Commandments are a light.   They illuminate our path, giving us the ability to see down the dark trails of life and avoid those things that would make us stumble. They guide us when there is a fork in the road of moral choice and keep us off the paths of destruction. Real fulfillment comes only when we live life as God intended. When we try to determine our own path alone, we are sure to stray onto the path of emptiness. Paul exhorts us,

> Therefore be careful how you walk, not as unwise men, but as wise, making the most of your time, because the days are evil. So then do not be foolish, but understand what the will of the Lord is.
>
> EPHESIANS 5:15–17

In these verses, Paul paints a picture of two individuals, one wondering aimlessly, carelessly, a servant of his foolish choices. The other lives cautiously, choosing each path with skill and insight. He calls the first one foolish—no insight, no skill at distinguishing right from wrong. He calls the other one wise—skilled, clever, able to tell the truth from a lie, able to counsel himself and others. His mind is enlightened and his eyes opened so that he is able to choose the path that pleases God and to live in harmony with Him. The Ten Commandments allow us to carefully examine and evaluate the path we and our children walk. We wouldn't send our children on a camping trip without a flashlight. We must not send them on their way in life without knowing the light the Ten Commandments can provide. Without their light, it is easy to succumb to foolishness.

The light that the Ten Commandments sheds on our path keeps us from three dangers. First, it keeps us from rationalization, from fuzzy thinking about the evil of sin. When we focus on other people's character and actions, our sinful behavior and flawed character doesn't look as bad. Its easy to rationalize, "Everyone else is doing it. It's not so bad." The Ten Commandments clear the fog. They remind us that no matter what everyone else is doing, no matter where society might draw the line, some things are always wrong. They remind us that the standard for behavior is not what our peers think, but what God thinks.

Second, the Ten Commandments keep us from compartmentalization, from allowing truth to remain theory in our minds—partitioned off and unapplied. The objective of the Ten Commandments is to change our hearts and behavior, not merely our minds. They give us concrete ways to determine if we are obeying the Great Commandment to love God and our neighbor or if we are merely paying lip service.

Third, the Ten Commandments shed light on our complacency. With the aid of their light I can help my children see the potholes and obstacles in the road ahead. There are forces constantly trying to lead us down the wrong path or, worse, keep us from moving at all for fear of falling. We need not live in fear. The path is firm and well lit.

The Ten Commandments are a leash. They remind us of our limits. They help restrain us and keep us from moral compromise and falling into sin. We all need to know where the boundaries are. We once had a blind Labrador retriever who found her way around familiar territory just fine. But whenever we took her out of the yard, we put her on a leash. We didn't do this because we didn't want her to run free. We did it because we didn't want her to run in front of a truck. In the same manner, the Ten Commandments keep us from hurting ourselves *and* allow us to live in freedom.

But there is something in us that says that rules and freedom don't mix. The fact is that true freedom must have boundaries. Think for a moment. When is a pianist free? When he ignores the laws of rhythm and scale? When he is ignorant of music theory? No, he is bound by the chaos of ignorance. The only sounds he is able to produce is cacophony, not music. But if he masters the fundamentals of rhythm, disciplines of scales, and rules of theory, then, and only then, can he move from noise to music and from performing someone else's composition to the freedom of creating his own.

Although the negative flavor of the commands tends to draw attention to the limitations, it is equally important to see the tremendous territory of freedom that is open to us without encroachment. One would hardly think of the Bill of Rights as a document limiting freedom, but it has the same negative flavor. *No, not,* and *nor* appear more than fifteen times in the Bill of Rights.

In the same way that the Bill of Rights both limits and guarantees our political freedom, the Ten Commandments describe our boundaries—the demands of justice in relationship with God and others—and outline our personal freedom, our God-given liberty and rights. For example, the first three commandments limit our freedom of worship, but they also guarantee that another person cannot coerce us to worship improperly. If nothing is to displace God as the ultimate authority in our lives, then each of us is responsible and must be given the liberty to worship God in the way we believe He requires.

We will talk about these rights more specifically as we deal with each individual command. Suffice it to say now that there cannot be freedom without limitations. Freedom without limitations brings only anarchy.

The Ten Commandments are a level. They give us a clear standard to evaluate our behavior. They tell us what is right or wrong without debate. Just like a carpenter's level shows when a board is straight, the commandments clearly tell us when our life is contrary to God's character. They let us know when our moral choices are wrong, when we are misaligned with God's will. Once in a while, a carpenter, priding himself on being able to judge a straight line without a level, will find one corner of his house is lower than the others. Just like everything in the carpenter's house will roll downhill, when one of the "corners" of our life is misaligned, our life will be out of balance. When we pride ourselves on being able to judge our moral choices by our own standards, our lives go off kilter. Then pride causes us to defend ourselves. We dig ourselves into an indefensible position even deeper, when all we'd have to do is measure our actions against the standards and make a few adjustments.

If we could just set our own standards, we might appear to be straight. We might look pretty good compared with some less exemplary people. Fallen televangelists did wonders for the pride of a large number of self-righteous Christians. At times, kids resort to comparisons as well. A few months ago ten-year-old James asked if he could do something he knew we would probably question. "The other kids are all doing it," he reasoned. I replied, "If all the other kids jumped off a bridge, would you?" Our kids need to understand that comparisons are inaccurate. They just won't do for quality work. We might get close, but it will never be perfect. And perfect is what God requires if we are going to present our own righteousness to Him for acceptance. God's standard for our behavior is His behavior.

In what seems like an attempt to outdo God, the Pharisees added 613 rules to the Ten Commandments. They tried to cover every contingency. But Jesus said,

> For I tell you that unless your righteousness surpasses that of the Pharisees and the teachers of the law, you will certainly not enter the kingdom of heaven.
> MATTHEW 5:20

He went on to say,

> Be perfect, therefore, as your heavenly Father is perfect.
> MATTHEW 5:48

In Ephesians 5:1, Paul commands us,

> Be imitators of God, therefore, as dearly loved children.

God's predetermined plan is that we be conformed into the image of Christ. Nothing less will do.

If we can't perform up to that standard, all we can do is appeal to God's mercy—which is exactly what He wants us to do. The quicker we place the level of God's law on our lives, the quicker we will see our sin and know our need for forgiveness. In fact, the Ten Commandments were never meant to provide a way to God, but to get us on the road by exposing our crookedness. Paul tells us how this worked in his own life.

> Indeed I would not have known what sin was except through the law. For I would not have known what coveting really was if the law had not said, "Do not covet."
>
> ROMANS 7:7

Paul later called the law a tutor.

> Therefore the Law has become our tutor to lead us to Christ, that we may be justified by faith.
>
> GALATIANS 3:24, NASB

The law silences every mouth that cries, "I am righteous and deserve a blessing from God." Then it directs us to the only place we can find forgiveness—God's mercy and grace.

Lessons for Parents and Children

The older I get, and the older our kids get, the more amazed I am that God keeps teaching me the same lessons over and over. He sure is patient. When I was a young mother with one child in sixth grade, one in first grade, and an infant, I often felt like my days consisted of jumping through one hoop after another. For a long time I kept putting off my personal goals and aspirations because I had to drive the carpool, do the laundry, clean the bathrooms, take the kids to the doctor and the dog to the vet, shop for groceries, prepare a Sunday school lesson, organize field trips, cook dinner, and clean the dryer lint catcher. Yes, it came down to that. One day as I was cleaning the oven with an ice pick—there was so much carbonized food stuck to it I couldn't get it off any other way—I stopped in my tracks. The more truthful way to say that is "God stopped me in my tracks."

I finally saw that I couldn't put my own spiritual life in the background, that while what I was doing was important, something was missing. I spent eighteen hours a day jumping through hoops of my own and others' making, following what I thought were the rules for being a good wife and mother. That day I realized that jumping through hoops was not want God wanted me to do.

Now when I have too much that I absolutely have to do, when I'm tempted to be short with my children, my husband, myself, or my God because I'm busy and tired, I think of that day I was cleaning my oven. Sometimes I work myself so far down into a hole it's hard to see the light at the top. That's when I forget that what's right to do has nothing to do with how many times I polish the silver each year or what kinds of awards my kids win in school or how many magazine articles I write. There's one litmus test and one only about whether it's right or wrong to do something. It's right if it fits in with God's character and His plan for me. It's wrong if it doesn't. So I ask myself a simple question: What would Jesus do in this situation? This is a tape I need to play over and over again.

Kathy has a way of learning from life's experiences that I will always cherish. In fact, the Ten Commandments teach us three lessons that we need to learn over and over again. The reason is embedded in the first lesson: They show us that we are sinful and fall short of God's standard. Both the Greek and the Hebrew words for sin mean to miss the mark. With the mark clearly drawn in God's law, we have an objective standard we can use to see that we fall short.

The second lesson is that we are totally helpless to deal with this problem. We are morally deficient and have no way to supply that which is lacking. We will never achieve perfection by ourselves. That's the bad news.

The good news, and the third lesson, is that the law points to God's solution through the perfect righteousness of Jesus Christ. Although the law reveals sin, it cannot deal with it. All three points are stated clearly in the Book of Romans.

> Now we know that whatever the law says, it says to those who are under the law, so that every mouth may be silenced and the whole world held accountable to God. Therefore no one will be declared righteous in his sight by observing the law; rather, through the law we become conscious of sin.

But now a righteousness from God, apart from law, has been made known, to which the Law and the Prophets testify. This righteousness from God comes through faith in Jesus Christ to all who believe. There is no difference, for all have sinned and fall short of the glory of God, and are justified freely by his grace through the redemption that came by Christ Jesus. God presented him as a sacrifice of atonement, through faith in his blood. He did this to demonstrate his justice, because in his forbearance he had left the sins committed beforehand unpunished—he did it to demonstrate his justice at the present time, so as to be just and the one who justifies those who have faith in Jesus.

Where, then, is boasting? It is excluded. On what principle? On that of observing the law? No, but on that of faith. For we maintain that a man is justified by faith apart from observing the law.

ROMANS 3:19–28

The law exposes our sin and takes us from the dead-end street of self-justification and opens the door to the gift of righteousness given by Christ.

For what the law was powerless to do in that it was weakened by the sinful nature, God did by sending his own Son in the likeness of sinful man to be a sin offering. And so he condemned sin in sinful man, in order that the righteous requirements of the law might be fully met in us, who do not live according to the sinful nature but according to the Spirit.

ROMANS 8:3–4

The law is only my enemy if I try to make it the road to righteousness and God's acceptance. Far from limiting us, the Ten Commandments point the way to freedom.

This is how free men and women live—and how they teach their children to live. God's example of love is one we would do well to follow. He gave us the Mosaic Law, and He gave us His Son because He loves us. We can do no less for our own children. And God also gave us the means, the ultimate child-rearing manual, to do so.

Aiming High

We all need to be reminded every once in a while of the critical importance of teaching our children the Ten Commandments— God's rules for free living. Our children must understand that God didn't give us the Ten Commandments to frustrate us. He did not look down and say, "Hmmm, how can I make those people more miserable? If they enjoy something, I think I'll make a law against it!" The laws of God are not illogical ordinances written by some power-hungry, sadistic god. They are sensible rules, given by a wise and loving God for the greatest good of His people. Maybe you feel your children—not to mention you yourself—are frustrated because the limits and rules you've been living by have not been clear. Today could be a turning point in your family. Think about the following ideas and act upon one or two you feel might make a difference.

∞

Make sure you explain the rules—yours and God's—to your children. Show them that your rules will help them be safe. Use age-appropriate examples, such as playing with matches, crossing the street, keeping a curfew.

∞

"Nothing in the world can take the place of persistence. Talent will not: nothing is more common than unsuccessful men with talent. Genius will not: unrewarded genius is almost a proverb. Education will not: the world is full of educated derelicts. Persistence and determination alone are omnipotent"—Calvin Coolidge. Persist in teaching your kids the values of the Ten Commandments.

∞

"Let us not become weary in doing good, for at the proper time we will reap a harvest if we do not give up" (Gal. 6:9). Ask God to help you hang in there when you feel like giving up.

∞

Be aware you're in a battle with irresponsible media for teaching values to your kids that are blatantly against the principles of the Ten Commandments. Movies and especially television tend to portray Judeo-Christian ethics and family values as subjects for ridicule and contempt. Discuss and learn from what you watch by asking questions such as: What was the message of this program? What were the values of the characters? What would you do to help any of the characters? Was there anything in the program you did not agree with? Did this show portray life as it really is? What in the program uplifted you or motivated you to be a better person? Was it worth your time to watch it?

∞

Start a collection of good kids' videos and audiocassette tapes that entertain your kids and teach them values at the same time. Kids ages five to thirteen will enjoy the *Secret Adventures* video series produced by Broadman & Holman. The "McGee & Me" video series produced by Focus on the Family and Tyndale House Publishers is also very good. When we're in the car, our ten-year-old enjoys listening to the *Adventures in Odyssey* cassette tape series produced by Focus on the Family.

∞

Make a list of how you can use the Ten Commandments as a light, a leash, and a level. Share your list with your kids.

∞

"First I make my decisions, then my decisions make me"— Howard Hendricks. Teach your children that God does not force us to obey His rules. But the decisions we make daily form us into what we will be tomorrow. Small decisions can have a big result—for good or for bad. It's a good idea to begin letting children as young as toddlers make decisions they can handle, for example, "Do you want Cherrios or oatmeal for breakfast?" As kids get older, it's also good to begin establishing a pattern of discussing the decisions they made after the consequences become clear. Don't berate. Don't dictate. Talk. If your child decides not to do his homework, what are the consequences? Is he happy with his decision? If he decides to do an extra-credit project and gets all sorts of praise from his teacher, again, talk with him about it. Is he glad he decided to do it?

∞

"How can a young man keep his way pure? By living according to your word" (Ps. 119:9). We know of no better way to help our children keep their way pure than by instilling God's word in their minds and hearts. The Ten Commandments are a good place to start.

Read good books that reiterate the teachings of the Ten Commandments. Learn together from the lives of the characters. Every night before his bedtime, we read a short portion of William Bennett's *The Book of Virtues* to our ten-year-old.

∞

Discuss a current event at dinner and how it relates to the Ten Commandments. Unfortunately, you don't have to read the paper or watch the news for very long for perfect illustrations.

∞

Use the following questions as a springboard for communication with older children about the teachings of the Ten Commandments.

∞

Ask your children, What would you do if . . .
* you are in a store with a friend, and you see him or her take something and not pay for it?
* you go to a party and alcoholic beverages and drugs are being offered?
* your friend tells you she cheated on the test she just finished.
* your crowd of friends makes fun of someone?
* you're invited to watch a television program or movie at a friend's house that would not be allowed at home?
* a friend tells you he or she is having sex with someone?
* someone asks you to go someplace with him or her, but warns you not to tell your parents?
* your friend is talking about committing suicide?

∞

Be involved in your child's schooling. Read their textbooks and watch for principles and ideas that may be opposed to God's values. Talk about what is the truth.

∞

Sing songs that underscore the truths you want your children to embrace as you put them to bed at night.

∞

Teach your kids this: You're not necessarily on the right track just because it's a well-beaten path. Talk about what this means.

It has been said that it's not what happens to you, but how you react to what happens to you that separates the winners from the losers and the successful from the unsuccessful. Our reactions, to a large degree, depend on the values we hold. Help your kids react wisely when they face hard situations in life, using the Ten Commandments as a guideline.

∞

Turn your stumbling blocks into steppingstones. When you go through a difficult time in your life, share with your children how you are trying to use the Ten Commandments as a light to give you wisdom. If you're struggling to respect a difficult boss at your office, talk about how the same principles apply to respecting difficult teachers at school.

∞

Make sure your kids know that if they have to do the wrong thing to stay on the team, they are on the wrong team.

∞

"Trust in the LORD with all your heart, and do not lean on your own understanding; in all your ways acknowledge him, and he will make your paths straight" (Prov. 3:5–6). Teach your children to ask God for guidance by praying with them daily.

∞

Buy your children their own modern translation of the Bible.

THE FIRST COMMANDMENT

I AM THE LORD YOUR GOD, WHO BROUGHT YOU OUT OF
EGYPT, OUT OF THE LAND OF SLAVERY. YOU SHALL HAVE NO
OTHER GODS BEFORE ME.

DEUTERONOMY 5:6–7

*God cannot give us happiness and peace apart from himself,
because it is not there.*

—C. S. LEWIS

Chapter 3

MAKING GOD
NUMERO UNO

AFTER FLYING NINETEEN HOURS ACROSS the Pacific to Seoul, Korea, I was relieved to see the airport. For six months I had looked forward to this mid-January trip to speak to wives whose husbands were stationed at Yongsan military post. But when the time came for me to go, I had a problem. I couldn't find my winter clothes.

As it happened, when I accepted this invitation, I didn't know that three days before I was scheduled to leave for Seoul our family would be moving from Texas to Tennessee. The moving crew finished unloading the van late on a Saturday night. Tuesday we were still buried in boxes. "Oh, well, how cold could it be in Korea in January?" I said, trying to see the silver lining in the cloud. Now that I was in Seoul, it was a bit difficult to maintain this attitude in a light jacket in minus twelve degree weather.

When I arrived at the base, the lovely officer's wife who had arranged for my being there said that she hoped to make my stay a memorable one. She wanted me to get a feel for the people and the culture—go where they go, eat what they eat, shop where they shop.

"Shop" is the operative word here. Had Bill known anything about the markets in Korea, he would have had me confined to quarters.

Forget after Christmas, twice yearly, preinventory, full moon, or founder's birthday sales. There is nothing, absolutely nothing, to compare with the rush that went through my body when I was let loose at It'aewon market in Seoul.

Designer names—at a fraction of their cost in the States. Silk scarves, leather jackets, designer jewelry, luggage—you name it, the merchants had it. Street after street of stalls and tiny shops stuffed with merchandise. Merchants in Seoul have raised selling to an art form. I'm sure they go to sales school to learn various approaches to use on naive tourists like me.

The first one I fell for was the "Search for Truth" approach. A merchant eyed me walking down the sidewalk and called out, "I've been holding a silk dress for just the right woman. I knew I would recognize her because of the aura around her." (Only he can see it.) He took my hand, and a worshipful look came across his face. "My spiritual adviser warned me that I was not to sell this dress to anyone but you." (He has three hundred more in the back room just like it.)

The merchant explained to me that he didn't sell clothes "just to sell them." It is a spiritual experience—matching the garment with the person for whom it was made.

I paid him for the dress and left feeling as though I was special, which is, of course, how he wanted me to feel, even though deep in my heart I knew he'd used this line before and he'd use it again. And, although I like the dress, I also left with the nagging feeling that while a dress in which I think I look good is a rare gift, no dress can really change the way I feel about myself.

Then there was the "Haven't I Seen You Before?" approach. As I was walking by a stall, a man grabbed me by the arm and said, "Excuse me, may I have your autograph? I've seen you in those American magazines. Here," he holds out a designer leather purse, "would you give me the honor of holding this purse and letting me take your picture?" (Although my best shots are with the lens cap on, I never turn down a chance to be a star.) Because of who I was, he said that he would give me a deal on the purse. "I have many purses," he says, "for your friends in Hollywood." He also ships.

Every woman in my family received a purse for her birthday.

I also fell for the "You Deserve a Break" approach. I was looking at a case of watches when a merchant dressed in a silk suit and enough gold to plate Colorado said in broken English, "Is hard for you to live in America? Everyting berry spensive—yes? Here we tink people use hard-worked-for money to buy reward for self. You like reward? Here—Rolex watch is nice reward. You buy in America for $2,000; my price $20."

I bought the watch.

One would think that a reasonably intelligent woman who has a college degree and runs a company might think to ask why a watch that sells for $2,000 in America goes for $20 in Korea. I didn't. I simply lived by the motto, "Buy now, repent later." Two days into the trip, my credit card number was embossed in the palm of my hand. That was also the day my new watch stopped running.

When it was time to return to the States, I stuffed two new, huge suitcases to the brim with my shopping trophies. Suddenly, and embarrassingly, I saw that I was living proof that materialism is the god of this age. I realized I had fallen into the American culture trap of depending on what we have for our significance and security. Designer clothes, bigger houses, faster cars: the more we have the more we'll know we're important and safe.

Not that there's anything wrong with shopping and getting a good deal. But when we go to extremes, just like the ancient Israelites, we threaten our freedom by turning our allegiance from the Creator to things in His creation.

Yes, I came back from my trip with some things my family and I could use and enjoy. And one of the things we need to teach our children about God's creation is that He created it for us. But I also came back with a renewed and profound sense of what is and isn't the most important thing in life.

I thank God that my shopping spree taught me a lesson. Twenty dollars wasn't too big a price to pay for the lesson that materialism can be an idol.

On the flight home, I began thinking about how much I missed my family. Traveling for work, as I do, can be interesting and stimulating. I meet hundreds of people each year, and I am continually impressed by their devotion to God. One of the side benefits, not the least by any means, of traveling is the opportunity I have to share with my children. I didn't exactly know what I was going to tell them about my experience in Korea. But I knew that I was feeling a lot like a kid myself, a kid who'd wanted and gotten a bunch of cheap toys that had predictably broken and/or not pleased me the way I thought they would.

In the end, I didn't say anything specifically about my experience right then. But I did remember it when James thought he couldn't live without a special action figure that was advertised on television. He scraped together every penny he had and bought the toy. Two days later it broke, and I shared with him the story of my watch.

When Bill picked me up at the airport, he wondered why I not only had new suitcases, but why they were so much heavier than the ones had been on the trip out. When he calmed down, I shared with him how embarrassed I truly was to have gotten carried away by the god of materialism. And I told him how grateful I was that God took the opportunity to teach me a lesson.

Making Room for God

Kathy's story reminded me that the First Commandment serves not only as an injunction, but as a warning. We do well to think of it any time we allow God to be crowded out of first place in our lives. After four hundred years of slavery, the Israelites were free at last, delivered from the harsh rule of Egyptians by the mighty hand of God. Their deliverance had been dramatic, miraculous, and total. Now, as they prepared to enter the Promised Land, they were about to face a serious threat to the freedom God had given. Wandering through the desert, the Israelites had not faced a great deal of competition for their allegiance to God. Entering Canaan would present a different challenge.

God knew that it would be easy for His people to be seduced by the physical, earthy representations of Canaanite deities and their promises of temporal satisfaction. In wandering away from the God who delivered them, they could willingly enslave themselves again. The Egyptians had forced slavery on the Jews. Now they would be tempted to voluntarily reenslave themselves by creating alliances with other influences in their lives. God wanted His people to know that freedom demanded an exclusive relationship with Him. He told them in the First Commandment,

> I am the LORD your God, who brought you out of Egypt, out of the land of slavery. You shall have no other gods before me.
>
> DEUTERONOMY 5:6–7

The land of Canaan was populated by a people who had created a god to solve every problem they had. The Israelites faced a full-blown pagan culture with a way of life dominated by the worship of some of the most incredibly debased gods ever invented by the human mind. Where did these gods come from?

As long as men and women have looked into the heavens, they have known that there is something bigger than themselves that they had better pay attention to. David writes,

> The heavens declare the glory of God;
>   the skies proclaim the work of his hands.
> Day after day they pour forth speech;
>   night after night they display knowledge.
>
> PSALM 19:1–2

Unfortunately, sin has also fogged the focus of most people, causing them to pervert what they see.

In spite of the incredible revelation in creation, people's perverted imagination distorts their interpretation of nature. Rather than letting nature point them to the Creator, they want gods of a more manageable size. So people deified creatures, constructing idols and using them to represent the natural forces.

As with primitive people everywhere, the Canaanites knew how dependent they were on the forces of nature—the sun, rain, seed, and soil—for survival

In deifying these forces, they sought to identify and control the forces that dramatically affected their life. When they needed rain, they appealed to the rain god. When their crops were about to wash away, they appeased the sun god. When they wanted a good harvest or more children, they worshiped the goddess of fertility. Over the years these rituals developed into sophisticated systems of belief and the worship of hundreds of little deities hungry for attention. In attempting to be free of an overly awesome Creator, they had actually created a religious bondage of their own making, under deities with the worst characteristics. Their worship included perverted, abusive sexual practices and even human sacrifice. Everywhere they turned, they found another hungry god demanding blood. No wonder their whole society was corrupt beyond repair. While seeking freedom, the Canaanites became enslaved to their own system.

The same thing can happen to us. Every time we move our allegiance from the Creator to the creature, we end up in bondage. Look at the downward cycle of ruin and bondage described in Romans.

> Therefore God gave them over in the sinful desires of
> their hearts to sexual impurity for the degrading of their

bodies with one another. They exchanged the truth of God for a lie, and worshiped and served created things rather than the Creator—who is forever praised. Amen.

Because of this, God gave them over to shameful lusts. Even their women exchanged natural relations for unnatural ones. In the same way the men also abandoned natural relations with women and were inflamed with lust for one another. Men committed indecent acts with other men, and received in themselves the due penalty for their perversion.

Furthermore, since they did not think it worthwhile to retain the knowledge of God, he gave them over to a depraved mind, to do what ought not to be done. They have become filled with every kind of wickedness, evil, greed and depravity. They are full of envy, murder, strife, deceit and malice. They are gossips, slanderers, God-haters, insolent, arrogant and boastful; they invent ways of doing evil; they disobey their parents; they are senseless, faithless, heartless, ruthless. Although they know God's righteous decree that those who do such things deserve death, they not only continue to do these very things but also approve of those who practice them.

ROMANS 1:24–32

The Competition in America

They worshiped their idols,
which became a snare to them.

PSALM 106:36

Obviously we live in a much different culture than the Israelites were about to enter. The gods of Canaan are only an ancient curiosity to our sophisticated culture. We don't pray to the rain god when we want our grass to grow. We turn our sprinklers. We don't sacrifice to the fertility god when we want to eat; we go to the grocery store. We wholeheartedly agree with Jeremiah. Idol worship is less than intelligent.

For the customs of the peoples are worthless;
they cut a tree out of the forest,
and a craftsman shapes it with his chisel.

46

They adorn it with silver and gold;
>   they fasten it with hammer and nails
>   so it will not totter.
Like a scarecrow in a melon patch,
>   their idols cannot speak;
they must be carried
>   because they cannot walk.
Do not fear them;
>   they can do no harm
>   nor can they do any good.

JEREMIAH 10:3–5

Yet for all our sophistication, Americans still trifle with other gods. As we drift further into secularism, some men and women are actually filling the vacuum with the worship of pagan deities or occult practices. Most Americans, however, take a more subtle approach. Although they aren't made of wood, stone, or metal, America has a host of popular gods. Whatever takes first place in our lives, that is the god we worship.

Sociologists tell us that something is a god, an object of worship, when it becomes the source of our self-worth and the ultimate consideration in decision-making. A man's job becomes his god when he determines his value by how high he can climb, and he is willing to sacrifice health, family, and even ethical standards to get to the top. A woman's social status becomes her god when she chooses to snub old friends who can't help her get into a certain club or organization in favor of those who can. We can only put one thing in the top slot of our priority system. Whatever is in that position dominates everything else in our life.

A wealthy friend of mine had a private consulting session with a top management expert. Using a pyramid, together they worked through Sam's priorities until only two remained, God and money. Looking at the top of the pyramid, the consultant asked Sam, "OK, which one goes in the top slot? There's only room for one. It's time for you to decide." Having never faced this question so directly, my friend asked to sleep on it. He realized that he had been trying to make room for both at the top and this had caused a great deal of conflict in both his business and personal life. After a sleepless night, he realized what Christ said was true, "You cannot serve God and money." The next morning God went at the top of the pyramid. My

47

friend continues to do well in business. The decision hasn't affected his net worth positively or negatively, but it has certainly affected his peace of mind.

It's important that our children understand that whatever has priority in their life is the god they serve. A young athlete makes winning his god when he will sacrifice anything to win. A teenage girl makes beauty her god when all she thinks about is her hair and make-up and if her clothes are "right." And if we let our children think that getting straight A's, winning the speech contest, or behaving "nicely" in front of our "important friends" is what makes us love them and makes them worthwhile in the eyes of God, we pass our own false gods on to them.

The Trinity of American Culture

The marketplace has imprinted three unmistakable gods on the psyche of American culture. They are the "must haves" if you call yourself successful, and many men and women will do anything to get them. The first is position. People must look up to and envy the station you have achieved. Even children begin to see the importance of position early in life. They want to be the most popular or the class president. When we ask them why these positions are so important, many times we find out it's so that other people will think well of them, which is not where they should get their self-worth. That can only come from God.

The second is possessions. We must own a bigger house, faster car, and more expensive clothes than everyone else. Even if we aren't really "into" possessions, our kids see the value our society places on them early in life. Certainly we can discuss the value of possessions when a child wants something we're not sure is good for her, or if she wants it for the wrong reasons. But there are other times to talk about the place of possessions in our lives. Buying a new car, for instance, can be a perfect time to talk to school-age children about our values. Why did we choose this particular car? Because it had features that would make our daily lives easier? Because it's rated high on performance and gas mileage? Or because it's a status symbol?

Third, we must have power. We calculate our success by how many people say, "How high?" when we say, "Jump!" We teach our kids by our example that power is or is not a god in our life. Would our kids call us a loving leader or a power monger? It's important that we don't "lord" it over anybody—including our kids. "Because I said so" is probably the worst way to explain to an older child why he or she is expected to do something.

Incredibly, the most precious gifts of God can also become false gods when we place them before God Himself. For example, it is possible for our family to take the place of God when we seek our sense of self-worth from our children or sense of security from a mate. Ministry can even become a god when I am impressed by the number of souls I have saved or books I have sold. Even God's own word can become a god if my sense of self-worth is based on how much I know or how precise my doctrine is, rather than on God Himself.

People who really know God are not impressed with such. He is far too big to be compared to even His best gifts. Then why would we or ancient Israel or anyone trade a fake for the real thing? The answer is very simple. We want a god who will serve us, so we create one to our proportion and liking. But all too soon we discover that this god is not able to take us through the difficulties of life.

Why Must God Be First?

When I demand to be first, it is usually an act of selfishness. Then why is it different for God to demand first place? The key to this question hangs at the front door of the commandments. God says,

> I am the LORD your God, who brought you out of Egypt, out of the land of slavery.
>
> DEUTERONOMY 5:6

The first reason He is to be first lies in His person. He is "the LORD your God." Loving God means accepting Him as He is—without cosmetic surgery. It means giving Him the place in our lives which He, in reality, occupies in the universe, the place of absolute authority. He is without peer in His creation. He is "numero uno." To put anyone or anything on the same plane with the same importance in our lives is to demote God. Listen to the Psalmist:

> For who in the skies above can compare with the LORD?
> Who is like the LORD among the heavenly beings?
> In the council of the holy ones God is greatly feared;
> he is more awesome than all who surround him.

O LORD God Almighty, who is like you?
>You are mighty, O LORD, and your faithfulness
>surrounds you.
You rule over the surging sea;
>when its waves mount up, you still them.
You crushed Rahab like one of the slain;
>with your strong arm you scattered your enemies.
The heavens are yours, and yours also the earth;
>you founded the world and all that is in it.
You created the north and the south;
>Tabor and Hermon sing for joy at your name.
Your arm is endued with power;
>your hand is strong, your right hand exalted.
Righteousness and justice are the foundation of your
>throne;
>love and faithfulness go before you.
Blessed are those who have learned to acclaim you,
>who walk in the light of your presence, O LORD.
They rejoice in your name all day long;
>they exult in your righteousness.
For you are their glory and strength,
>and by your favor you exalt our horn.
Indeed, our shield belongs to the LORD,
>our king to the Holy One of Israel.

PSALM 89:6–18

If He is Lord over all creation, He certainly belongs as Lord over our lives.

Making God number one in my life not only gives Him the place He deserves in creation, but it also gives Him the place He deserves by right of redemption. Before God states the first command, He reminds the Hebrews of His action on their behalf. They were free not because of their strength or the benevolence of some king or other god or quirk of circumstance. They were free because He "brought them out of the land of slavery." They owed everything to Him. God is not only exalted, He is active. He graciously reaches down to act on behalf of His people. Psalm 113 calls us to praise the Lord because of this.

Praise the LORD.
Praise, O servants of the LORD,
>praise the name of the LORD.

> Let the name of the LORD be praised,
>   both now and forevermore.
> From the rising of the sun to the place where it sets,
>   the name of the LORD is to be praised.
> The LORD is exalted over all the nations,
>   his glory above the heavens.
> Who is like the LORD our God,
>   the One who sits enthroned on high,
> who stoops down to look
>   on the heavens and the earth?
> He raises the poor from the dust
>   and lifts the needy from the ash heap;
> he seats them with princes,
>   with the princes of their people.
> He settles the barren woman in her home
>   as a happy mother of children.
> Praise the LORD.

For the Israelites, and for us, to place any deity on equal footing with God would be to deny their—or our—mighty deliverance.

God not only willingly acts on our behalf in the physical world, He is also the source of our spiritual freedom. As New Testament believers, we have all the more reason to make God first in our lives. Our deliverance took on cosmic proportion as Jesus Christ set us free from bondage to sin. Our deliverance affects our eternity. To place anything else on an equal par with God is to act in utter disregard for the greatest act of love and power ever known to man. Paul reminds us of this.

> But now that you have been set free from sin and have become slaves to God, the benefit you reap leads to holiness, and the result is eternal life. For the wages of sin is death, but the gift of God is eternal life in Christ Jesus our Lord.
>
> ROMANS 6:22–23

How Do We Make God First?

What is the proper response to God's exalted place and merciful action? Paul tells us clearly.

Therefore, I urge you, brothers, in view of God's mercy, to offer your bodies as living sacrifices, holy and pleasing to God—this is your spiritual act of worship. Do not conform any longer to the pattern of this world, but be transformed by the renewing of your mind. Then you will be able to test and approve what God's will is—his good, pleasing and perfect will.

ROMANS 12:1–2

Stop to worship. Remember the awesome God who has condescended to have a relationship with you. Cultivate the wonder of God. Thomas Carlyle said, "Wonder is the basis of worship." Too often in our scientific age we have lost the wonder of not only the world but also its Creator. G. K. Chesterton predicted, "The world will never be starved for want of wonders but only from want of wonder." One of Israel's problems was that they allowed God to become commonplace.

> Your wickedness will punish you;
> your backsliding will rebuke you.
> Consider then and realize
> how evil and bitter it is for you
> when you forsake the LORD your God
> and have no awe of me,"
> declares the Lord, the LORD Almighty.

JEREMIAH 2:19

One of the things we do as a family every year is make sure we get to the mountains. There is something about the grandeur of the Rockies that slaps us awake to the majesty of God. I am awed by their beauty and by the God who formed them. In the same way, every time I get on an airplane, I am amazed that we are being lifted up. Sure I know the laws of aerodynamics, but I don't want to forget the One who wrote those laws and keeps them in force. Every time I take off, I think about being lifted by the hand of God. I know that if He should become distracted, we would fall like a rock.

Not only do we need to take time to worship God and cultivate wonder. We need to capitalize on our children's innate sense of wonder. They come into this world with it. Our job is to see that they know where it comes from and learn how to keep it. Once when I was going through a rough passage in life, James was riding with me in the car late in the afternoon. All of a sudden he pointed to the sky and said, "Look at the sunset, Dad! God sure is a good artist." I was taken back by the fact that my preoccupation had prevented me from recognizing this awesome display of beauty. It took a child to remind me of the One who has a purpose in my seemingly adverse circumstances, and just as He created a beautiful painted sky, He was painting a beautiful picture with my life.

Remember what God has done. We need to take time to remember God's mercy and grace. It is easy in this day to forget just where we would be but for the grace of God. God's mercies need to be ever "in view" to us. Every Christian needs to reflect regularly on the distance he or she has come by God's grace. Ephesians 2 sets the beautiful gem that God has made us in Christ against the black backdrop of sin. We were dead spiritually, totally dominated by worldly philosophies, doomed to an eternity apart from God. But,

> because of his great love for us, God, who is rich in mercy, made us alive with Christ even when we were dead in transgressions—it is by grace you have been saved. And God raised us up with Christ and seated us with him in the heavenly realms in Christ Jesus, in order that in the coming ages he might show the incomparable riches of his grace, expressed in his kindness to us in Christ Jesus. For it is by grace you have been saved, through faith—and this not from yourselves, it is the gift of God—not by works, so that no one can boast.
>
> EPHESIANS 2:4–9

We need to remember out loud what God has done for us and to make that a regular part of our family devotions, as well as naturally throughout the course of the day. The habit of gratitude is built a day at a time. We can teach our children the virtue of gratitude by being grateful ourselves—often and conspicuously. There are many natural times—at the breakfast table, at bedtime, and spontaneously through the day—to pray prayers of thanksgiving with our children. When a grade improves on a report card, stop and thank God for His help in learning. Before an athletic event, thank God together for your child's strong body and for the privilege of playing on a team.

When you feel the first chill of winter, take a minute as a family to thank God for the heat in your home.

Recognize the competition. Do you know what is likely to come between you and God? What pressures do you feel trying to squeeze you into the world's mold? Prestige, power, and money easily become dominant forces in our lives if we are not careful. I find it helpful to ask regularly what has a grip on me more than anything else? Whatever my heart clings to is my god.

> Do not love the world or anything in the world. If anyone loves the world, the love of the Father is not in him. For everything in the world—the cravings of sinful man, the lust of his eyes and the boasting of what he has and does—comes not from the Father but from the world. The world and its desires pass away, but the man who does the will of God lives forever.
>
> 1 JOHN 2:15–17

What are we telling our children when we tell them that they are important to us and that God is important to us? If we tell them this and then miss a family outing for an important business meeting, what is the message? If we tell them that things aren't important and God is, and then live our lives as if the opposite were true, what are we telling them? If we tell them that all people are equal in the eyes of God and put down certain groups or individuals, what are we telling them?

Recognize the threat. Whatever comes between God and us is a threat to our freedom. To let anything else occupy even level ground with God not only reduces His place, but puts us in grave danger. The freedom Christ purchased on the cross is easily sacrificed experientially when we set our affection on worldly substitutes. God created us with a huge hunger for significance and security that can only be met by Him. Whenever we seek to fill that vacuum with anything other than God, it will ultimately lead to slavery.

The Israelites certainly learned this the hard way. After hundreds of years of continually playing footloose with this commandment and thumbing their nose at God's warnings, they were carried into captivity again. This time to Assyria and Babylon. Asaph the ancient Hebrew hymn writer warned,

"Hear, O my people, and I will warn you—
    if you would but listen to me, O Israel!
You shall have no foreign god among you;
    you shall not bow down to an alien god.
I am the LORD your God,
    who brought you up out of Egypt.
Open wide your mouth and I will fill it.
But my people would not listen to me;
    Israel would not submit to me.
So I gave them over to their stubborn hearts
    to follow their own devices.

PSALM 81:8–12

It's too bad that the Israelites didn't understand that far from being a limitation, the First Commandment is a call to freedom. We can and must learn to turn a deaf ear to our own stubborn hearts and teach our children to do the same. Not too long ago, Joel was invited to go to a concert. He just wanted to go because his friends were going. When we looked into it, we realized that we weren't sure of the values of the band or of their songs. We talked about this venture, and it turned out that he was feeling pressured, but really didn't want to go at all. Instead we all went as a family to a good movie. Following the First Commandment not only gives us the strength to turn a deaf ear, it also gives us the guidance to hear our true heart's desire, what God really has in mind for us.

Aiming High

There's a lot of competition in the world for our allegiance. We find it necessary to evaluate God's place in our lives regularly. It's all too easy to allow other things to crowd into our lives and knock Him down a few notches on our list of priorities. Let the following ideas spur your thinking about how you and your kids can put God in His rightful place in your lives.

∞

Realize we're in stiff competition with a pagan culture for what our children will worship. Don't bury your head in the sand. Listen to your children's music with them. Question the lyrics. Keep up with what your kids are hearing on the radio. Ask if they understand what the song is deifying.

55

"Where your treasure is, there will your heart be also" (Matt. 6:21). We know what we worship by what we spend our money and our time on. Make a family plan to spend some time and money on something that reflects what you worship. Do without something your family wants and donate that money to a worthy cause.

∞

Set aside a special family prayer time. Make a list of each family members' prayer requests and photocopy the list for each person. Continue praying individually during the week, remembering to pray that each person would put God first in all things.

∞

"When I fed them, they were satisfied; when they were satisfied, they became proud; then they forgot me" (Hosea 13:6). If you have been abundantly blessed with material possessions, regularly acknowledge as a family the source of your blessings that you might not forget God.

∞

Teach your children that God is the source of everything we have. Although we work and earn money, unless God gives us air to breathe and our bodies and minds to use, we would have nothing. Talk about how everything—our bodies, possessions, talents—belongs to God and we are His stewards.

∞

If you have a personal accomplishment, let your kids know how good you feel about it *and* that you know you were able to do this because of God.

∞

"Put in its proper place, money is not man's enemy, not his undoing, nor his master. It is his servant, and it must be made to serve him well"—Henry C. Alexander. Talk together as a family about how money can serve you well so you won't serve money.

∞

"All that I have seen teaches me to trust the Creator for all I have not seen"—Ralph Waldo Emerson. Take a walk in the woods with your child. Learn to identify different trees, animals, and birds. Talk about God's being the Lord of all creation.

Visit a farmers' market or roadside stand and delight in the various fruits and vegetables God made.

∞

Take advantage of changing seasons to remind children about God's good earth. Go apple picking in the fall and make homemade applesauce; make snow ice cream in the winter; fly kites in March winds; go fishing in the summer.

∞

On a star-filled evening, lay on a quilt in your backyard and look at the heavens God created.

∞

Whatever your kids are studying—math, biology, literature —remind them that all truth is God's truth.

∞

When you're swimming, running, or riding bikes together, comment about how good it is that God gave us muscles to enjoy these sports. Thank Him spontaneously.

∞

When they grow up, what will your children remember that was important in your life? Bill remembers that his dad faithfully prayed for fifty people every day.

∞

Help your children get involved in a church youth group or Bible study. Peers with like values can encourage each other to live up to high standards.

∞

"Neutral men are the devil's allies"—E. Chapin. Tell your kids that if we don't stand for something, we may fall for anything. Talk about what you stand for as family.

∞

Send your kids to a good summer camp that embraces the values you hold. It's good for kids to hear someone else besides mom and dad talking about what's right and wrong.

∞

Help your kids start their day remembering that God is always with them. Schedule your morning so you can have a peaceful breakfast and pray together about your day.

∞

Read a passage of Scripture aloud at the breakfast table from a modern translation of the Bible. Get into the habit of starting your day by acknowledging your Creator and his word.

∞

See to it that your own spiritual life is growing so you will have something to offer your children. Pray regularly. Get involved in studying the Bible—on your own or in a group. Fellowship with spiritually minded people.

∞

"All scripture is God-breathed and is useful for teaching, rebuking, correcting, and training in righteousness, so that the man of God may be thoroughly equipped for every good work" (2 Tim. 3:16–17). Teach your kids to respect the Bible—that it is God's word to His children and relevant to every issue in life.

∞

If we say God is in first place in our life, remember that the test of our love for God is the love we have for one another. Do we pass?

THE SECOND COMMANDMENT

YOU SHALL NOT MAKE FOR YOURSELF AN IDOL
IN THE FORM OF ANYTHING IN HEAVEN ABOVE OR
ON THE EARTH BENEATH OR IN THE WATERS BELOW.
YOU SHALL NOT BOW DOWN TO THEM OR WORSHIP THEM;
FOR I, THE LORD YOUR GOD, AM A JEALOUS GOD,
PUNISHING THE CHILDREN FOR THE SIN OF THE FATHERS
TO THE THIRD AND FOURTH GENERATION OF
THOSE WHO HATE ME, BUT SHOWING LOVE
TO A THOUSAND GENERATIONS OF
THOSE WHO LOVE ME AND KEEP MY COMMANDMENTS.

DEUTERONOMY 5:8–10

*What comes to mind when we think of God
is the most important thing about us. . . .
The most portentous fact about any man is not
what he at a given time may say or do,
but what he in his deep heart conceives God to be like.
We tend by some secret law of the soul
to move toward our mental image of God.*

—A. W. TOZER

Chapter 4

THE REAL THING

I DON'T KNOW ABOUT YOUR SUNDAY MORNINGS, but Bill and I think that how we begin that morning sets the tone for the rest of the day. A typical Sunday morning might go like this.

Our music alarm goes off, and we hear a two-hundred voice choir singing "Great is Thy faithfulness . . . Morning by morning new mercies I see . . ." Bill rolls over, kisses me gently on the cheek, and with mint-fresh breath says, "I hate to disturb such a beautiful picture, my love, but God is calling us. It's time to get up."

I kiss him back and leap out of bed. I touch my toes twenty times and do one hundred sit-ups. Barely winded, I walk into the bathroom and splash a little water to freshen my rested face and brush my hair, which has hardly moved during the night. I gracefully descend the stairs wearing a flowing robe and matching slippers. I pour two cups of coffee, and we sit in our favorite early-morning spot for an hour of quiet prayer before it's time for breakfast and to leave for church. Our time together with God ends only when our fully dressed children appear, Sunday school materials in hand. We work together to make a Sunday breakfast of homemade waffles, with preserves we made last summer, sausage, and freshly squeezed orange juice. As we cook, we all recite memory verses. And as we eat, we listen to inspirational music.

The key word in this story is "might." In reality, our music alarm does go off. As a matter of fact, it's the first alarm to go off. I usually sleep through it, but the music wakes Bill enough to realize he's freezing (I have stolen all the covers again). What he says isn't about his hesitation to disturb a beautiful sight. Some mornings he mumbles about blanket hogs, others he just mumbles. Then he announces that it's time for me to get up.

Having learned long ago that the best defense is a good offense, I retort, "There's no way I'm getting out of bed. I haven't had enough sleep. You kept me up half the night with your snoring."

Bill turns his head away, takes two deep breaths of fresh air to recover from my donkey breath, and shoots back, "I do not snore."

"Right. You don't snore, and Arnold Schwarzenegger doesn't work out. Get a grip. Your snoring blows lamps off the tables, pictures off the wall, and makes the dog across the street howl."

We're saved from a full-blown argument by the bell. The second alarm—the one on Bill's wristwatch—goes off. Now there's music and beeping, and we're still in bed.

Five minutes later the third alarm buzzes. Bill has positioned this clock so he can stretch over to the bookshelf where it sits and turn the alarm off without getting out of bed.

Finally, the fourth goes off in the bathroom, which means I have to get out of bed to turn it off. This clock says it's six-forty, but it's actually six-thirty—the time I want to get up.

Once in the bathroom I struggle to unstick my eyelids and stare into the mirror. Not a pretty sight. My hair lies flat, plastered to my face on one side. On the other side, it sticks out at a right angle. I throw on a robe and manage to clear a path down the hall. Every morning is an adventure. Will I trip over the dog? The schoolbooks? The laundry basket? Will I live to see the kitchen?

Ah, there it is at last! And . . . I'm out of coffee—again. Now where did I put that grocery list? About this time, the dog barks to be let out. Bill wanders in and wants to know what I've done with his blue tie?

"What blue tie?" I snap. "How can you worry about a stupid tie when we're out of coffee?" Any minute, the boys will begin their morning litany: where is my _____? You name it, they've lost it, and they need it for Sunday school today. No wonder I'm tempted to go back to bed.

Okay, I'm exaggerating, just a tiny bit. But you get the picture. I'm not at my best early in the morning. However, I've learned over the years that "not at my best" can continue through the day if I don't put first things first. And that's why Bill and I do get up early most days, and especially Sundays.

Something Is Missing

Kathy does tend to exaggerate. And I do know where my own ties are, most of the time at least. But try as we might, sometimes our Sunday mornings do leave something to be desired—like an encounter with the living God.

If you had to rate your Sunday morning experience on a scale of one to ten, what would you say? Have you ever wondered what happens to us on Sunday mornings? Sometimes it seems that Christianity is at its worst on the Lord's day.

Think about your average Sunday morning for a moment. When did you get up? Was there sufficient time or did you have to rush? What was the general atmosphere in your house before leaving? Can you remember the conversation on your way to church? Was anyone upset? During the whole process, was there any time to spend alone with God? What were you thinking about when the worship service began? How about after church? What did you talk about on the way home? Was the general nature of the conversation self-centered or God-centered? And perhaps most importantly, was there any attempt to see the morning from the Lord's eyes? Did you ever stop to ask what He thought?

I try to ask myself questions like this regularly. It helps me focus on making Sunday morning a worshipful experience for me and for our children.

No doubt something is missing from the worship of most Christians in America. Not often do churchgoers find themselves face to face with the living God. If we did there would be a renewed sense of His holiness. We would be absolutely awed by His grace. We would be struck with joy and amazed that God wants to spend time with us, much less use us for His glory. Warren Wiersbe, the former pastor of Moody Memorial Church in Chicago, presided over countless Sunday worship services. He suggested that we have all lost touch with who God is. He postulates, "Rather than an encounter with the living God, we are toying with an image of our own imagination." If God is more of a figure in history than a real person to be dealt with on a daily basis, it's easy for our minds to stray from reality.

I remember the first time I fell in love. I was seven years old when I saw the movie *Toby Tyler* and fell head over heels with the little blonde girl in the circus. She was the girl of my dreams, and I knew I would marry her some day. Of course, I didn't really know her, but I just "knew" that she was perfect—that when we met she'd be interested in everything I had to say, that she'd know just what to say back, that she'd like the same games, books, and sports I did. As it turned out, the girl I created in my imagination probably had very little in common with the person she really was.

The Verge of Idolatry

If we are not careful, our minds can play the same make-believe game with God, and when we do, our worship can border on a violation of the Second Commandment not to engage in idolatry. Not that we were sculpting an idol, but we are forming an image of God in our minds that is convenient, even if not very compelling. How else can we explain the reaction of so many who come before the Lord? Beth can sing perfect alto in the church choir without missing note, beat, or word, all the while plotting her strategy for tomorrow's sales meeting. Mike sits through the sermon seemingly focused on what is being said, but all the while he's frustrated because he'll miss the beginning of the game on television by at least fifteen minutes; that is, unless he can beat everyone else out of the parking lot. By 11:30 he is plotting his exit. Jim and Kate look like the perfect couple, all smiles and impeccably dressed. No one knows that their relationship is about to fracture. They use so much emotional energy to keep up the facade, the spirit of God would have to crack them on the head to get through.

If you asked any of these people, or countless others, they'd tell you they were worshiping on Sunday, taking part in church activities, making sure their children do the same. But what message do you suppose Beth's daughter has gotten when her mother missed every soccer game this season and the band recital because she had sales meetings and choir practice? Does Mike think his son doesn't know that he values football—which he talks about every minute he's not working—more than he values God? And how can Jim and Kate teach their children about a loving God in a hostile household?

What Is Idolatry?

The word *idolatry* can bring up all kinds of images to us. Since I recently spent a week with medical missionaries from Nepal, the image that comes to my mind is of a Nepali woman presenting an offering to Kali, the blood-thirsty Hindu goddess. Like many of the Eastern countries influenced by Hinduism and its pantheon of gods, Nepal has literally hundreds of gods all clamoring for their due from these poor people. Their worship not only perpetuates the poverty of the land, but it also nurtures a settled despair.

The First Commandment addresses the worship of false images—the false gods of the Canaanites, the images of pantheism, as well as the idolatry of money, status, and power. But there is another form of idolatry that is much more subtle in its expression and thus much more dangerous. It's this subtle idolatry that the Second Commandment addresses.

> You shall not make for yourself an idol in the form of any-
> thing in heaven above or on the earth beneath or in the
> waters below. You shall not bow down to them or worship
> them; for I, the LORD your God, am a jealous God, punish-
> ing the children for the sin of the fathers to the third and
> fourth generation of those who hate me, but showing love
> to a thousand generations of those who love me and keep
> my commandments.
>
> DEUTERONOMY 5:8–10

It is not the worship of false gods that is condemned here. Otherwise this would be a repeat of the First Commandment. Rather this commandment refers to inadequate and inaccurate images of the true God and their use in worship. It is possible to worship false gods. It is also possible to worship the true God falsely.

The episode of the golden calf at Mount Sinai is actually a violation of the Second Commandment, not the first. The Israelites were not reverting to the worship of Egyptian gods but attempting to create a picture of God to aid them in their worship—a picture of the virile strength of God who had just delivered them. The account in Exodus 32:4–6 makes this clear.

And he took this from their hand, and fashioned it with a graving tool, and made it into a molten calf; and they said, "This is your god, O Israel, who brought you up from the land of Egypt." Now when Aaron saw this, he built an altar before it; and Aaron made a proclamation and said, "Tomorrow shall be a feast to the LORD." So the next day they rose early and offered burnt offerings, and brought peace offerings; and the people sat down to eat and to drink, and rose up to play.

An Encounter with the Real Thing

When men and women encounter the living God, a different reaction occurs. We either fall in worship or cower in awe, aware of the foulness of our hearts in the presence of a holy God. Here is Isaiah's response to being in God's presence.

> In the year that King Uzziah died, I saw the Lord seated on a throne, high and exalted, and the train of his robe filled the temple. Above him were seraphs, each with six wings: With two wings they covered their faces, with two they covered their feet, and with two they were flying. And they were calling to one another:
>
> > "Holy, holy, holy is the LORD Almighty;
> > the whole earth is full of his glory."
>
> At the sound of their voices the doorposts and thresholds shook and the temple was filled with smoke.
> "Woe to me!" I cried. "I am ruined! For I am a man of unclean lips, and I live among a people of unclean lips, and my eyes have seen the King, the LORD Almighty."
> Then one of the seraphs flew to me with a live coal in his hand, which he had taken with tongs from the altar. With it he touched my mouth and said, "See, this has touched your lips; your guilt is taken away and your sin atoned for."
> Then I heard the voice of the Lord saying, "Whom shall I send? And who will go for us?"
> And I said, "Here am I. Send me!"
>
> ISAIAH 6:1–8

An encounter with the living God shakes us awake, arrests our attention from football games, sales meetings, self-pity, and smug self-righteousness. It awakens us to the greatness of the person we are meeting and the sheer grace it takes to allow us into His holy presence. It interrupts our plans and confronts us with God's claim on our lives. In short, it is not something that we can walk away from and return to business as usual.

The Importance of the Second Commandment

God's reaction to attempts to form images of Him in the Exodus account and in the Ten Commandments is extreme. If the sheer number of words means anything, then this problem weighs heavy on His heart. The content of this command leaves no doubt as to what He thinks about this idolatrous tendency among His people. He reserves His severest judgment for those who tamper with His identity and glory. His anger reverberates through generations as the effects of idolatry impair the worship of children and grandchildren. Idolatry in any form has a multigenerational impact. That explains why God is so upset with the Jews in Jeremiah's time eight hundred years later. The harvest of idolatry in the prophet's time was sown with seeds planted generations before.

> The LORD said, "It is because they have forsaken my law, which I set before them; they have not obeyed me or followed my law. Instead, they have followed the stubbornness of their hearts; they have followed the Baals, as their fathers taught them."
>
> JEREMIAH 9:13–14

Why is it that God is so concerned about this danger? What's wrong with using visual representations if they help us worship the true God? Why is this so important? It's because the glory of God and the spiritual well-being of His people are inextricably bound together.

In his classic book *Knowing God*, J. I. Packer offers two devastating results of idolatry. First, it obscures God's glory. John Calvin, a French leader who helped rescue the church from the corruption of the superstitious idolatry of the sixteenth century wrote,

> A true image of God is not found in all the world; and hence . . . His glory is defiled, and His truth corrupted by

the lie, whenever He is set before our eyes in a visible form.
... Therefore, to devise any image of God is itself impious;
because by this corruption His majesty is adulterated, and
He is figured to be other than He is.[1]

The point is not just representing God, who is spirit, as a body with
parts. The problem is that images conceal more than they reveal.
Although Aaron meant to honor God by portraying His might with
the golden calf, the representation hid more than it revealed. It
obscured God's moral character, His wisdom, His patience, and His
goodness.

Second, God ferociously opposes idolatry because idols mislead
us, conveying false ideas about who He is. Images affect our thoughts
about God. With huge chunks of God's true identity concealed by
Aaron's calf, men and women were left to their imagination about
God's true character and divine being. This had immediate results
on their worship.

> When Aaron saw this, he built an altar in front of the calf
> and announced, "Tomorrow there will be a festival to the
> LORD." So the next day the people rose early and sacrificed
> burnt offerings and presented fellowship offerings.
> Afterward they sat down to eat and drink and got up to
> indulge in revelry.
>
> EXODUS 32:5–6

Their worship followed the animalistic instincts of the calf they worshiped. Make no mistake, this was no Sunday School picnic, but a
drunken orgy—a form of worship regularly used by the Canaanites
to revere their false gods. It was only one small step from the worship
of the image of God the Israelites had formed in their minds to the
worship of false gods of Canaan.

Thinking of God As We Like

Although we are not likely to form golden calves to represent God,
the idolatry God speaks of in the Second Commandment grips
American Christians by the spiritual throat. Today men and women
might occasionally use pictures or statues of Jesus in unhealthy ways,
but the real problem is not molten calves, but rather mental images.

It is a particularly deadly form of idolatry because it is self-deluding. While thinking we worship the true God, by adjusting His attributes in our minds, in reality, we create a different god altogether. Images, whether molten or mental, are still idolatrous and destructive. I've seen two distinct forms of mental idolatry in America.

When we don't take the Bible and God's self-revelation seriously, we pick and choose those attributes of God we like, much as someone makes choices from a cafeteria line. One person says, "I like to think of God as a God of love, not justice." Another prefers the gracious "God of the New Testament" to the "judgmental, vengeful God of the Old Testament." Still others, who are fed up with the softness of our society, love to focus on the God who really lays down the law with sinners. Some Christians even feel compelled to be God's press agent, remaking His image so that He will appeal to popular culture. Others impart ideas from Eastern religions and combine them with selected biblical images.

The images of God coming from Hollywood are a great example of this cafeteria approach. God, angels, and heavenly beings are hotter than "bodies" in Hollywood this year, according to Jeff Gorninier, a reporter for *Entertainment Weekly*. He goes on to say, however,

> Seekers of the day are apt to peel away through theological stuff and pluck out the most dulcet elements of faith coming up with a soothing sampler of Judeo-Christian imagery (monks and angels, sans the righteous anger and guilt), Eastern meditation, self-help lingo, a vaguely conservative craving for "virtue" and a loopy New Age pursuit of "peace." This happy free-for-all, appealing to Baptists and stargazers alike, comes off more like Forrest Gump's ubiquitous "box of chocolates" than any real system of belief.[2]

The danger of course is that they create a god who has no basis in reality. This is offensive to God. To look at God this way is to be like a man who sees his wife as the most beautiful creature on earth. You might say that he idolizes her. But does he see that she is also brilliant? He objectifies her as a sex object and ignores her mind and emotions. He does not really know her, and their relationship suffers. We don't need a facade or a projection in our minds. We need a real God who is alive and active in the affairs of men. We are real people with real problems who need a real God, not a placebo.

Re-creating God in our minds not only angers God, it sets us up for disappointment. God will not remold Himself for us. And when we go looking in a time of need for the god we have created, he will not be there—because he does not exist.

On the conservative side of the spiritual spectrum, those who take the Bible seriously often develop rather wooden pictures of what God is like in their minds. Just like modern science has lost God in the wonders of His creation, it is possible for Christians to lose God in the wonders of His word. We can be captivated by the ideas of Scripture and miss God in the process.

Kathy and I believe that God's self-revelation in the Bible is absolutely accurate. However, it does not tell the totality. How could it? It describes God, but does not define Him. Thinking that we somehow have a handle on God is to dishonor Him as much as those who manhandle His identity. We forget that He has revealed Himself as bigger than our minds can conceive. Paul reminds us that God—

> is able to do immeasurably more than all we ask or imagine.
>
> EPHESIANS 3:20

Human language and thought can accurately describe what God is like, but there is no way our language or our finite minds can capture Him. Whether we try to capture God in a box or construct a god in our minds who pleases us, we have a relationship with a false god.

Why do we play so loosely with God's identity and mental idolatry? The goal of our mental gymnastics is to whittle God down to a manageable size. A. W. Tozer put it this way,

> Left to ourselves we tend immediately to reduce God to manageable terms. We want to get Him where we can use Him or a least know where He is when we need Him. We want a God we can in some measure control.[3]

We want a god that is safe and comfortable—who will not disrupt our lives, who serves our needs and leaves us alone when we don't want to bother with him. C. S. Lewis accurately observed that we don't want a heavenly Father so much as a heavenly grandfather who lets us do as we like and wants to say at the end of the day that a good time was had by all. This is not the God of the Scriptures.

70

What is our image of God? What image are we passing on to our children? Until and unless we can begin to worship a God who knocks our socks off, we haven't grasped what it means to follow the Second Commandment. We're toying with an image of our own imagination, and we're teaching our children to do the same thing. This experience of God is built over time, through knowledge and relationship. As we build our own knowledge of and relationship with God, we build our children's, mostly by immersing them in our own true worship experience.

How Can We Get to Know God?

Although the Second Commandment limits our pursuit to God's self-revelation, not our speculation, it is a positive invitation to know God as He is, as He is revealed Himself to men. It's as if God is saying to us, "Don't think of me as you like. Don't put me in a box. Know me in all my power and glory as I have revealed myself."

Is it really possible to know God? If you are talking about totally understanding Him, the answer is obviously no. But He is knowable. We can discover Him where He has revealed Himself to us. Just because we can't swallow the lake, doesn't mean we can't drink what we are able to contain.

This is what the LORD says:

> "Let not the wise man boast of his wisdom
>   or the strong man boast of his strength
>   or the rich man boast of his riches,
> but let him who boasts boast about this:
>   that he understands and knows me,
> that I am the LORD, who exercises kindness,
>   justice and righteousness on earth,
> for in these I delight,"
> declares the LORD.
>
> JEREMIAH 9:23–24

The Bible is filled with examples of individuals who knew God, and whose hearts hungered for more. Moses prayed,

> If you are pleased with me, teach me your ways so I may know you and continue to find favor with you.
>
> EXODUS 33:13

71

David cried out,

> My soul thirsts for God, for the living God.
> When can I go and meet with God?
>
> PSALM 42:2

Paul proclaimed,

> What is more, I consider everything a loss compared to the
> surpassing greatness of knowing Christ Jesus my Lord, for
> whose sake I have lost all things. I consider them rubbish,
> that I may gain Christ.
>
> PHILIPPIANS 3:8

"Wait a minute," you say. "These people were prophets and
apostles. They saw God do miraculous things. I can't know God like
they did." You are right. Actually we have an advantage. God is as
knowable today as ever. In fact, we not only have the accurate record
of the prophets' and apostles' encounters with the living God, but we
have the active ministry of the Holy Spirit dwelling within us, leading
us to the truth.

So where do we go for this knowledge? Men and women have
found five sources of information helpful in their quest to know God.

History.   The recorded acts of God and man provide a rich trail of
information. Some have proclaimed history as "His Story."

Tradition.   The recorded and remembered beliefs and experiences
of believers passed down from generation to generation.

Experience.   Our own personal encounters with God and His world.

Reason.   Human evaluation of our world and our experience in it.
As the author of intellect and reason, God invites us to bring all our
intellectual abilities into our faith.

Revelation.   God's own disclosure of Himself. God reveals Himself
in three unmistakable ways. Through creation,

> *The heavens declare the glory of God;*
>   *the skies proclaim the work of his hands.*
>
> PSALM 19:1

in Scripture,

> All Scripture is God-breathed and is useful for teaching, rebuking, correcting and training in righteousness, so that the man of God may be thoroughly equipped for every good work.
>
> 2 TIMOTHY 3:16–17

and in Christ.

> For in Christ all the fullness of the Deity lives in bodily form.
>
> COLOSSIANS 2:9

In the past God spoke to our forefathers through the prophets at many times and in various ways, but in these last days he has spoken to us by his Son, whom he appointed heir of all things, and through whom he made the universe. The Son is the radiance of God's glory and the exact representation of his being, sustaining all things by his powerful word.

> HEBREWS 1:1–3

Evaluating the Information. All five sources of knowledge are helpful, but not all are equally helpful. Some can even be contradictory. Since our reason isn't infallible, every source of information about God must be checked for accuracy against what He tells us about Himself in Scripture. Even our interpretation of what we see in the Creation is subject to error. The other sources might be like an unauthorized biography. They contain some truth and some error. The only way to distinguish truth from error is to go to the person himself. When we go to the Scripture, we are going to God's authoritative revelation of Himself. The principle is simple: we must take our thoughts about God from God.

If we truly want to know God, we are dependent on His revelation. The same person who wrote,

> "I consider everything a loss compared to the surpassing greatness of knowing Christ Jesus my Lord."

also wrote,

> Oh, the depth of the riches of the wisdom and
> knowledge of God!
>> How unsearchable his judgments,
>> and his paths beyond tracing out!
>
> ROMANS 11:33

Please don't misunderstand. It is not as if God is hiding. He wants to be found more than we want to find Him. But He has not obligated Himself to skeptics or promised to reveal Himself to rebels. He has, though, promised honest seekers satisfaction for their effort. Jesus gave us this principle when we seek good things from God,

> Ask and it will be given to you; seek and you will find; knock and the door will be opened to you. For everyone who asks receives; he who seeks finds; and to him who knocks, the door will be opened.
>
> MATTHEW 7:7–8

If we really want to know God, we can pursue Him with the confidence that our search will be satisfied.

Developing a Relationship with God

When we talk about knowing God we're not referring to some special emotion or tingle down our spine. We're not talking about hearing voices or seeing visions. God is a person, and He can be known as a person in the same way a son knows his father, a wife knows her husband, or a friend knows a friend—relationships that the Bible uses as analogies for our relationship with God.

Knowing God begins with faith. The prerequisite to a relationship with God is reconciliation. The fact is that no one can approach God and hope to know Him while still in rebellion. Fortunately, God made the first move to end our rebellion by sending Christ. Paul says,

> For if, when we were God's enemies, we were reconciled to him through the death of his Son, how much more, having been reconciled, shall we be saved through his life! Not only is this so, but we also rejoice in God through our Lord Jesus Christ, through whom we have now received reconciliation.
>
> ROMANS 5:10–11

Our relationship with God is established through Christ. Through Christ our sin—which is a barrier—is removed, and our place in God's family is secured. Once this initial barrier is cleared, we come to know God as we do any other person.

Knowing God takes time. It's a universal rule: If it's valuable, it takes time. Few things of significance are automatic. This is true of any relationship. Time invested in another is part of every quality relationship. It is only as I spend time with a person that I come to know her, see what she sees, learn what she likes and dislikes, see how she responds in a crisis. There is no knowing, no growing without time.

It is not a surprise that we should want to spend time with God, but it is amazing that He wants to spend time with us. Mark 3:14 is one of the most remarkable verses in the Bible because it reveals this desire of God.

> He appointed twelve—designating them apostles—that they might be with him and that he might send them out to preach.

Imagine! The Sovereign Creator of the universe wants to "be" with me and me with Him!

Knowing God demands communication. God has given us the capacity to convey thoughts. And as with any two persons, communication has two elements: listening and talking. As with most of our relationships, we need to listen a lot more than we talk. We listen to God speak through His word. The books of the Bible are more than a dusty set of ancient manuscripts; they are the living word of God.

> For the word of God is living and active. Sharper than any double-edged sword, it penetrates even to dividing soul and spirit, joints and marrow; it judges the thoughts and attitudes of the heart.
>
> HEBREWS 4:12

Every time we pick up the Bible, it's as if God speaks afresh to us. In His word He tells me what He is like, what He promises, and how He wants me to live. Listen to how Paul says it.

> All Scripture is God-breathed and is useful for teaching, rebuking, correcting and training in righteousness, so that

the man of God may be thoroughly equipped for every
good work.

2 TIMOTHY 3:16–17

As we grow in our knowledge of God we can listen to Him speak to us
in our thoughts and recognize His voice amidst all the mental activity.

Communication also involves speaking. Our conversation
should be characterized by honest words and honest praise. Open
acknowledgment of your desires and feelings before God is essential
for intimacy. Paul presses for this kind of prayer in advice to the early
church.

> Do not be anxious about anything, but in everything, by
> prayer and petition, with thanksgiving, present your
> requests to God. And the peace of God, which transcends
> all understanding, will guard your hearts and your minds
> in Christ Jesus.
>
> PHILIPPIANS 4:6–7

We are chief beneficiaries here, of course, not God. If we are hiding
true feelings for whatever reason, our relationship will remain shallow.

Communication also involves honest praise. Worship is the natural
response to God. Everything about Him is worth of praise. Worship
may very well be the true barometer of our knowledge of Him.

Knowing God takes commitment. Commitment is the foundation
for any relationship. Without commitment, communication will
remain shallow and relationships will be superficial. When we reveal
ourselves to someone else, we become vulnerable. In every deep and
intimate relationship there is a mutual commitment. We know God's
level of commitment from His Word.

> But God demonstrates his own love for us in this: While we
> were still sinners, Christ died for us.
>
> ROMANS 5:8

> He who did not spare his own Son, but gave him up for us
> all—how will he not also, along with him, graciously give us
> all things?
>
> ROMANS 8:32

God's commitment to us is undeserved, unconditional, and total. He holds nothing back. Although God's love is not dependent on our response, He asks for that same level of commitment from us in response. As we commit ourselves to Him, He is able to open more of Himself up to us.

> Therefore, I urge you, brothers, in view of God's mercy, to offer your bodies as living sacrifices, holy and pleasing to God—this is your spiritual [or reasonable] act of worship. Do not conform any longer to the pattern of this world, but be transformed by the renewing of your mind. Then you will be able to test and approve what God's will is—his good, pleasing and perfect will.
>
> ROMANS 12:1–2

No one will make that kind of commitment to a contrived image of God. But because of who God is and what He has done, Paul calls this a reasonable act of worship. As I open myself to God, He reveals Himself more and more intimately to me. It is impossible to know God intimately apart from an obedient heart.

Knowing God demands risk.   Unfortunately, it's all too easy to accumulate fascinating facts about God without coming face to face with Him. We can know all about God theoretically without really knowing Him experientially. Knowledge about who God is only becomes knowledge of God Himself when we step out and put what we have been told on the line of reality. We won't know the Lord is good until we "taste and see" for ourselves as He invites us in Psalm 34:8. We won't know that God is faithful until we act as if He is present, even when it seems He is far away. We won't know that God accepts us totally by grace and on the merits of Christ alone until we come expecting God to bless us, even though we know we are unworthy. We won't know Christ and what He gives us is all we need until we turn away from and relinquish our demands for others to love us and until we learn to rest in His love alone.

Knowing God is a matter of grace.   Lest we forget, let me remind you that God is the initiator of intimacy. If He did not want to be known, we would never find Him. Incredibly, God pursues us into the darkest pits of humanity and shines the knowledge of Himself. Jesus told the woman at the well,

Yet a time is coming and has now come when the true worshipers will worship the Father in spirit and truth, for they are the kind of worshipers the Father seeks.

JOHN 4:23

He is not seeking men and women who want to make their own gods in their minds or in their workshops. He is looking for men and women who are desperate for real answers and real life and real knowledge of the real God.

Aiming High

When we come to understand that there is no life in an artificial world and we're ready to stop manufacturing our own reality about God, we are ready for the truth and for the greatest adventure of life. It is only when we know the living God ourselves that we can introduce Him to our children. The following ideas are meant both to help you think about your own perception of God and how to pass on a correct perception of God to your children.

∞

Schedule time when you won't be uninterrupted to think about if and how God's word is important and relevant in your own life. Write down some ways that you can live your life so that your children see that importance.

∞

Make sure your children understand that knowing God does not mean turning off your mind. Create an atmosphere where they can ask questions and work through their beliefs openly. Honest questions and honest doubts deserve honest discussion and honest answers.

∞

Talk as a family about how you can make your Sunday morning experience a way to know God better. You might institute a tradition of going out for brunch after church and sharing one thing each person noticed. You might read Scripture together as a family before leaving for Church. You might decide to make your Sunday mornings less hectic by getting up earlier, having older children help get younger children ready, or any other ways you and your family can brainstorm together.

Pick a period of time, a month or so, over which you can read Scripture together as a family. As you read, begin a list of the attributes of God.

∞

Talk about what we idolize in our culture. Pick almost any magazine or hour of television to watch together. What does the content of the advertisements say about idols?

∞

If you have images of God or Jesus in your home, talk with your children about what they are and what they aren't.

∞

While your children are very young, begin to ask them who they think God is? Most children first and best experience God as a loving parent. But by asking them, you can direct their concept away from, for instance, the God who would punish a playmate who's hurt them or the God who belongs only to their church.

∞

Don't be shy about sharing your awe of God and His creation. Sometimes in this technological world we're not amazed by much of anything. Tell your children just how you feel about God.

∞

Read biographies of Christian forebears with your children. What can these men and women tell us about the real God?

∞

Sit near the front in church so your children can see what's happening and feel more involved in the worship service.

∞

Talk about other religions with your children and compare them with your own beliefs. Prepare older children getting ready to go off to college that their beliefs about God may be questioned and even ridiculed. Make sure they are grounded in what is true and are ready to defend their faith. Consider sending high school or college-bound kids to a Mind Games Conference sponsored by Probe Ministries. Call 800–899–7762 for information.

∞

Read J. I. Packer's *Knowing God* (Downers Grove, Ill.: Inter-Varsity Press, 1973).

Read A. W. Tozer's *The Knowledge of the Holy* (New York: Harper and Row, 1961).

∞

Buy a copy of Henry T. Blackaby and Claude V. King's *Experiencing God: How to Live the Full Adventure of Knowing and Doing the Will of God* (Nashville, Tenn.: Broadman & Holman Publishers, 1994) or the *Experiencing God: Knowing and Doing the Will of God* interactive study (Nashville, Tenn.: LifeWay Press, 1990). Work through it alone or with your older children.

∞

Look for something new about God you can learn every time you read His word. Teach your children to do the same.

∞

As a family, start your day at the breakfast table reminding each other to be alert for God. Expect to encounter God every day.

∞

Take a close look at who you think God is. Where did you get this information? Can it be confirmed in His word? Do you think you know the real thing or have you constructed a mental image on your own? Ask your children how they see God. Teach them what is true about Him.

∞

"The man who comes to a right belief about God is relieved of ten thousand temporal problems, for he sees at once that these have to do with matters which at the most cannot concern him for very long"—A. W. Tozer. Read this quote at dinner one night and talk about what it means to you.

THE THIRD COMMANDMENT

YOU SHALL NOT MISUSE THE NAME OF THE LORD YOUR
GOD, FOR THE LORD WILL NOT HOLD ANYONE GUILTLESS
WHO MISUSES HIS NAME.

DEUTERONOMY 5:11

A good name is more desirable than great riches;
to be esteemed is better than silver or gold.
—PROVERBS 22:1

Chapter 5

GREAT GOBS
OF MUD

I GREW UP DANCING ON THE EDGE OF etiquette, to say the least. Precocious boy that I was, at age five I was the first of my friends to learn challenging finger gestures. My problem was figuring out when the gestures were appropriate. The day I shot my Sunday school teacher "the bird," I found out that there were some places where freedom of expression had too high a price.

I also developed the fine art of cussing at an early age. It was the lingua franca of the locker room, and I became fluent before most. As a preacher's kid, it was the easiest way I could convince my friends that I was a regular guy.

My problem here was keeping my languages separate. I spoke one vernacular on the playground and another in the classroom, at home, and especially at church. One slip of the tongue could easily ruin my sterling image with the new Sunday school teachers. (Maybe that's why we moved so often.)

There are some situations when the most satisfying verbal response is just not available. In other places a person might get away with more colorful expressions, but not in Sunday school.

There was one thing I knew though. No matter how angry I was or how bad my hammered thumb hurt, using the Lord's name in vain was strictly off limits—no matter where I was or who I was with. Ironically, after using every four-letter word in the book, I would light into a friend who happened to use God's name in profanity. Quoting proper King James English, I'd intone, "Thou shalt not take the name of the LORD thy God in vain." Anyone growing up within shouting distance of a church knew that the Third Commandment prohibited using the Lord's name as a cuss word.

So "spiritual" people like me made slight alterations using linguistic acrobatics. We came up with gosh darn it, geessss, tarnation, good golly, holy cow, and heavenly days. My personal favorite was dad-gummit. I liked to live close to the edge.

In most circles you could get away with these expletives, even on the church steps. But the mom of one of my seventh-grade friends knew the true source of these vulgarisms. We were playing Ping-Pong in his backyard, and I was losing. He served, "Ten to five." I went for the ball and whipped the air, "Dad-gummit!" I really thought this was a safe enough phrase to utter in the house of the "righteous." I missed three more shots in a row, "Dad-gummit! Dad-gummit! Dad-gummit!"

That's when his mom came charging out of the house. The screen door slammed behind her, and she stood there with her hand on her hip. "Who out here is cursing?"

I looked guilty while we listened to a short sermon that would have made Jonathan Edward's "Sinners in the Hands of an Angry God" seem tame in comparison. I saw the wrath of Yahweh in her eyes and swore never to profane that hallowed abode again.

To this day Ping-Pong makes me search my soul for appropriate expletives.

There are other things that make Bill search his soul for the proper expletive. I ought to know. I've been married to him for twenty-three years, and I figure that makes at least 8,395 occasions I've given him to look for the right word. I was raised to be a lady. So I learned the right thing for what you might say is the wrong reason. Ladies never cuss—not that they aren't tempted.

In fact, I'm very grateful to Bill. He's a very clever man. The first time I heard him say "Great gobs of mud, Kathy, what were you thinking driving forty-nine miles an hour in a thirty-mile-an-hour zone?" I knew I had a lot to learn from him.

So over the years we've both developed a colorful repertoire and an understanding of not swearing for the right reasons, which I hope we've passed on to our children.

Misusing God's Name

As I grew from a boy to a man, I realized that cleaning up my speech was only a minor part of complying with the Third Commandment. This command speaks against any improper use of God's name, as most modern translations point out.

> You shall not misuse the name of the LORD your God, for the LORD will not hold anyone guiltless who misuses his name.
> DEUTERONOMY 5:11

The particular word the Lord chooses to describe this misuse, however, was translated well in the King James. Vain means empty, useless, for worthless purpose. Literally: You shall not lift up the name of YAHWEH without reason. It prohibits not only the casual approach to God's person, symbolized by His name, but also the prostitution of the power of God for personal gain and the abuse of our personal relationship with Him.

If we keep our language cleaned up, that's great. But that's a minor part of what God is saying here. There are a host of other ways we can daily misuse God's name. If we do, we can be sure our children will follow our lead.

What's in a Name?

Why all the fuss about a name? Sometimes people misunderstand the power of a name. As its most basic function, a name symbolizes a person. So when we use someone's name in an offensive way, we naturally offend the person symbolized. Our son John, for example, is offended by people who call a toilet the "john." How we use the name of God tells us something of who we know Him to be and how we value His person.

A name implies a particular character and reputation. When I mention Judas Iscariot or Benedict Arnold, certain strong images flash into most people's minds. These men's traitorous actions were so heinous that their names have become synonymous with betrayal. On the other hand, George Washington and Abraham Lincoln are synonymous with honesty.

The fact is, when your name or mine is mentioned among people who know us or have heard of us, certain things usually come to mind. Often they associate our name with a positive or negative image. That's why Solomon reminds us,

> A good name is more desirable than great riches;
> to be esteemed is better than silver or gold.
> PROVERBS 22:1

Most parents take time to pick a special name for a new child. Of course we want it to sound good. But more often than not, parents pick a name because it has special significance to them. They like the meaning of the name, or it reminds them of someone they respect or love. We chose the names of our first two boys partly because of what the names mean. John means "God Is Gracious," and Joel means "Jehovah Is God." We named our last son after my dad—James Carr Peel.

There were some names we didn't consider because they had unpleasant memories attached to them. Perhaps you've heard someone say, "Don't ever mention my name in the same breath with that person!" It is because that name carries a reputation. Names symbolize the character of a person, positively or negatively.

The way we use God's name either reflects His true character or is offensive to Him, much in the same way that my son John is offended when his name is used to refer to a bathroom fixture. Since so much of our welfare rides on our perception of God, anything we do to distort His reputation is destructive not only for us, but for others around us, especially our children. That's why using God's name so casually that it dishonors His character is so offensive. We obviously can't hurt God, but we sure can hurt ourselves, and our children pick up attitudes of disrespect quickly.

I'll never forget my son's response to a presidential campaign several years ago. As we were watching television, he shouted out angrily, "You fool!" I was shocked and corrected him immediately. Whether I disagreed with the man or not, I didn't want to hear that kind of disrespect for anyone, much less a potential leader of our country. As I thought about it though, he had picked up this attitude of disrespect from me. Even though I hadn't uttered his words, I was guilty of the same disrespect.

A name implies authority. When I want to make sure my older boys listen to their younger brother, I remind James to tell them, "Dad said . . ." My name gives James the power to move his larger brothers, power he does not possess in himself. I not only tell James he'll get better results if he uses my name, I point out this is how Jesus wants us to pray. Jesus instructs us to ask in His name. Not because it is the heavenly "open sesame" to God's storehouse, but because His name caries authority. He has given us the right to ask.

> And I will do whatever you ask in my name, so that the Son may bring glory to the Father. You may ask me for anything in my name, and I will do it.
>
> JOHN 14:13–14

Not only did giving James the authority to use my name get him to get his brothers to act, it gave me a perfect teaching opportunity to say, "It's like this James. When you use my name to tell Joel and John to do something, they do it, right?" Then I quoted John 14:13 to him. That verse is beautiful, so plain and straightforward that even a fourth-grader can understand it. I had an opportunity to share with James something I know to be true about God.

> In that day you will no longer ask me anything. I tell you the truth, my Father will give you whatever you ask in my name. Until now you have not asked for anything in my name. Ask and you will receive, and your joy will be complete.
>
> JOHN 16:23–24

To pray in Jesus' name means that I ask by the authority and power of the one who bears that name. Asking in Jesus' name also implies that I am under that authority, speaking for Him or what would be His will. When we try to manipulate God's power to our selfish desires in prayer we are misusing His name. It would be similar to James using my name to get his brothers to take him to the store so he could spend all his birthday money on candy, something for him that I did not and would not sanction.

A name implies a relationship. To know and use someone's name, especially their first name, implies that we have an equal relationship with that person. When we hear our name called across a crowded room, we expect to see someone we know.

Often when Kathy and I meet someone these days they refer to us as Mr. and Mrs. Peel. Kathy and I both turn around to see if my parents are standing behind us. We prefer to be called by our first names because we want a less formal, equal relationship with people. When we allow someone to use our first name, to some extent it makes them our peer. It says I'm here on your level, not a pedestal. In the same way, when God allows us to call Him by name, He is saying I'm here with you. I want a relationship with you. Without sacrificing His transcendence, He comes down to our level so we can have a relationship with Him.

Young children often ask how they're related to Cousin Sally, Aunt Alice, or Uncle Tom. They see that these are people we care about, and what they're really asking is how do they fit in with them? What's my relationship to them? These questions just might be another teachable moment, a time to talk about how we fit into the family of God as well as our biological families.

Interestingly, God did not reveal His name to Abraham, Isaac, Jacob, or Joseph. God spoke His proper name for the first time to Moses in the Sinai wilderness.

> God said to Moses, "I AM WHO I AM. This is what you are to say to the Israelites: 'I AM has sent me to you.'"
>
> EXODUS 3:14

> I appeared to Abraham, to Isaac and to Jacob as God Almighty, but by my name the LORD I did not make myself known to them.
>
> EXODUS 6:3

Most modern English Bibles have used the term LORD to represent God's Hebrew name YHWH (from the Hebrew verb meaning "to be"). But God was not communicating a title. He was revealing His proper name. Out of fear of blasphemy and violating the Third Commandment, the Israelites never spoke or read the name Yahweh, but substituted the word "Adonia," meaning "Lord," as they read. Since the vowels were not written in ancient Hebrew, we have lost the exact pronunciation, but it was probably Yahweh, meaning simply, "I am." He is the preeminently self-existent one, and so He named Himself appropriately.

The revelation of His personal name indicated a new level of relationship and commitment. It was indicative of the intimacy of the relationship God was entering into with Israel. That new level of revelation indicated a new level of responsibility. The people had a responsibility of not abusing that intimacy. The great danger of course in grasping the imminence of God, his presence right here in our daily lives, is that we can forget about transcendence, that He is the Creator and ruler of the universe, the Lord on high.

Set Free by the Third Commandment

People of the ancient Near East considered the name of a god to contain certain implicit power in and of itself apart from any relationship. As such, they often tried to harness the power of their gods by using their names in curses, incantations, and black magic.

This commandment set the Israelites free from fear of pagan magic. God's power could not be used against them by the magical use of His name; however, it also meant that they couldn't use that power flippantly for their own purposes. He was still God. The implications go far beyond magic and incantations for both ancient and modern times. Any attempt to manipulate God for personal ends and violating God's character falls directly under this prohibition. Linking God's name to some purely self-serving purpose, from declaring an unjust war in the name of God to simply trying to add weight to your word in an oath violates the Third Commandment.

To misuse the name of the Lord then means any use that distorts His image, abuses His authority, or abuses or presumes upon our relationship with God. History certainly reveals the necessity for this command.

The Useful and the Users

One of the ugliest realities of the history of faith is that there have always been people who used their religion as a means of getting ahead. The 1980s certainly did not have a lock on phony faith. As long as good men and women have tried to serve God from a pure heart, there have been those who have used their spiritual position or the hungry hearts of others to line their own pockets. There will always be those who want to use the name of God for their purposes and those whose heart's desire is to be useful. Christ told His disciples,

> Not everyone who says to me, "Lord, Lord," will enter the kingdom of heaven, but only he who does the will of my Father who is in heaven. Many will say to me on that day,

"Lord, Lord, did we not prophesy in your name, and in your name drive out demons and perform many miracles?" Then I will tell them plainly, "I never knew you. Away from me, you evildoers!"

MATTHEW 7:21–23

P. T. Barnum said, "There's a sucker born every minute." And the church has had no shortage of men and women ready to put on a show to relieve people short on discernment of their extra pocket change. As Christ says, we can know them by what they produce.

Watch out for false prophets. They come to you in sheep's clothing, but inwardly they are ferocious wolves. By their fruit you will recognize them.

MATTHEW 7:15–16

Each of us needs to be aware of certain fruits or characteristics of the users, not only for ourselves, but our children as well. Cult leaders prey on unsuspecting young people who have not been trained to spot phonies. Just because someone names the name of God and does dramatic or supernatural things does not mean that he or she is being used by God. Even mature people can be led astray by following a charlatan until they are able to compare it to the real thing.

That was the case in Samaria as the church spread from Jerusalem. When persecution grew, early Christians began to evacuate Jerusalem. What are the "fruits" of a man or ministry being used by God? Follow Philip to Samaria.

Those who had been scattered preached the word wherever they went. Philip went down to a city in Samaria and proclaimed the Christ there. When the crowds heard Philip and saw the miraculous signs he did, they all paid close attention to what he said. With shrieks, evil spirits came out of many, and many paralytics and cripples were healed. So there was great joy in that city.

ACTS 8:4–8

Users want God to make them rich. There never seems to be a shortage of people who want to use God to get rich. In Samaria it was

90

a fellow known as Simon the Magician. Notice the "fruit" of a user in contrast to Philip as the account continues.

> Now for some time a man named Simon had practiced sorcery in the city and amazed all the people of Samaria. He boasted that he was someone great, and all the people, both high and low, gave him their attention and exclaimed, "This man is the divine power known as the Great Power." They followed him because he had amazed them for a long time with his magic. But when they believed Philip as he preached the good news of the kingdom of God and the name of Jesus Christ, they were baptized, both men and women. Simon himself believed and was baptized. And he followed Philip everywhere, astonished by the great signs and miracles he saw.
>
> When the apostles in Jerusalem heard that Samaria had accepted the word of God, they sent Peter and John to them. When they arrived, they prayed for them that they might receive the Holy Spirit, because the Holy Spirit had not yet come upon any of them; they had simply been baptized into the name of the Lord Jesus. Then Peter and John placed their hands on them, and they received the Holy Spirit.
>
> When Simon saw that the Spirit was given at the laying on of the apostles' hands, he offered them money and said, "Give me also this ability so that everyone on whom I lay my hands may receive the Holy Spirit."
>
> Peter answered: "May your money perish with you, because you thought you could buy the gift of God with money! You have no part or share in this ministry, because your heart is not right before God. Repent of this wickedness and pray to the Lord. Perhaps he will forgive you for having such a thought in your heart. For I see that you are full of bitterness and captive to sin."
>
> Then Simon answered, "Pray to the Lord for me so that nothing you have said may happen to me."
>
> ACTS 8:9–24

Simon was in the religion racket, and he wanted in on the deal when the genuine article came to town. There was a buck to be made. Teachers have debated whether Simon was a true believer or not for centuries. Whatever the case, Dr. Luke places the story here to contrast the faithful work of God with the phony—the person who is used by God and the person who wants to use God—or misuse Him. Since so many people mistake the staged for the spontaneous, it's helpful to contrast Philip and Simon.

Since many people have such a difficult time distinguishing the useful from the users, several questions emerge that we should ask of every ministry.

Who is the center of attention?   In the authentic work of God, He is always the focus. Notice who is on center stage in Philip's ministry— he proclaimed Christ. Mark this well. Jesus Christ is the focus, not a man or woman, not an experience, not a method, not a church, not even the miraculous. If you are drawn to Christ, you've got the genuine article.

That was certainly not the case with Simon the Magician. Even though he had "the Great Power" and claimed it was divine, the focus is on Simon, not God. There was supernatural power, there was even God talk, but God was not in it. Men who know God don't claim to be "someone great." All of us need to beware of the lure to center stage and of men and women who demand to be the center of attention. History is dotted with examples who have led hundreds, even thousands away from the truth: Joseph Smith, Mary Baker Eddie, Herbert Armstrong, Jim Jones, and David Koresh all took the place in their ministry where only Christ belongs. Many less radical have also plagued the church, individuals enamored with themselves and their success. They build a following around themselves. They hold themselves up as God's representative and call people to follow. But if their focus is not Christ, they are not following God. They're using Him. Don't follow them.

What happens to people?   As is always the case in God's work, people are set free. That was certainly true in Samaria when Philip brought the good news of Jesus Christ. The miracles performed here were not just signs and wonders. Satan lost his grip on these people. They were set free spiritually from sin and death and many of the physical effects of the fall of man—people were healed and released from demonic power.

Those men and women being used by God set people free. They didn't bind them up in legalism or authoritarian relationships.

Where Christ is, there is freedom, power, and real joy. When you see someone setting up a code of man-made rules, saying, "Do this and God will love you," no matter how good the action might be, that person is not speaking for God. God's love is unconditional and unilateral. Rather than bind you, God wants you to be free. Christ said,

> Come to me, all you who are weary and burdened, and I will give you rest. Take my yoke upon you and learn from me, for I am gentle and humble in heart, and you will find rest for your souls. For my yoke is easy and my burden is light.
> MATTHEW 11:28–30

That kind of freedom produces joy. A deep inner sense of inner satisfaction in response to the freedom we have in Christ. That's the work of authentic ministry.

What is the method? Users are often preoccupied with the spectacular rather than the basic. Even though Philip was doing spectacular miracles, the preoccupation was never the person or his power, but Christ. The miracles had no meaning apart from the message of Christ's redemption. They were present in Philip's ministry to authenticate the man and his message, not as an end in themselves. In fact, there is no such thing as a faith healer in the New Testament. Healing was always given to authenticate, to attract attention to something greater, never as an end in itself. The men who performed miracles were not known as miracle workers but evangelists.

If the method is predominant, even though the stated objective is to glorify Christ, He is not in the work. Christ does not take a backseat even to the work of His own power. When people are encouraged to be enamored by the person or seduced by the spectacular, and not with God, watch out. Men and women used by God don't put on a show—they exalt Christ. Paul's ministry was authentic. Listen to how he describes it.

> When I came to you, brothers, I did not come with eloquence or superior wisdom as I proclaimed to you the testimony about God. For I resolved to know nothing while I was with you except Jesus Christ and him crucified. I came to you in weakness and fear, and with much trembling. My message and my preaching were not with wise and persuasive words, but with a demonstration of the Spirit's power,

so that your faith might not rest on men's wisdom, but on God's power.

1 CORINTHIANS 2:1–5

What happens when things get tough? What happens during adversity is a good gauge of authenticity. The genuine, those used by God, flourish under persecution. Disappointment will thin the ranks of the users. A person committed to his or her own prosperity simply won't hang tight when things get tough. On the other hand to those seeking God's glory, adversity serves to deepen their resolve to go deeper into the wealth they have in Christ.

Users are generally preoccupied with things and money. When the cost gets too high, you can expect the users to get packing, but not so the useful. They are willing to endure hardship and deprivation to serve Christ.

You know we never used flattery, nor did we put on a mask to cover up greed—God is our witness. We were not looking for praise from men, not from you or anyone else. . . . We loved you so much that we were delighted to share with you not only the gospel of God but our lives as well, because you had become so dear to us. Surely you remember, brothers, our toil and hardship; we worked night and day in order not to be a burden to anyone while we preached the gospel of God to you.

1 THESSALONIANS 2:5–9

Who are they trying to please? Although we are commanded to be gracious, we are never called by God to compromise the truth to gain acceptance. Sin is sin, no matter how politically incorrect it is to identify it as such. Are problems overlooked or passed over because the price of confrontation is too high? The user will always serve his or her advantage first. If the word of God is offensive, it will be softened so as not to offend. The man or woman useful to God understands the need to call it as God sees it and speak the truth in love. Peter confronted Simon with the truth and called him to repent. Paul said it like this,

We proclaim him [Christ], admonishing and teaching everyone with all wisdom, so that we may present everyone perfect in Christ. To this end I labor, struggling with all his energy, which so powerfully works in me.

COLOSSIANS 1:28–29

In contrast, read how Paul describes the users we can expect in the later days.

For the time will come when men will not put up with sound doctrine. Instead, to suit their own desires, they will gather around them a great number of teachers to say what their itching ears want to hear. They will turn their ears away from the truth and turn aside to myths.

2 TIMOTHY 4:3–4

Unfortunately there will be men and women committed to their own prosperity and success who will accommodate them.

Who is the audience?   Users fail at a number of places, not the least of which is exclusivism. If you are in it for yourself, you serve only those who can serve to advance your cause in some way. Those useful to God serve anyone with an open heart. There is never an elite group, no spiritual aristocracy, no select group of the enlightened (which you can join for the right price). God's truth is open for every man and woman with a sincere desire to know Him. Note the words I've italicized in Colossians 1:28. "We proclaim *him*, admonishing and teaching *everyone* with *all* wisdom, so that we may present *everyone* perfect in Christ." *All* truth for *all* people so that *everyone* can reach the *ultimate* level of maturity.

We need to be aware of the characteristics of the godly and the godless, those who truly want to be used by God as opposed to those who want to use God for their own ends. If we don't, we may be caught up in their delusion. We need to teach our children to be healthy skeptics. They need to be wary of users, but ready to embrace the genuine works of God. They'll learn that from us.

We've all heard of brokenhearted parents whose young adult children have joined a cult. It's no guarantee, but one way to prevent our children from doing this is to make them aware of what a true relationship is from early childhood on. We can do this a variety of ways. We might help them see that it matters what happens to people, and we help them out even when it would be more convenient not to.

95

We might help them see that no matter how much they might idolize their church youth director, as young teens often do, the reason to participate in the group is to grow spiritually. We also need to ask ourselves why we go to church? Is it to worship God and grow spiritually, or because our pastor has a magnetic personality. It's not bad for a pastor to have a great personality, but our attitudes do rub off on our children. If our conversation around the Sunday dinner table is focused on something petty rather than on what we are learning personally, we might confuse our children. Unfortunately, it seems that some spiritual leaders use the wrong motives to get people involved and fall into the Simon trap. Or they soft-pedal real religion and substitute some kind of false feel-good group experience.

And we might, as always, share our understanding on a day-to-day basis about what our own relationship with God is really all about.

We're All Tempted to Become Users

Not everyone who has a user mentality starts a religious movement or hold himself up as a teacher. There is a much more subtle form of using God of which we need to be aware. It's easy for American Christians to develop a consumer mentality toward God. Here are some questions that will tell us if we are users or useful to God.

What is the major focus of my life? If anyone or anything takes the place of God at the center of our lives, we will have a tendency to view God as a useful resource to help us achieve our goals in some area of our lives. In fact, we will tend to see everything in our lives as subservient to whatever we put in the center. If our career and success are our central focus, God will be important only to the extent that He is helpful to us in getting us where we want to go. Christian symbols can be used and intended to say loud and clear that this business is run on Christian principles to honor God. Or they can be used because its good business in some parts of the country to advertise the fact that you are a Christian. The latter is just an advertising gimmick to attract business. I know business people who will walk out of a deal if someone mentions early on that they are a Christian. It seems that far too many men and women have used the name of Christ to create an opportunity but had no scruples when it came to honesty, much less ethical standards that honored Christ. They are flatly in violation of the Third Commandment.

Kids can use God, too. They might wear a cross necklace to get in good with a teacher who keeps a Bible on her desk. They might attend a Christian club meeting and go to youth Bible studies just to impress a certain classmate they'd like to date. Sad but true, no one is exempt from using God.

How do you respond when things don't go your way? What you do when circumstances run counter to your expectations tells a lot about whether you are keeping the Third Commandment. If you name Christ as your Lord and then become angry when He interrupts your plans, you're not only being hypocritical, you are misusing the Lord's name. If God is who He claims to be, then He has an absolute right to exercise sovereignty over your life. I have no right or authority to call Him to account for what He does.

The problem with most of us is that we want to be the master and use God as our servant. We have reversed the roles. We want Him to be like the genie of the lamp. Rub Him the right way, and He does what we want. When things don't go exactly to our liking, we shake our fist and demand to know why God is so unfair. This is one of the most destructive mind-sets we can develop.

We foster this in our children if we let them get away with the idea that we parents are here to serve them. I am amazed at the disrespect and selfishness that parents allow from their children today. Too many young people view their parents as servants. If they don't get what they want there's sure to be an explosion. Children who grow up thinking this way toward their parents will also think this way toward their God.

One of the most incredible attributes of God is that He does desire to serve us. Christ said Himself,

> For even the Son of Man did not come to be served, but to serve, and to give his life as a ransom for many.
>
> MARK 10:45

Just because our Father is committed as a good God to meet our needs, does not mean that we can treat Him as a servant though. The fact that He wants to meet our needs does not mean that He is required to do so. We must never lose sight of this fact. Late in his ministry, Paul wrote to his protégé Timothy concerning men who used religion to pad their bank accounts.

> But godliness with contentment is great gain. For we brought nothing into the world, and we can take nothing out of it. If we have food and clothing, we will be content with that. People who want to get rich fall into temptation and a trap and into many foolish and harmful desires that plunge men into ruin and destruction. For the love of money is a root of all kinds of evil. Some people, eager for money, have wandered from the faith and pierced themselves with many griefs.
>
> 1 TIMOTHY 6:5–10

The greatest of these temptations is to use God. When we do, we can expect God in His goodness to apply the correct amount of pain to help us relinquish this strategy.

How valuable is your word?   One of the most common ways men and women have used God's name is to reinforce the value of their word. According to Christ, however, if you have to use God's name to get people to believe you, you are not worthy to use His name at all.

> Again, you have heard that it was said to the people long ago, "Do not break your oath, but keep the oaths you have made to the Lord." But I tell you, Do not swear at all: either by heaven, for it is God's throne; or by the earth, for it is his footstool; or by Jerusalem, for it is the city of the Great King. And do not swear by your head, for you cannot make even one hair white or black. Simply let your "Yes" be "Yes," and your "No," "No"; anything beyond this comes from the evil one.
>
> MATTHEW 5:33–37;
> SEE ALSO JAMES 5:12

Godly character should stand behind everything we say. If we have to invoke the name of God to make someone believe us, then we are abusing our relationship with God.

Not too long ago, we had a good, but painful opportunity to teach our kids about the importance of keeping our word. We naively entered into a business deal that left us, quite surprisingly, with a huge loan to pay off. When we realized what had happened, we had two choices. We could choose to tell the bank that we had no idea we would end up being responsible for the loan, then have an attorney legally find a way for us to get out of it. Or we could cut back on our lifestyle, use our savings and anything else we could scrape together to pay back the loan. We chose the latter, and when the kids felt the pain of the lifestyle change, we were able to say that "a good name is more important than silver and gold." They understood our commitment to keep our word and stood by us in our decision not to dishonor God's name.

Does your walk keep step with your talk? One of the other ways we commonly use God is through spiritual talk to impress someone else. Most of us want other people to like and respect us, but when we put on a show to make people think we are spiritual, we are in trouble. But be sure, when my talk outsteps my walk, I'm not only making a fool of myself, I'm using God for my own purposes. Jesus said,

> Be careful not to do your 'acts of righteousness' before men, to be seen by them. If you do, you will have no reward from your Father in heaven.
>
> MATTHEW 6:1

This warning about the Third Commandment hangs over all these endeavors:

> the LORD will not hold anyone guiltless who misuses his name.
>
> DEUTERONOMY 5:11

Rather than deceit and abuse, God calls us to use His name in a worthy manner. Over and over we are called to sing praises to His holy name.

Aiming High

Forbidding our children to use swearwords and to take the name of God in vain is pretty easy. We simply lay down the law, and the result is probably that they don't use those words or expressions in front of us, unless they're trying to get our attention any way they can. It can and will take a lifetime to fully comprehend what this commandment is really about—discovering who God is to us and learning to talk to Him in the way that reflects our relationship with Him. Teaching opportunities abound in this area. For instance, when a child wants to know why Grandpa is called Big Papa. Or when a child calls a sibling "Stupid." This chapter is really about beginning to recognize those opportunities in our daily lives. Let the following ideas inspire your own ability to recognize the opportunities in your life.

∞

"It is not fair to ask of others what you are not willing to do yourself"—Eleanor Roosevelt. What would your children say about your choice of words when something unpleasant happens to you. Are you modeling responses you want your children to repeat?

∞

Talk with your children about why you wear a cross on a necklace or have pictures of Christ in your home. Even small children can understand this as a way of making God the center of attention. Ask them to help you think of other ways you can make God the center of attention in your family life.

∞

Let your children decide what they want to pray for, but talk with them about their desires. Is asking God for a brand new, zillion-speed, expensive bicycle a way of asking God to make them rich?

∞

Point out the small ways God is at work in your life. A miracle is not always spectacular. It might be a miracle that you get through a three-hour car trip without sibling arguments. It might be a miracle that you finish a project on time. Make sure you and your children take time to thank God for these small miracles.

∞

Take inventory of your own behavior. Have you been tempted to call someone un-Christian because she did not fit into your idea of who belongs to the family of God? Do you trot your religion out when it's convenient or might get you someplace and leave it hidden at other times?

∞

When things aren't going well for a child, take time to discuss the situation with her. Even a small child can have some pretty creative ideas about what God might be trying to teach her when her friends shun her because she's bossy.

Don't make promises to your children that you can't keep. This is probably the best way to teach them the value of your word. It's tempting and easier to say, "We'll take a family trip to Florida next year," when your kids are nagging you. But if you can't afford a trip to Florida or have no real intention of ever taking such a trip, explain that to them and tell them why.

∞

Swearing or cussing is often used to release emotion. If your child uses a word you don't approve of when he loses a game, talk with him about how he really feels. Talk about the value of discovering and articulating our true emotions, rather than hiding behind cliched expletives.

∞

Make up your own silly substitutes for swearwords for those situations, like stubbing one's toe, that just seem to demand them. Involve the whole family, and post your list on the refrigerator.

∞

Talk with your children about their names. Tell them why you chose them, perhaps what their names mean. (You can find this out from most baby name books.)

∞

Use a family dinner table discussion for each person to be able to say what he'd like to be remembered for in life. Parents can use this opportunity to talk about how their relationship with God affects their desires.

∞

Make a family tree showing more than the usual relationships—grandparents, parents, siblings, cousins, etc. Begin at the top with God, showing that the whole family are children of God. You might also include spiritual relatives, people from the Bible with whom you and your family particularly identify. For example, perhaps if you had a hard time conceiving a child you might identify with Sarah. Or as parents facing your child's departure from home, you might identify with Mary and Joseph after Jesus told them He had to be about His Father's business.

∞

Talk with your older children and teenagers about examples of people in the news linking God's name to their self-serving purposes.

Get in the habit of ending your family prayers with a phrase like, "We ask this in the name of Jesus."

∞

Choose nicknames for yourselves that reflect your relationship with God. These don't have to be names you come to use on a regular basis. They can be silly or serious. A daughter who is grateful for what God has given her might be Princess Full of Thanks. A father who spends much time in prayer might be called Harry Hotline.

∞

Get in the habit of singing God's praises by praying the Psalms together on a regular basis.

∞

We all make mistakes. A word you felt like saying, but didn't mean to say, might slip out. Turn this into a teachable moment.

∞

Talk honestly as a family about ways you could be using God.

THE FOURTH COMMANDMENT

OBSERVE THE SABBATH DAY BY KEEPING IT HOLY,
AS THE LORD YOUR GOD HAS COMMANDED YOU.
SIX DAYS YOU SHALL LABOR AND DO ALL YOUR WORK,
BUT THE SEVENTH DAY IS A SABBATH TO THE LORD YOUR GOD.
ON IT YOU SHALL NOT DO ANY WORK,
NEITHER YOU, NOR YOUR SON OR DAUGHTER,
NOR YOUR MANSERVANT OR MAIDSERVANT,
NOR YOUR OX, YOUR DONKEY OR ANY OF YOUR ANIMALS,
NOR THE ALIEN WITHIN YOUR GATES,
SO THAT YOUR MANSERVANT AND MAIDSERVANT MAY REST,
AS YOU DO.
REMEMBER THAT YOU WERE SLAVES IN EGYPT AND
THAT THE LORD YOUR GOD BROUGHT YOU OUT OF THERE
WITH A MIGHTY HAND AND AN OUTSTRETCHED ARM.
THEREFORE THE LORD YOUR GOD HAS
COMMANDED YOU TO OBSERVE THE SABBATH DAY.

DEUTERONOMY 5:12–15

Do not wear yourself out to get rich;
have the wisdom to show restraint.
—PROVERBS 23:4

Chapter 6

DOWNTIME

THE FRONT PORCH LOOKED LIKE A CYCLONE had hit it—overturned chairs, bodies, and scattered playing cards flew in all directions. But it wasn't a strong wind that had caused the disturbance on the Peel porch that Sunday afternoon. It was the appearance down the dusty road of a familiar Model T. As the black car topped the hill, my dad knew instantly it was the preacher. The visit of the Methodist parson normally would not have brought panic to the heart of the Peel cousins, but it was Sunday and they were playing gin rummy in broad daylight on the front porch. The boys stuffed the cards in every conceivable hiding place, including boot tops and knicker pockets just as the preacher turned into the yard. Yes, they looked as guilty as the cat that swallowed the canary when Brother R. B. Gordon strolled across the grassless yard toward the house.

The boys were all standing, awaiting their judgment when Brother Gordon spoke, "Are Mr. and Mrs. Peel at home?"

"Papa and Mamma are taking a nap, but I'll get them," my dad blurted out. He escaped inside before anyone else could volunteer or Pastor Gordon could object. Of course they were asleep. Mamma and Papa, my grandparents and the patriarch and matriarch of the Peel clan in Central Texas, would never have allowed such foolishness as card playing anywhere in their house on the "Sabbath."

Even though the boys escaped, the memory of that close encounter was so etched on my father's twelve-year-old mind that he could paint the word picture to me in living color some forty years afterward. My dad grew up in a time when most Christians would have agreed with the seventeenth-century Westminster divines when it came to obeying the Fourth Commandment.

> The whole day is to be celebrated as holy to the Lord, both in public and private as being the Christian Sabbath. To which end, it is requisite, that there be a holy cessation or resting all that day from all unnecessary labors; and an abstaining, not only from all sports and pastimes, but also from all worldly words and thoughts. . . .
>
> What time is vacant, between or after the solemn meetings of the congregation in public, be spent in reading, meditation, repetition of sermons; especially by calling their families to an account of what they have heard, catechizing of them, holy conferences, prayer for a blessing upon the public ordinances, singing of psalms, visiting the sick, relieving the poor and such like duties of piety, charity and mercy accounting the Sabbath delight.[1]

Fortunately, by the time I came along, things had lightened up a bit, but Sunday was still considered the Sabbath and there were certain things you just didn't do. The central act of obedience to keeping the Sabbath was worship, which meant going to church. If you didn't go to church, you might as well forget it. You had broken the Fourth Commandment. So we never traveled anywhere where we couldn't get to a church on Sunday. I had a chain of attendance pins that was so long it was embarrassing. I hated going to a new church full of strangers on vacation, but by the time I was a teenager I had met more people than Will Rogers.

However, even a casual reading of the Fourth Commandment yields no reference to worship. There was no church, not even a synagogue at the time. The temple had not yet been built. This ought to stop and make us evaluate our understanding of what it means to keep the Sabbath. That's certainly not to say that church attendance is optional for Christians. Both the habit of Jewish believers and New Testament Christians, as well as passages like Hebrews 10:25, make this clear.

> Let us not give up meeting together, as some are in the

habit of doing, but let us encourage one another—and all the more as you see the Day approaching.

What Does It Mean to Keep the Sabbath?

The Fourth Commandment is much more far-reaching and profound than where we spend Sunday morning at 11:00 A.M. and whether we watch the Cowboys on Sunday afternoon. The subject of the Fourth Commandment is not worship, but work and leisure, their place in God's plan, and the proper balance. Listen carefully to God's words.

> Observe the Sabbath day by keeping it holy, as the LORD your God has commanded you. Six days you shall labor and do all your work, but the seventh day is a Sabbath to the LORD your God. On it you shall not do any work, neither you, nor your son or daughter, nor your manservant or maidservant, nor your ox, your donkey or any of your animals, nor the alien within your gates, so that your manservant and maidservant may rest, as you do. Remember that you were slaves in Egypt and that the LORD your God brought you out of there with a mighty hand and an outstretched arm. Therefore the LORD your God has commanded you to observe the Sabbath day.
>
> DEUTERONOMY 5:12–15

Keeping the Sabbath means balancing work and rest. That's what the Hebrew word *Sabbath* means, by the way, rest. Ironically, the Westminster description sounds anything but restful. I'm a fan of the Westminster divines on many issues, but they were also a product of their time—a time dominated by thinking that made artificial distinctions between the ordinary Monday-through-Saturday tasks of life and God's work.

We all recognize that work and leisure are integral parts of life. But what most people don't consider is the place they have in God's mind. Many Christian leaders unfortunately still consider work to be a worldly impediment to spiritual development. These individuals have not stopped to consider that the positive part of this commandment covers 87 percent of our lives and tells us emphatically that we are to spend that time working.

Work Is God's Idea

Six days you shall labor and do all your work.

DEUTERONOMY 5:13

Since this is God's will, work cannot by nature be in direct competition with our spiritual development. This may come as a shock to some, but work was not invented by the devil. It is not even a result of the fall. Work and labor were around before sin entered the picture, and it will be around after sin's exit—because man was created to work. That's obvious in the story of our origin in Genesis.

> Now the LORD God had planted a garden in the east, in Eden; and there he put the man he had formed. And the LORD God made all kinds of trees grow out of the ground —trees that were pleasing to the eye and good for food. . . . The LORD God took the man and put him in the Garden of Eden to work it and take care of it.
>
> GENESIS 2:8–15

This being the case, work is not by nature a competitor for our devotion to God. In fact, God uses the very same Hebrew words to describe His work and rest.

> By the seventh day God had finished the work he had been doing; so on the seventh day he rested from all his work. And God blessed the seventh day and made it holy, because on it he rested from all the work of creating that he had done.
>
> GENESIS 2:2–3

God not only made us to work, He Himself is a worker performing a variety of "worldly" sounding tasks. In Genesis 1 and 2 He is superintending the earth, planting a garden, providing food, delegating responsibilities, and monitoring and disciplining His subordinates. When we look at Christ's life and ministry, a secular-sacred mind-set would lead us to believe that Jesus squandered His time on earth engaging in worldly activities. With the world to save, how could He spend His limited time running a small business, selecting wood, sanding tables? And even in His ministry He was consumed in large part with meeting the physical needs of people.

Keeping All of Life Holy

The Sabbath is not primarily a day of worship or a retreat from world-liness to "holy" activities. It is a legislated time of rest. Part of the problem that we have in interpreting this commandment is that very early in the history of the church, the pagan idea that material things were inherently evil and spiritual things were holy crept into the thinking of the church. That, of course, meant that physical things like work and play were unholy. Spiritual activities like prayer, study, reading, meditation, listening to sermons, singing of psalms, visiting the sick, and other duties of charity were things that were *really* important to God. The implication is that if you were really spiritual, you would leave the secular world altogether and do "God's work" full time, because any job outside of ministry is a colossal waste of time.

As a result of this view, more often than not, men and women to this day labor under the assumption that their daily work means very little or nothing to God. One friend told me he grew up in a church where status was determined by your work.

> ★★★★ Missionaries
> ★★★ Pastors
> ★★ Christians who went to Bible College

If you were working in a "secular job" and had not redeemed your-self by going to Bible college, you were a lowly "one-star Christian."[2] Kathy related immediately to his story.

Truth be known, being a church-staff wife had its good moments and its bad. Something that was particularly hard in one church where Bill served was the attitude that the church board held about women, especially women who were full-time family managers. In their minds, we were half-star Christians. If we did all the church volunteer work anyone asked us to do, we might work our way up to one star. If we happened to bring magazine-worthy hot dishes to fellowship dinners, we might gain another half-star. Sewing cross-stitch Bible verses for the church office could bring us up another half-star. I never made it past half a star. After years of feeling like a second-class Christian, I learned that all work—changing diapers, organizing pots and pans, and elder board meetings—was equally valuable.

Kathy and I both learned from that experience. All work is God's work. Paul makes that crystal clear in his words to the slaves at the Colossian church. Far from wasting our time, we need to see daily work not only as honorable, but as a matter of God's will.

> Slaves, obey your earthly masters in everything; and do it, not only when their eye is on you and to win their favor, but with sincerity of heart and reverence for the Lord. Whatever you do, work at it with all your heart, as working for the Lord, not for men, since you know that you will receive an inheritance from the Lord as a reward. It is the Lord Christ you are serving.
>
> COLOSSIANS 3:22–24

Notice the inclusive words—"everything" and "whatever." Mark it—if our work meets legitimate needs, we're working for God. In fact, only work that is inherently sinful is truly secular. Prostitution, bank robbery, and drug running are truly secular. Any other distinctions are not only unbiblical, but destructive. Hear what Paul is saying. We can go to work for the same reason we go to church—as an act of worship.

We have developed some rather strange ideas about God's will. If we think that the only way we can follow God fully is by going into vocational ministry or volunteering our lives away at church, most of us will miss our destiny. Think what would have happened if William Wilberforce, the man credited for almost single-handedly stopping the British slave trade, had left politics for "ministry."

When Wilberforce made a serious commitment to Christ, he went to John Newton to discuss whether he should leave Parliament and enroll in seminary. Newton, a pastor, wisely reminded Wilberforce, "Maybe God has you there for a purpose." Because Wilberforce remained in his "secular" calling, he not only became one of the strongest forces for Christ in his generation, but slavery was ended in the British Empire, largely because of his personal crusade —something that would have been impossible from the pulpit.

Equal to his passion to suppress the slave trade, and unknown to many, was Wilberforce's passion to impact British "manners"— not etiquette, but moral values. He had been born to a life of careless privilege, but when he came to Christ, he was tireless in his efforts to address the moral decay of his country. Again he chose to do this, not from the sidelines, but as one heavily involved in the so-called secular institutions of his culture. Os Guinness catalogs his impact like this.

> When he died, people acclaimed William Wilberforce not only as a great liberator, but as the arbiter of Europe. As one person put it, Wilberforce was not only the George Washington of his own country, but of humankind. Equally, when Wilberforce died, his own distinctive tradition of faith, evangelicalism—which was always a minority tradition in England—could be described as the single most decisive force in Britain and the rock on which the nineteenth-century English character was formed.[3]

When the church pulls away from the marketplace, bad things happen. Not only are future Wilberforces discouraged from the most strategic arenas of impact, but the marketplace, which drives American values today, is deprived of godly influence.

The Difference Between Worldly Work and Worldly Values

Even though work itself is not worldly, no one would question that the workplace today is dominated by worldly values. Christians need to beware of the potential temptations. That's why it's important not only for the church to reclaim a biblical theology of work, but for men and women to recognize that their daily work falls into God's jurisdiction as much as the preacher's work. Christ is as much Lord of the marketplace as He is Lord of the place of worship. If this is true, then my daily work—whatever it is—is His work. If it is His work, then it should be done in a way the glorifies Him. And if He is indeed Lord, the results are His as well.

My friend Doug Sherman, who has championed Christianity in the workplace for years, sums it up like this: His work—His way—His results.

Embarrassingly for overenergized, commit-now-pay-later women like me, Doug's paradigm ends up my work—my way—my results. Although I've learned a lot over the years about what types of requests to decline, I still catch myself saying yes to too many good requests. If I were honest, I would have to confess that sometimes my yeses are spoken from lack of trust in God. Will we be able to pay the bills? Will I ever have opportunities like this again? If I say no, what will they think of me? When I'm in this kind of mind-set, doing my work in my way, the results are usually mediocre.

What does this mode of operation say to my children? When I overbook and overschedule my life with work, I'm not sure exactly how many, but I'm breaking a number of the commandments. I'm stealing time that I should be giving to my children; my work rules my life, dethroning God from His rightful place as ruler of my life; and I'm certainly not taking time out to rest as God commands me to. I'm quite sure this is not what God has in mind for me, and it's not the example He wants me to set for my children.

Any man or woman who goes to work uninformed by a biblical view of work, is not only unaware of the necessity to carry out work under God's ethical standards, but is unconscious of the resources available with God as his or her partner. Both ethically, morally, and functionally he or she goes to work underinformed, and underempowered.

For the Ancient Israelites and for Us

The Fourth Commandment was a constant reminder to the Jews that their work belonged to God along with its results. It serves as the same reminder to us. God is a partner in everything we achieve. The purpose of the Fourth Commandment is not to get us to think about God one day a week, but to remind us that all of life in under His control. By placing the limit on work to six days, He proclaimed Himself Lord of the Israelites' work, as well as their rest in no uncertain terms. The full impact of this command might be lost to us if we don't stop to think about it from the viewpoint of an agrarian society.

For those of us, especially if we're men who want the world to know we're taking care of our families and living in twentieth-century America, success often means more prestige, a newer car, a bigger home, designer clothes, and better educational opportunities for our children. But for ancient Israel, the recipients of the command, success meant survival in a hostile wilderness. Individuals in developing countries today would understand immediately what it means. To work is to eat, to survive. Therefore, to take a day of work away from them might be a threat to their survival.

Imagine for a moment Isaac and Miriam ben Judah and their four children, a typical family settling in the Promised Land. They've set up their household, plowed their field, and planted a crop that they are counting on to be food for the winter. They work six days a week doing backbreaking tasks, and they are glad to set one day a week aside to rest. But it's now harvest time. It's Friday afternoon and the clouds begin to roll in just hours before the Sabbath begins. The whole family works feverishly, but there is no way to complete the job. Leaving the crops in the field could mean they will be ruined and the family will go hungry halfway through the winter.

There is little doubt what most of us would do in a similar situation. We'd work until the job was done. But the ben Judahs don't have that option. In obedience to the Fourth Commandment, they walk away, leaving their crop in the field. If God is not their partner, if He cares only for their spiritual welfare and not their physical welfare, they are in trouble. On the other hand, if He is as much the Lord of their work as their worship, the safest thing they can do is live in obedience to their Provider. That's why Moses reminded them,

> Be careful to follow every command I am giving you today, so that you may live and increase and may enter and possess the land that the LORD promised on oath to your forefathers. Remember how the LORD your God led you all the way in the desert these forty years, to humble you and to test you in order to know what was in your heart, whether or not you would keep his commands. He humbled you, causing you to hunger and then feeding you with manna, which neither you nor your fathers had known, to teach you that man does not live on bread alone but on every word that comes from the mouth of the LORD. Your clothes did not wear out and your feet did not swell during these forty years.
>
> DEUTERONOMY 8:1–4

It would be easy for the Israelites, just delivered from the devastating seven-day-a-week labor of Egyptian slavery, to reenslave themselves to work attempting to ensure their survival. But their survival was not dependent on them, but on God. Man does not live on bread alone—what we can produce—but on every word that comes from the mouth of the LORD—that is what He decrees and provides. Even though we may try, we cannot sustain life on our own, even working seven days a week. God must intervene. We can't do it on our own.

David said it like this.

> Unless the LORD builds the house,
> They labor in vain who build it;
> Unless the LORD guards the city,
> The watchman keeps awake in vain.
> It is vain for you to rise up early,
> To retire late,
> To eat the bread of painful labors;
> For He gives to His beloved even in his sleep.
>
> PSALM 127:1–2, NASB

Then to leave work one day a week was a act of obedience that reminded them that their work, its rewards, and their entire welfare was in God's hands. Today most of us don't worry about starving this winter. And being out from under the law, we are free from this sign of the covenant. But given the option, many of us end up working ourselves to death trying to ensure our success.

Working Ourselves to Death

It had been a busy morning. I had risen at 4:30 A.M., showered, and enjoyed a brief quiet time before heading down the road ninety miles to lead a small group meeting in Nacogdoches, Texas. Every Thursday morning at 7:00 A.M. I gathered with seven other men to discuss God, the Bible, and what in the world it had to do with their careers. After the meeting, I stayed to visit one of the group members. I left to head back to my office in Tyler with just ninety minutes to make a noon appointment.

It was just thirty minutes later, 11:05 A.M. Tuesday morning, May 26, according to the accident report, that I woke with the loud crash as shattered glass and torn metal were flying by my left side. I had fallen asleep and drifted to the other side of the highway. Instinctively, I threw on the brakes somehow stopping without leaving the narrow highway. I was covered with glass. My face stung and my shoulder ached as I opened what was left of my door. The entire upper half of the left side of my car was gone, scattered up and down the lonely stretch of East Texas farm road.

In the road behind me was a pickup truck with a large gooseneck trailer. The driver, who had been able to keep most of his truck and trailer out of my encroaching path, was unhurt. He told me by the looks of things he expected to find me as well as pieces of my car scattered along the road. I was actually fortunate he had been there. The road was lined with huge pine trees. If I hit one, I would have had little chance of surviving. As torn up as my car was, it could have been a lot worse. And miraculously my body had defied the laws of physics—rather than being thrown into the path of devastation, I was pulled by someone in the opposite direction.

As I rode in the ambulance the fifteen miles to the Cherokee County Medical Center, all I could think of was that I had nearly killed a man. I had neglected some of my own best advice.

We have an expression, "He's working himself to death." I almost did just that. While working harder and harder to ensure my success, I was slack in responsibilities I could not afford to neglect. I allowed my work to consume my heart and cloud my judgment. The bill came due that day in a series of poor decisions I made: decisions to rob myself of sleep, to crowd too much into my schedule, and to not stop and rest a few moments. After all, someone's eternal destiny back in Tyler rested on my shoulders.

God graciously interrupted my frantic flight that day and reminded me of the limitations of my humanness. The fact is that there is never enough of me to go around to do all of the things that need to be done and never enough time to do them. It seems that God has designed this world to remind us that we can't live without Him. This is what Moses was saying in Deuteronomy 8. It's also what Paul meant in 1 Corinthians when he wrote,

> I planted the seed, Apollos watered it, but God made it grow. So neither he who plants nor he who waters is anything, but only God, who makes things grow.
> 1 CORINTHIANS 3:6–7

No matter what your work, whether its business, government, medicine, or church, God causes the increase. This confidence brings us tremendous freedom to enjoy life rather than be consumed by it.

In the Gospels, we constantly see Jesus retiring across the sea, into the wilderness, or taking some time to rest. Here is a man on the most important mission ever conceived, with a three-year fuse, and there is never any rushing. Conspicuously lacking are the urgent agendas that fill so much of my life. If God would have sent me on

Christ's mission, I'm sure I would have died of exhaustion, not crucifixion.

In the Old Testament, God legislated rest on the Sabbath not only so man would rest, but so that he would have to trust God for his success for at least twenty-four hours every week. Today He has set us free from the law, and I can work myself to death if I choose. Or I can trust Him with my success and walk away for the rest I need. I can include the other parts of life that God thinks are important like raising a family, caring for my neighbors, and developing my whole being intellectually, socially, physically, as well as spiritually. I can take time to enjoy and enhance the beauty of life all around me.

If I constantly arrive home late at the end of the day with nothing left for my family, physically or emotionally, I have given more to work than I can afford to give. If I think that closing a big deal is more important than fulfilling a promise to help my child warm up before a big game, then I'm off-base. If I think arriving at the office early and staying late is better use of my time than helping with homework, then I don't know what's important. Far from contributing to my success, I have guaranteed my failure where it counts most, before God.

Kathy and I are always fighting for balance in our lives. It's all too easy for us to be consumed with work. We have to make a conscious effort to rest, relax, and spend time with our kids. Shooting basketball, playing Monopoly, building model cars, and reading a good book are equally as important as finishing a magazine article, being interviewed on a radio show, or speaking to five hundred people.

Keeping the Sabbath Holy

What about the seventh day? If the keeping the Sabbath didn't require synagogue attendance, what did it mean? The commandment itself seems to make God's intention perfectly clear.

It meant no work. For six days God wants people to work, but one in seven was to be set aside for a period devoid of the daily routines of life. He says clearly,

> the seventh day is a Sabbath to the LORD your God. On it
> you shall not do any work.

That's how they kept it holy—not by doing spiritual things, but refraining from work. Holy means separate, set apart. The Sabbath was set apart from the other six days by the absence of work—not because work was unholy, but because there is more to life than work.

It involved everyone. Everyone stopped work from the highest to the lowest. God makes this clear. Nobody works:

> neither you, nor your son or daughter, nor your manservant or maidservant, nor your ox, your donkey or any of your animals, nor the alien within your gates.

No one had a right to work or rest more than anyone else. No one could say, "When I gain financial security, then I'll take a day off."

It demanded rest. Interestingly, the Bible is not specific about the form that this rest is to take. That probably has to do with the fact that different people would choose different activities to fill their nonwork time. Inherent in the word *rest* is refreshment and replenishment. Life is filled with a rhythm of expenditure and replacement. The obvious implication is that men and women are not just machines constantly working, constantly producing. We must take time, even in a subsistence environment, to develop the other parts of our lives.

It was a statement of faith. It states clearly, that the one who keeps this commandment is trusting in God for his or her welfare.

> Remember that you were slaves in Egypt and that the LORD your God brought you out of there with a mighty hand and an outstretched arm.

Just as God was faithful in Egypt, He will continue to protect and keep His people.

It was a sign of the covenant. As circumcision was the sign of the covenant with Abraham, so observing the Sabbath was a sign of the Mosaic Covenant. It was a public acknowledgment that they belonged to Yahweh, and He was their God.

> Therefore the LORD your God has commanded you to observe the Sabbath day.

When other cultures saw this sign, they marveled at the Israelites' faith and commitment.

Keeping the Sabbath Today

Obviously a great deal of debate has gone on over whether individuals today are still required to keep the Sabbath. The answer lies in whether one is still under the Mosaic Covenant. In the New Testament Paul makes it clear that Christians are no longer bound legally to the Mosaic Law. In fact, he tells us that we should not let someone require us to make one day honored over the other.

> Therefore do not let anyone judge you by what you eat or drink, or with regard to a religious festival, a New Moon celebration or a Sabbath day. These are a shadow of the things that were to come; the reality, however, is found in Christ.
> COLOSSIANS 2:16–17;
> SEE ALSO ROMANS 14:5–6

How was the Sabbath a shadow and Christ the reality? Jesus brings us rest. The Book of Hebrews speaks of Christ as our ultimate rest.

> There remains, then, a Sabbath-rest for the people of God; for anyone who enters God's rest also rests from his own work, just as God did from his.
> HEBREWS 4:9–19

Christ said Himself,

> Come to me, all you who are weary and burdened, and I will give you rest. Take my yoke upon you and learn from me, for I am gentle and humble in heart, and you will find rest for your souls. For my yoke is easy and my burden is light.
> MATTHEW 11:28–30

In Christ we have been set free from the requirements of the law and the treadmill of good works as a way to gain God's acceptance. God has given us rest in His Son; the rest that we could never gain ourselves. So we can relax!

The Spirit of the Law

Even though Christians are not bound by the law, the principles of work, rest, and leisure still need to be applied to our lives. These are some of the most important things in life we need to teach our children.

Every day belongs to the Lord. Every day is holy, set apart to the Lord because He is the Lord of all life, work, leisure, rest, vacation, entertainment. The question of God's will should come up every day of our lives, not just on Sunday.

> And whatever you do, whether in word or deed, do it all in the name of the Lord Jesus, giving thanks to God the Father through him.
>
> COLOSSIANS 3:17

We can underscore this truth in our children's minds by starting each day praying together at the breakfast table and acknowledging that the day belongs to the Lord and that everything we do is for Him. We can thank Him out loud spontaneously during the day for our child's mind and ability to study, participate in a sport, or play an instrument. We can end the day by recapping the day's events and thanking God for what happened and praying for concerns we have about the days ahead.

If it's wrong on Sunday, it's wrong every other day. I don't have two sets of language, behaviors, or manners. One of the most destructive things we do to ourselves and our children is to foster the idea that life is divided into the secular and the sacred. If God is the Lord of Monday through Saturday, as well as Sunday, then we need one set of moral values.

If we aren't comfortable participating in something as a family or an individual on Sunday, we shouldn't participate in that activity any other day of the week either. The converse is also true. If we feel good about doing something on any day, Monday through Saturday, then we should feel equally as free to do it on Sunday. Each day is just as holy as the other, and every activity should be as pleasing to God on one day as on the other.

We can't guarantee our success. We shouldn't work ourselves to death. No matter how hard we work, we cannot guarantee our success. There are too many things out of our control. Market conditions, economics, government, health, co-workers, and even the weather affect our success.

Americans had a much more spiritual attitude when most of us lived on the farm. Men and women who made their living from the soil knew that much of their success was absolutely beyond their control. Right soil conditions mixed with the right combination of sun and rain, along with a lot of backbreaking work and help from their neighbors was required for a good harvest. After completing their work, most of our ancestors fell on their knees and asked God to send the sun and rain in the correct proportions. They knew their success required God's intervention.

Make it a habit to pray as a family and thank God for His provision for your life. When you have a big success at work, talk to your children about how God made it possible. Remind them that He is the source of your paycheck.

Take time to enjoy life along the way. You can afford to take a little time off if God is in control. None of us is safer than when we place ourselves in God's hands. Schedule some specific time to spend with your kids one-on-one and doing something fun together as a family. If you say you don't have time to do this, ask yourself if you really believe that God is Lord of your work.

The goal of life is not to retire. A life of careless leisure is not a worthy goal for a child of God. We were made to work and be productive. We also need to take time to enjoy life all along the way. To wait until the end of life to relax a little is destructive. Too many men drop dead the same year they retire. Even if they don't, they often find they have let their work eat the center out of their life, leaving them only the crusts. In other words, they have nothing to live for.

We need to teach and model for our kids that work is a good and healthy part of living created by God. If the time comes in later years to retire from a company job, we can ask God to give us work to do someplace else. It might be volunteering at a church or community service agency, it might be helping family members or neighbors who don't have the extra time that we do, or it may be starting a new profession. There are countless stories of men and women who started a new career in the later years of their lives and succeeded beyond their wildest dreams.

Life needs to be balanced. It's important that we try to balance the areas of our life—grow spiritually, develop intellectually, branch out socially, grow stronger emotionally, take care of ourselves physically, hone our talents, explore the arts, enjoy our family, and play with our kids. We can't lead a balanced life if we're working ourselves to death.

Leisure needs to be evaluated. Keeping the Sabbath (rest and leisure) holy not only means not contaminating it with work, but keeping those things that are *truly* worldly off the plate in our leisure diet. We need to ask ourselves if the leisure activity we're engaged in is morally pure? The lines between entertainment and indoctrination have been blurred today by sitcoms with a moral agenda. Hollywood has gotten us to laugh at and condone sin. This kind of leisure is probably not what God had in mind for us or our children.

Aiming High

If this chapter was as convicting for you to read as it was for us to write, we should evaluate our work and our schedules. Are we doing God's work in God's way, trusting in His results? Or are we doing our work our own way, trying desperately to control the results. Perhaps we all need to sit down, take a deep breath, and think about implementing some of the following ideas.

∞

"What shall it profit a man, if he shall gain the whole world, and lose his own soul?" (Mark 8:36). Evaluate how much you work and what it's worth to you and your family.

∞

Plan individual regular outings with your children. They each need some one-on-one time with you when you're not looking at your watch every five minutes or afraid you'll miss an important call.

∞

"Every man's work, whether it be literature, or music, or pictures, or architecture, or anything else, is always a portrait of himself"—Samuel Butler. What does your work say about you and your relationship to God?

∞

There are twenty-eight Proverbs that talk about the glory or benefits of hard work. Read one a day at breakfast and talk about how God feels about work and rest.

∞

Remember that all of life is sacred, whether you're washing clothes, driving a carpool, or writing a sales contract. Remind your kids that everything they do is sacred as well —playing in a soccer game, taking a math test, doing the dishes.

∞

121

Talk about this verse as a family: "Do not wear yourself out to get rich; have the wisdom to show restraint. Cast but a glance at riches, and they are gone, for they will surely sprout wings and fly off to the sky like an eagle." (Prov. 23:4)

∞

Take time to evaluate how you spend your time. Record for two weeks how much time you spend with each child individually and together as a family in meaningful relaxation and recreation. If you see it's not enough, schedule some time on your calendar to do this.

∞

Brainstorm as a family about recreational and relaxing activities you enjoy. Make a list of thirty-minute, two-hour, and all-day activities that you can do together. The list can be as long as you desire. Keep it handy, and try to do at least one or two things a week. Depending on the ages of your children, the list might include:

* Thirty-minute activities: Take a walk around the block. Work a crossword puzzle. Relax on the porch with a cold drink and take turns reading a good book aloud. Play cards or a board game.
* Two-hour activities: Build a model. Go shopping. Go garage-saling. Go on a long bike ride, or hike in a nearby wood. Peruse a museum.
* All-day activities: Go hunting or fishing. Go to a lake or beach.

∞

"That man is the richest whose pleasures are the cheapest" —Henry David Thoreau. Don't wait until you have a fat bank account to start scheduling some time off with your family. It doesn't take a lot of money to have fun together. Go on a family campout, take advantage of free community functions, plan an old-fashioned picnic.

∞

Look at the money and time you spend for recreation and relaxation with your family as an important investment.

∞

Make it a priority to do fun things together as a family. Get involved in a hobby or project with your kids—build a doghouse, have a family garage sale, train for a 10K run, breed and raise dogs, keep a giant jigsaw puzzle going.

Consider planning a family trip that includes work and relaxation. Plan to go someplace where you can be involved in a mission project for a few days, then spend the rest of your time at a vacation site.

∞

"Whoever trusts in his riches will fall" (Prov. 11:28). Whatever you are trusting in is probably obvious to your spouse and children. If you need to be honest with yourself and with them about being out of balance, do so.

∞

If you are not involved in worshiping together at church as a family, talk about why you're not. Consider adding this balance to your life.

∞

"I come to the office each morning and stay for long hours doing what has to be done to the best of my ability. And when you've done the best you can, you can't do any better. So when I go to sleep I turn everything over to the Lord and forget it."—Harry S. Truman. Try to make this your attitude.

∞

Ask yourself some honest questions to see if your life is out of balance.

* Can you find ample time for rest and leisure?
* Do you have a variety of outside interests in your life?
* Do you feel that your sense of personal responsibility has become so strong that you feel you must press yourself beyond your limit or the project, business, or relationship will fail?
* Are you consistently exhausted when you reach home and all you want to do is watch television?
* Do you find yourself getting irritated with your family when they make demands at the end of the day?
* Do you consistently take back jobs you have delegated?
* Do you take more than your load because you believe it won't get done unless you do it?
* When you finally plan leisure time, do you have a hard time relaxing?

THE FIFTH COMMANDMENT

HONOR YOUR FATHER AND YOUR MOTHER, AS THE LORD
YOUR GOD HAS COMMANDED YOU, SO THAT YOU MAY LIVE
LONG AND THAT IT MAY GO WELL WITH YOU IN THE LAND
THE LORD YOUR GOD IS GIVING YOU.

DEUTERONOMY 5:16

When you have children,
you begin to understand what you owe your parents.
—JAPANESE SAYING

Chapter 7

THE SECRET TO LONGEVITY

IT'S TOO LATE NOW, BUT WHEN TWO OF OUR children became teenagers, I realized we were foolish not to limit our family to a French poodle. I figure I could have maintained my dignity, self-respect, and a bank balance.

When our kids were young, I deluded myself into believing they would automatically grow up with a sense of awe and respect for us, their loving, self-sacrificing parents. After all, we're the ones who hocked the family jewels so they could go to the "right" preschool, gave up a cruise so they could have straight teeth, and lived without furniture in our living room so they could have furnishings in their tree house. (Note: Children's interest in a tree house lasts about as long as it takes to build it.)

Surely they would rise up and call us blessed, we thought, thanking God for giving them such sensible, virtuous, infallible parents. Surely John would thank me when I grounded him from television for watching more than his allowed time. After all, he was the oldest, he knew the rules, he knew the Fifth Commandment, and he knew his responsibility to set a good example for his younger brothers. I didn't expect him to ask me why his father didn't get grounded when he watched more television than usual. I kept my cool, and John and I had a little chat about nobody being perfect. That is, after all why God gave us parents, expectations, and rules.

As a matter of fact, all our children are quick to point out all the mistakes we've made, and I don't think that's all bad. After all, we're aiming high with them. They should expect the same of us. And they are, most of the time, gracious and polite kids. Since Bill and I have written books about parenting, they've promised (as long as we maintain their open line of credit at the electronics store) not to chronicle our faux paus to any network reporters.

It's not that we have a lot of dirty family laundry to hang out; it's just that since Bill and I harp on the importance of other parents practicing what they preach to their kids, our own kids are quick to pick up on inconsistencies in our behavior. Sometimes I think God is cooperating in their efforts. It seems that He has a way of holding me accountable in my own life for whatever virtue or character trait I'm trying to build into my children. What a drag.

When I get to heaven, I want to ask Him a few things. If He wants children to obey the Fifth Commandment and honor their parents, I'd like to know why the very day I'm teaching my children the importance of being good stewards of our money and resources, my banker calls to suggest I disconnect my private line to the shopping network. Or if I'm stressing the importance of being considerate of other people, why my kids happen to be with me at the grocery store when the clerk tallies my two carts of groceries, deducts my fifty-eight coupons, then has to wait while I send the kids running in three directions to get the items I forgot, only to discover that I left my checkbook at home. As James pointed out, the checker and the lady behind me were more considerate than I was. So I guess my lesson wasn't entirely lost.

But most embarrassing is when I'm in the car, waxing eloquent about how teenage drivers should learn early on to obey the laws. More than once a car with pretty lights on its roof has pulled me over—and it wasn't to tell me my car needed washing.

Although I make it hard sometimes for my children to obey the Fifth Commandment, they are still required to do so, as am I. Even at age fortysomething I would be foolish not to listen when my parents give me advice. They've been around longer and have wisdom about some things that only comes with years.

Grandparents, parents, kids—the family is God's idea. It is the foundation block for any culture. No civilization that has let this foundation crumble has been able to stand. Strong families make strong communities, strong communities make strong cultures, strong cultures make strong countries, strong countries make strong civilizations. And as I see it, that's really what the Fifth Commandment is about.

Importance of the Family

Kathy couldn't be more right about this one. She has a great sense of humor, but she's dead serious when it comes to talking about families. I thank God every day we didn't limit our family to that French poodle. Families are important. We've heard that line so much lately that we risk not paying attention to it. Or, worse, we risk shouting it from a bandwagon of one sort or another, without realizing what it means— why families are important and what our God-given responsibilities are to keep them that way. (Hint: It's not because kids should do what parents say so parents can feel better about being limited by God's rules, which is how some people seem to act.)

Families provide emotional stability. Everyone has a need to belong. As painful as relationships might be for some of us, we all want to know and be known by someone else. We call it intimacy, and it is essential for stable emotional development. The problem is that all of us, at some level, want to hide. We're afraid to be found out for fear of rejection. The family is the place that God created to shelter us from the stresses and demands of daily life, one place where it's safe. It's a place where we can get close to someone else, be loved and accepted for simply being a part of a family, not because of what we look like, what we do, or how smart we are. When a family provides this kind of emotional strength, children and parents have an incredibly stable platform from which to engage a shaky world. Without it, most of us would become lonely and depressed. We would be ill-equipped to master life's crises. When we experience this loving stability, we can also accept constructive criticism and soul-searching. It's much easier to accept criticism when we know it's coming from someone who really cares about us.

As I get older, I wonder how much longer I'll have the energy and stamina to continue wrestling with my three sons, two of whom are stronger and more agile than me. I can still hold my own with them one-on-one, but if they gang up on me, I'm dead meat. They completely drain my energy.

Many days, though, the boys have a way of serendipitously renewing my energy. A few weeks ago I was having a bad day. I was emotionally and physically drained. John called home from college to tell me that he was reading my book *Living in the Lions' Den Without Being Eaten* and that the book was really helping him through a hard time. Now this may not sound like a big deal, but believe me, an author's children usually don't care about their parents' books. An author's children, like all children, just want to know if there's food in the refrigerator, if their jeans are clean, and if their friends can come over Friday night. John's affirmation about my book renewed my energy to engage the world.

Families provide economic viability. The closer men and women live to subsistence, the more they need each other. It takes everyone working together for anyone to make it. That is one of the reasons that this commandment and the prohibition of adultery were so important to the Israelites entering the Promised Land. The family had to stick together if they were going to make it. Any force that threatened family stability also threatened their survival. Likewise, in early America, large harmonious family units were an important key to survival on the American frontier.

Today the economic forces that threaten the family are slightly different. We don't all have to work together on the farm. Many of us are blessed with more money and material goods than we really need. And that can be hard on families, because we put an emphasis on wanting and having things rather than working together to survive as a unit. If the family isn't used to working and pulling together, it can be catastrophic when hard times come. Rather than pulling together, our tendency is to blame, and we blame each other, society, our bosses, or whoever we think is responsible for our circumstances.

Families hand down cultural training. Home is where life charts its path. It's where young minds are shaped and the traditions and customs of a people are passed on from one generation to another. At various times in history it has been the chief place of education. Mothers taught children to read; fathers taught arithmetic. Mothers taught daughters to spin, weave, sew, and cook. Fathers apprenticed their sons as farmers, tinkers, and tailors.

At all times, the family is the place where faith is passed from parent to child. The key place where God intended His truth to be taught is the home, with mom and dad as the teachers. Edith Schaeffer compared it to "a perpetual relay of truth."

The primary place for the flag of truth to be handed on is in the family. The truth was meant to be given from generation to generation.[1]

If one generation fails, the relay is broken.

Families are a relational training center. We learn how to treat each other as human beings at home. Whether we treat others with respect and dignity or disregard and indifference is largely a matter of how we learned to relate to our own family members while we're growing up. How we settle conflicts, how we express love and affection, anger and frustration to each other, whether we respect authority figures—all of these things we learned at home.

The most potent force in a child's life is the modeled behavior he sees in his parents. C. S. Lewis's wife, Joy Davidman, recounted one of Grimm's fairy tales that illustrates this point in her book *Smoke on the Mountain*. It seems that a mother, father, their four-year-old son, and aging grandfather all lived together. The grandfather's hands were unsteady, and at mealtimes he often missed his mouth. Eventually they removed him from their table to eat in the corner, alone and in disgrace. After dropping his bowl one day, they took away his utensils, leaving him with his hands to feed himself from a trough. The parents shouldn't have been surprised, but they were when the father found their son doing a little woodworking in the shed. "What are you doing?" the father asked. "I am making a trough," he said smiling up for approval, "to feed you and mamma out of when I get big." Soon the old man was back at his place at the table eating from a plate. No one ever scolded him again.[2]

That kind of gives the Golden Rule—"Do unto others as you would have them do unto you"—a new relevance to us as parents. Children learn how to treat others, including how to honor father and mother, at home. We would do well to never forget that our children will do as we do, not as we say. If that isn't reason enough for us to treat our own mother and father with honor as they age, then the Bible gives us four other reasons.

Why Should I Honor My Parents?

This is the first commandment that comes with a promise. Several blessings are promised to children who honor their parents.

Residence in the Promised Land.   In the first recording of the Ten Commandments in Exodus, God told the Israelites,

> Honor your father and your mother, so that you may live long in the land the LORD your God is giving you.
>
> EXODUS 20:12

The continued privilege of living in the Promised Land was based on obedience. Playing footloose with the rules invited a deportation slip, which is exactly what happened several hundred years later when they continued to thumb their nose at God. Since the family is the primary source for revelation to be passed on from one generation to the next, and since parents are the key transmitters, dishonoring parents had a double impact. When children of whatever age dishonored their parents, not only was that act sinful itself, but they cut themselves off from the prime source of truth and God's will. To dishonor one's parents invited spiritual ignorance as well as judgment.

Prosperity in the land.   In the restatement of the Ten Commandments in Deuteronomy, as the Israelites were about to enter the Promised Land, Moses, under God's guidance, added to the original statement,

> Honor your father and your mother, as the LORD your God has commanded you, so that you may live long and that it may go well with you in the land the LORD your God is giving you.
>
> DEUTERONOMY 5:15–16

This is simple. If you cut yourself off from your parents, you cut yourself off from a full life. The Fifth Commandment not only guarantees that aging parents will be respected and cared for in their less productive years, it ensures that succeeding generations will not lose the wisdom learned about God as well as life in general. The generation that cuts itself off from the previous generation is destined to repeat the mistakes of its forefathers, thwarting progress and ultimately inviting economic demise and spiritual disaster. Dishonoring one's parents is economic and spiritual suicide.

Longevity.   When we come to the New Testament, the direct relationship of the Old Testament between obedience and prosperity has changed. Yet there is still an enduring universal principle that is applicable for all ages and all men and women. In Ephesians, Paul writes,

> Children, obey your parents in the Lord, for this is right. "Honor your father and mother"—which is the First Commandment with a promise—"that it may go well with you and that you may enjoy long life on the earth."
>
> EPHESIANS 6:1–3

Plain and simple, this verse promises longevity—long life on the Earth. Certainly there are times when the good die young—factors of disease or accident that are beyond our understanding or control. The important kernel of truth here is that those with rebellious attitudes toward their parents often live undisciplined lives that lead to destructive lifestyles. Moreover, even if a rebellious child enjoys the full length of days and economic prosperity, as long as he lives in rebellion, there will be no lasting peace of mind. God simply will not obligate Himself to bless persons who choose to live in rebellion either to Him or to their parents.

It's the right thing to do. Volumes, heavy tomes even, have been written to explain the dangers of disobedience, disrespect, and dishonor directed toward one's parents. More lengthy reasoning has gone into why it is in our best interest to heap honor on them, but the bottom line is pretty simple: we obey because it is the right thing to do. It pleases God. Paul gets down to it in Colossians 3:20,

> Children, obey your parents in everything, for this pleases the Lord.

The ultimate reason I honor my parents is not to be blessed and avoid problems, but because God tells me to.

How Do I Honor My Parents?

For children, honoring parents means more than obeying their rules grudgingly. For adults, honoring parents means more than hosting a party for them on their fiftieth wedding anniversary. Honoring one's mother and father means at least three things.

An attitude of respect.   As with all obedience, God is more interested in attitude than anything else—what's going on in our heart. To honor our parents then means, first, that we have an inner attitude of respect. Authority in general is at issue here, of which parental authority is the most basic. If we fail to respect our parents, it is unlikely that we will respect any authority at any level. In fact, Paul makes it clear that the one who rebels against authority is in rebellion against God Himself. The reason is that God is the source of all authority.

> there is no authority except that which God has established. The authorities that exist have been established by God. Consequently, he who rebels against the authority is rebelling against what God has instituted, and those who do so will bring judgment on themselves.
>
> ROMANS 13:1–2

This was no light statement, since Paul lived under the rule of the Roman Empire. He recognized that even Caesar's authority was from God. That did not mean that Paul had to obey Caesar when Caesar abused that power by requiring Paul to disobey God. Nor does it mean that children are required to obey parents when they ask their children to sin. It does mean that all of us owe a deep attitude of respect toward all authority—beginning with our parents.

That respect is based on our obedient attitude toward God rather than the personal character of the parent or other person in authority. It is an obligation that arises out of our devotion to God, not the person's worthiness for office.

Make no mistake. We are constantly sending messages to our children about how they should view authority, not only in how we treat our own parents, but how we respond to our leaders in general. If they see us constantly belittling church leaders, government officials, or superiors at work, they pick up attitudes that are dishonoring to God, the source of all authority.

Kathy and I have been through some ugly church fights. There were times I wanted to give more than a few people a piece of my mind, which I couldn't afford to lose. But I knew that even though these leaders hurt us, they were in authority over us and we needed to respond as respectfully as possible. We decided, though, to not share with our children all our struggles and disappointments. We felt that this would only cause our boys to take up the offense for us against the leaders and become angry and maybe disillusioned with the church as a whole. We asked God to help us remember that if we scorned the authorities over us, we were scorning Him and teaching our children by example to do the same. We find this principle in the Book of Acts.

When a member of the Jewish Sanhedrin ordered Paul to be struck, the apostle responded,

> God will strike you, you whitewashed wall! You sit there to judge me according to the law, yet you yourself violate the law by commanding that I be struck!
>
> ACTS 23:3

Paul was certainly justified in confronting the hypocrisy of this man, and yet when he discovered the authority this man had (even though he was abusing it), Paul changed his tune.

> Those who were standing near Paul said, "You dare to insult God's high priest?"
>
> Paul replied, "Brothers, I did not realize that he was the high priest; for it is written: 'Do not speak evil about the ruler of your people.'"
>
> ACTS 23:4–5

An attitude of respect for parents takes different forms depending on the age of the child. For young children, it means obedience. Short of sin, it means that mom and dad set the rules and kids have to obey them whether they like it or not, whether they agree with the rules or not. Personally, I've never known a child who automatically respected authority. It's something that they learn from parents, primarily in the way mom and dad kindly, but firmly, assert their right to rule. When we as parents refuse to set boundaries or enforce consequences for violating them, we are not doing our children any favors. We actually teach them that they are their own authority—a deadly attitude, not only spiritually, but socially and even physically. Nor are we doing them a favor by bullying them into submission. That may be an even surer way to guarantee their rebellion against authority.

Every one of us is born with passions that cannot be allowed to run wild. If they do, we will not be able to learn the self-discipline needed for adult freedom.

As children grow, parents must move from control to teaching self-control. As children become young adults, they need expanding freedom as they begin to exercise self-discipline to be in charge of their own attitude of respect. As we relinquish control, we teach our children to apply the principles of living we've been trying to teach them all along. The relationship is more like a player and a coach. The coach is still in charge, but the player begins to run the plays on his own. During this time, the coach gives basic training, correction, and encouragement. Young adults display an attitude of respect by heeding the coach's rules on their own, but not because they fear reprisal. They honor their parents by taking their words of correction seriously.

When young people move into adulthood, they move from their parents' authority to a personal authority of their own. Now they step away from their parents' responsibility toward a direct responsibility to God. As adults we honor our parents, not by obedience, but by respecting their advice, seeking their wisdom, and asking for their counsel. God requires me to make my own choices before Him. But parents ideally remain a tremendous source of wisdom and spiritual truth for their adult children when the parents are seeking to honor God themselves. Proverbs reminds us,

> My son, if you accept my words
>   and store up my commands within you,
> turning your ear to wisdom
>   and applying your heart to understanding,
> and if you call out for insight
>   and cry aloud for understanding,
> and if you look for it as for silver
>   and search for it as for hidden treasure,
> then you will understand the fear of the LORD
>   and find the knowledge of God.
>
> PROVERBS 2:1–5

Kathy and I have found our parents to be a tremendous source of wisdom. When we were young adults, we sought their advice about the timing of our marriage. We listened to their advice, and it seemed to us to reflect wisdom. When I chose a seminary, I consulted with my father again. I listened to his opinions and came to a different conclusion than he advised. My father honestly thought I was making a mistake, but I was convinced that God wanted me to go to a different school than my father had recommended. Although he had strong feelings, my father never tried to pull rank on me. I, on the other hand, honored him by asking for his blessing to follow the path I felt God was leading me down. He, in turn, honored me with that blessing even though he personally would not have taken that particular path.

If parents are not a source of spiritual wisdom, adult children must take responsibility for themselves to follow God. Adults are not commanded to obey their parents. Of course, some parents are not above sinful manipulative techniques to maintain a debilitating control over their adult children. Christ recognized this reality when He warned His followers,

> Anyone who loves his father or mother more than me is not worthy of me; anyone who loves his son or daughter more than me is not worthy of me.
>
> MATTHEW 10:34–37

Even in this circumstance, we owe parents honor, not contempt. We can disagree with our parents, not give in to their manipulation, and still show them an attitude of respect. Even if we have parents who don't show us respect, even if we have parents who abuse their authority, who abuse God's will, who live a less than godly life, we can be respectful in our disagreements with them. And we can respect them by forgiving them in our hearts.

Expressions of appreciation.   A second way we show honor to our parents is by expressing our appreciation for them. No matter how bad a job we think our parents did in raising us, there are probably things that they did right.

Like a lot of the sixties generation, Kathy didn't always have a proper appreciation for her mom and dad. I watched her attitude change, though. See if you can relate to her story.

One of the great privileges of Bill's four years at Dallas Theological Seminary was getting to sit under the instruction of Dr. Howard Hendricks. During one particular class he taught for the wives of seminary students, Dr. Hendricks gave us an assignment I'll never forget. He asked that we make two lists: one list of all the ways our parents influenced us for good, the other all the ways we felt that they failed us. Well, I didn't have enough space to list what my parents had done wrong. When I finished the assignment, I smugly sat back thinking what a miracle it was I had turned out as well as I had, considering their performance.

Dr. Hendricks then said if there were people in the class who couldn't list anything positive their parents did, they were operating from a base of extreme immaturity. I tried not to slink down in my chair too far.

That night in class I came face to face with my own immaturity and self-righteousness. Dr. Hendricks helped me change my perspective and begin to look for the good things in my parents instead of the bad.

Shortly after that class, I ran across a little poem that became my life philosophy, not only about my parents, but about everything else. I've tried unsuccessfully for years to locate the source. It goes like this.

> As you travel my brother
> Whatever be your goal,
> Keep your eye upon the donut,
> And not upon the hole.

Striving to live by this philosophy in relation to my parents has made all the difference in the world. As I've focused on the positive characteristics they built into me—a strong work ethic, the importance of honesty, the ability to look at problems as opportunities—our relationship has gotten better and better over the years. I came away from that course with three principles about honoring parents:

1. We honor our mother and father by first giving thanks to God for the parents He gave us.

2. We honor them by praising them and thanking them personally. Everyone needs to feel appreciated.

3. We honor them by forgiving them—just like we want our children to forgive us. No one, except God, is a perfect parent.

I'm just as grateful as Kathy is that she took that course. Through her growing understanding and changed behavior, she changed me. I think it's no secret that by becoming better children, we become better parents. And as with other things in life, it's not enough to learn new principles. We must act on them.

We can perform acts of service. Honor means more than attitude and appreciation. There is a concrete aspect to this command that cannot be escaped. The form of the Hebrew word "to honor" indicates "to effectively convey." This is the third way we honor our parents.

Obedience to this commandment means that children must meet their parents' needs in tangible ways, not just with words. Our parents have needs, and we as children are required to address those needs as God enables us, even to sacrifice if necessary.

One of the most important ways that we serve our parents is to remember that they have emotional needs like everyone else. As parents grow older, their world changes, and they lose more and more autonomy. Important decision-makers often find that few people pay attention to them after awhile. As children, we need to pay attention to our parents. This, of course, was less of a problem in ancient Israel where extended families lived together or in close proximity. Today we pay attention to our parents in different ways, such as writing letters, phoning them, asking their advice, spending time with them, participating in their hobbies, including them in holiday celebrations, taking them shopping, remembering special occasions, and trying to understand their world.

We serve our parents when we meet their emotional needs by continuing to treat them like adults. We should let them be autonomous as long as possible. One of the saddest commentaries on America today is the wholesale discarding of the elderly. As soon as we can, we park them in institutions where they often mentally and physically rot away. They deserve better than that. Children who discard their parents in such a manner, for no reason other than their own convenience, can be sure they have violated the Fifth Commandment.

A third important way that we serve our parents, obvious to the ancient Israelites, but often missed by us today is our obligation to make provisions for their basic needs. The materialistic culture of ancient Rome also had a problem of discarding its older citizens. This so angered Paul that he counseled Timothy,

> If anyone does not provide for his relatives, and especially
> for his immediate family, he has denied the faith and is
> worse than an unbeliever.
>
> 1 TIMOTHY 5:8

Our Lord Jesus had little patience with this either. He confronted the greed of the Pharisees head on.

> For God said, "Honor your father and mother" and "Anyone who curses his father or mother must be put to death." But you say that if a man says to his father or mother, "Whatever help you might otherwise have received from me is a gift devoted to God," he is not to "honor his father" with it. Thus you nullify the word of God for the sake of your tradition.
>
> MATTHEW 15:4–6

Taking care of our parents' physical and material needs in their old age, when their productive time is past, is more important to God than our gifts to Him. Even if it means personal sacrifice, we owe this debt of honor to our parents, if not as a act of love for them, as an act of love and devotion to God.

When, as adults, we honor our parents with acts of service, we are teaching our children to do the same, using the principle of incarnation. There is another important way we can teach our children this principle. We can see to it that they take part in the life of the family. Beginning in their early years, they have family responsibilities. They need to know that mom and dad are not their servants. You can put a sock on a two-year-old's hand and tell him to help mommy clean house by wiping off the baseboards. No, he won't do a very good job, but that's not important. What is important is that he understands that he's part of a family, and everyone in the family helps each other out. Sure it's easier to set the table ourselves than to teach a four-year-old to do it. But the young child who has everything done for him or her becomes the adult who doesn't understand what an act of service is and is likely never to perform one.

One of the saddest situations we know of is a beautiful forty-year-old woman whose parents spoiled her to the extent that she can hardly function now as an adult. Growing up, she had no responsibilities other than making herself beautiful every day. She treated her parents like servants, and they thought they were doing her a favor by revolving their lives around her every beck and call. She never had to serve anyone but herself, and she became completely self-absorbed. She never learned the importance of respect and service to others. Her inability to serve anyone other than herself has cost her three marriages, and at this writing she very well may lose custody of her children.

Aiming High

How good a job we do of teaching our children to honor their parents has a lot to do with our being the kind of parents that our children want to honor. It's hard for children not to honor parents who love them with unqualified love, who serve them and teach them to serve, who are obviously on their team, helping them develop into all God created them to be, and who are committed to placing themselves under God's authority, drawing on His wisdom and guidance for leading the family. Our children will respect us more if we are not afraid to set standards and rules for our family to abide by. See if some of the following ideas spur your thinking about teaching your children to respect you and about your being a parent worthy of respect.

∞

"Being powerful is like being a lady. If you have to tell people you are, you aren't"—Margaret Thatcher. Stop and think when you're tempted to scream and demand respect from your children. This is not an effective way to get it.

∞

Ask yourself this question about your young child's behavior: What disrespectful behavior am I laughing at today that I do not want to see repeated and exaggerated when my child gets older?

∞

Remember, if we want our children to honor us, we need to model this behavior by honoring our own parents. Do something together today to honor your parents, their grandparents. It might be as simple as picking out a no-occasion card to send them.

∞

When your kids push the limits—sassing, using terms like "my old man" or "my old lady," lacking gratitude, obeying with a resentful attitude—use the occasion as a teachable moment, not a time to lose your temper. Talk with them about the Fifth Commandment, about their responsibilities to you.

"Youth today loves luxury. They have bad manners, contempt for authority, no respect for older people, and talk nonsense when they should work. Young people do not stand up any longer when adults enter the room. They contradict their parents, talk too much in company, guzzle their food, lay their legs on the table, and tyrannize their elders"—Socrates, indicting the young people of Athens in 500 B.C. Take comfort in the fact that our children probably don't have less respect than any other children in the history of the time. On the other hand, don't lower your standards for your children.

∞

"Build for your team a feeling of oneness, of dependence on one another and of strength to be derived by unity"— Vince Lombardi. Teach your kids that a family is a team, each sharing privileges and responsibilities, each member giving due respect to the other, on each other's side and committed to each other's good.

∞

Foster an attitude of servanthood toward each other in your home.

∞

Take a look at yourself from your teenagers' perspective. Do they look up to you as the type of adult they want to be some day? Is there anything in your life that is causing them to disrespect you?

∞

"Yield to a man's tastes, and he will yield to your interests" —Edward Bulwar-Lytton. Think about these words. How might you work with your kids to let them know that your interests include their best interests? It is hard for a child to disrespect an adult who shows sincere interest in his world.

∞

Create opportunities for your children to spend time with their grandparents. Research shows that it's through knowing our grandparents—or not knowing them—that we develop our attitudes about what it means to grow old. Teach them a healthy respect for old age.

∞

If your child invites a disrespectful guest over to your home, when the guest leaves, instruct your child in private about respectful behavior.

∞

We were raised by imperfect parents. We are imperfect parents, raising imperfect children in an imperfect society. "Love covers a multitude of sins" (1 Peter 4:8).

∞

Be considerate of your spouse's needs to stay in touch with his or her parents.

∞

Everyone wins when grandparents are active in the lives of their grandchildren. They understand life's transience and can reinforce the continuity of love and spiritual values through the wisdom gained by experience. If you don't have parents or grandparents, adopt a senior citizen as a family.

∞

If you, as an adult, are at war with either of your parents, do what you can to make peace.

∞

Do not excuse children's rudeness or disrespect toward you just because they are angry or upset. If a child is rude or insensitive, insist on a sincere apology.

∞

Let your children see you having the courage and humility to admit mistakes and to take the blame when you are wrong. They will respect you more for it.

∞

Thank your parents for their input in your life.

∞

Remember, when you must inflict a little pain in the short run to teach your kids respect for authority, you are paving the way for your child to be successful in the long run.

∞

Be vigilant about your teenagers' friends. If they ask to spend time with someone you know has a high disrespect for authority, let them have the friend over to your house. If you see that the relationship would not be a healthy one for your child and that your child may not be strong enough to be the leader, talk about this openly. When one of our boys wanted to pursue a friendship with a boy we knew was headed for trouble because of his attitude toward authority, we had a great opportunity to talk about the importance of choosing good friends and the effect they have on our lives.

∞

Teaching respect for parental authority begins early. A two-year-old, if undisciplined, will become a disrespectful, surly six-year-old. If left untamed, he will become a scornful teenager.

∞

As parents, make lists similar to the one Kathy did in class. Use two headings, "Ways My Parents Helped Me" and "Ways My Parents Failed Me." Share your lists with your children. Invite them to make similar lists and share them with you.

THE SIXTH COMMANDMENT

YOU SHALL NOT MURDER.

DEUTERONOMY 5:17

*Raised voices lower esteem. Hot tempers cool friendships.
Loose tongues stretch truth. Swelled heads shrink influence.
Sharp words dull respect.*

—WILLIAM A. WARD

Chapter 8

WARNING: GROWING UP MAY BE HAZARDOUS TO YOUR HEALTH

LIVING WITH A RESIDENT THEOLOGIAN IS a stretch for a woman like me. I mean, I can't get away with anything. Don't get me wrong, I don't want to run drugs, rob a jewelry store, or stab the woman who cuts in front of me at the grocery store checkout line. It's just always having a constant reminder that what I think—my attitude—is just the same as my actions when it comes to breaking a commandment. This cramps my style a bit, especially when it comes to the Sixth Commandment. When Captain Bible tells me that anger and hatred rank right up there with murdering, I'm in trouble. Here's a case in point.

Over the past few years I've developed a love-hate relationship with airlines. I love them when they arrive on time with me and my luggage aboard, which is about once every presidential election year. I hate them the rest of the time.

I've thought about starting a skyways lottery. Each week participants would buy tickets for certain flight arrival times. Whoever picks the time slot for the flight that arrives on time that week, with the correct number of bags for all passengers, wins the grand prize. If there is no grand-prize winner (and many weeks, of course, there wouldn't be) the grand prize grows. Judging from my experience, a few lucky people would become independently wealthy.

Airline personnel can be especially insensitive to this problem of arriving late to a banquet with only the jeans in which you're traveling.

Recently I asked a ticket agent if he could route my suitcase through Portland, Phoenix, and Detroit before arriving in Tampa.

"Of course we can't do that," he responded indignantly.

"That's interesting, you sent it that way last week," I smiled, envisioning this guy's body outlined in chalk.

It was bad enough that I arrived at my speaking engagement without my suitcase and clothing. Then the airline refused to pay for me to purchase a few items I desperately needed before going on stage (antiwrinkle cream, cover-up for the dark circles under my eyes, blusher so I wouldn't look anemic, sealer to protect my lipstick from seeping into the wrinkles around my mouth). Just because I told the agent the topic of my speech was "God Looks on the Heart," he responded, "Then why do you need your clothes?" The nerve.

Sometimes our anger seems easy to justify. When our seven-year-old son came home with a note from his teacher saying that he'd cornered another kid on the playground and shouted, "Nanny, nanny, boo-boo, Stick your head in doo-doo," we were justifiably angry with him. What we didn't realize was that he was feeling left out and unloved. When everybody calmed down, we were able to discuss alternate ways of handling anger—his and ours. Sometimes anger seems insignificant. The littlest things will set us off. But Jesus says that anger and hatred are the same as murder, and that's very serious. Obviously, if I want my children to embrace the spirit of this commandment, I'd best get myself in gear.

What the Sixth Commandment Is Really About

Not long ago I read a story out loud with my morning coffee about a murder in Chicago. The police, after searching for nearly a year, solved the brutal murder of an elderly woman who had been beaten and had her throat slashed. The killer turned out to be an eleven-year-old boy. This was the second story within a few days that involved a child murderer in Chicago.

I think of my own young son and myself as a young boy. The horror of this story is shocking to most of us. The worst injury that most of our kids give or receive is a black eye. Increasingly, though, we're hearing about children and teenagers murdering adults and each other. To a growing number of young people, growing up is becoming hazardous to their health.

The Sixth Commandment, "You shall not murder," demands that we respect life. It refers only to the willful taking of another person's life—murder. Many of us may sit back smugly and ponder the evil in a person's heart that might lead him to take another's life. This commandment is something we relax about, "Finally, a commandment I don't have to worry about violating!" Well, we may have succeeded in keeping the letter of the law by never taking another's life in cold blood, but Jesus presses the implications of God's will past our behavior. We may not have blood on our hands, but do we have blood on our hearts? Christ hits us hard with these words from the Sermon on the Mount.

> You have heard that it was said to the people long ago, "Do not murder, and anyone who murders will be subject to judgment." But I tell you that anyone who is angry with his brother will be subject to judgment. Again, anyone who says to his brother, "Raca," is answerable to the Sanhedrin. But anyone who says, "You fool!" will be in danger of the fire of hell.
>
> Therefore, if you are offering your gift at the altar and there remember that your brother has something against you, leave your gift there in front of the altar. First go and be reconciled to your brother; then come and offer your gift.
>
> MATTHEW 5:21–24

When we let hateful anger run out of control, we will also come under judgment. Our attitude gives away the evil in our hearts. When I let anger dominate my life, I become the victim of my own hatred. Embarrassingly, in just the past twenty-four hours, Kathy and I have been our own illustrations of this principle.

I was out of town yesterday, and as is my practice, I called home to touch base. I wanted to hear Kathy's smooth voice tell me how everything was running like clockwork, and she couldn't wait for me to get home. Instead, I heard a frustrated woman tell me how, because I didn't check the pilot light before I left town, the heater wouldn't work, and she and the children were freezing. She lost a chapter of this book because my computer crashed. And she had to have her car towed from the grocery store parking lot when it wouldn't start, which meant she had to drive my car, which she detests. She was frustrated because of the time and work she felt were lost. And she was angry, which was wrong.

In response, I basically had two options. Recognizing that this was very unusual behavior for her and she was probably fighting her hormones, I could gently guide her back to rational thinking. Or I could get angry too and respond to her with a buck-up-and-be-spiritual sermon. I chose the latter, which was not my best move.

Today she asked me to help her find some files and retrieve some documents that were stuck in e-mail. When I sat down at the computer, my pot began to boil. I realized that my very creative, predominately right-brained wife was living up to the reputation of blondes. She had renamed and misfiled chapters on three different disks so that there was no way to tell which chapter was the latest edit. I was angry, very angry, which was wrong. Now Kathy had two choices. She could remember that we had been through this same scenario before and ask my forgiveness for doing something that is extremely frustrating to me, then gently remind me that I tend to get compulsive about "a place for everything and everything in its place." Or she could get angry because after twenty-three years I still don't understand that creative people get so busy creating that they forget details, like where they put the things they create.

Thankfully, we recognized our wrongs. When James asked if I was going to send mom to her room without supper because she hadn't followed instructions, we decided it was time to cut each other some slack. Not only had we been in violation of the Sixth Commandment, but we weren't exactly setting a very good example for our kids.

Tonight we are once again living in peace. We've both escaped God's anger through Jesus Christ. But the question is, How will we escape our own? How will our children escape? If we are serious about being obedient to Jesus Christ, anger is something we need to admit and deal with. We can begin by understanding the nature of anger itself.

The Causes of Anger

Generally speaking, men, women, and children become angry for three reasons.

Righteous indignation. Hatred for sin, injustice, and cruelty angers most sensible individuals. For those of us who love the Lord, anything that brings reproach to His name angers us. When we see abuse of someone's person, name, or emotional well-being, we become angry. This goes for kids on the playground as well as adults in the business world.

Physical safety.   The natural response to danger or physical pain is anger. If we stub a toe, we get angry. It's probably a self-preservation response. Interestingly, we have the same response when our emotional safety is threatened.

Personal satisfaction.   We become angry when we are frustrated by unmet personal needs. Each of us has an emotional tank that holds feelings of well-being, security, wholeness, and significance. When it is full, we are satisfied. When it is empty, we focus our energies on filling it. When these attempts are frustrated, and our goals for satisfaction are blocked, we get angry. It seems even babies have this response.

Anger is a strong emotion of displeasure that originates deep within our unconscious mind. Its anatomy unknown, it erupts into our conscious mind with a force that can be either incredibly destructive or extraordinarily helpful. By nature, anger is neither good nor bad in itself. In fact, anger is a God-given part of our emotional constitution. It is part of God's nature as well. He has the full range of emotions, just as we do, including anger. Jesus expressed anger when some religious leaders used a handicapped man to try to trick him. He is furious with injustice and the cruel way men treat their fellowman.

> He looked around at them in anger, and deeply distressed at their stubborn hearts, He said to the man, "Stretch out your hand." He stretched it out, and his hand was completely restored.
>
> MARK 3:5

I'm glad God is angry with evil and will finally eradicate it. His anger with sin is our hope that there will indeed be a better day. That is our only hope.

The big difference between God's anger and my anger is that His is always justified and controlled. Anger by nature is like gunpowder. It can blast away injustice or do irreparable personal harm. The effect and the consequences depend on who uses it and how it is used.

Used positively, anger is a most effective motivator. Anger pushes us past our fears and feelings of inadequacy. It enables us to call on reserves of energy and will power we don't know we have. It can also provide the motivation for both personal and cultural change.

Negatively, out of control and arbitrarily unleashed, anger is the most destructive emotion on earth. It is the cause of wars, murders, alienations, assassinations of persons and character. Uncontrolled anger never solves problems. In fact, it usually makes them far worse. It is often as harmful to the emitter as it is to the recipient. It's like throwing cactus at someone barehanded. You might hurt them, but you're sure to inflict as much or more harm on yourself.

I can be angry, I should be angry, but I must deal with anger so that it does not lead me into sin. When I fail to deal with anger, I create an opportunity for Satan to lead me into a sinful response. In Ephesians 4, Paul gives us an important spiritual principle.

> "In your anger do not sin": Do not let the sun go down while you are still angry, and do not give the devil a foothold.
>
> EPHESIANS 4:26–27

Anger must be limited and terminated. If we don't deal with anger, we allow it to fester and erupt into sin. In other words, if we don't handle it, it will handle us.

Four Ways to Face Anger

Repress it. Men seem to be especially good at this response. Oftentimes we deny emotions even to ourselves. Anyone who has ever counseled men has encountered someone telling you he's not angry, all while he's shaking his fist in your face. By some defense mechanism, people are able to deny the presence of anger to themselves. This is, without a doubt, the most self-damaging response.

When we repress anger, our inner being works like a pressure cooker. It can take most of our emotional energy to keep the lid on. Repression is destructive emotionally and often leads to depression from the sheer emotional fatigue of keeping the lid on. It is destructive physically and can contribute to a whole array of physical problems including high blood pressure, ulcers, and heart attacks. And if we're repressors, we tend to pass this trait along to our kids. We don't tolerate their anger, and they don't learn healthy ways of dealing with it.

Repressed anger is also destructive spiritually. It's just a matter of time before it leaks out in sinful responses: critical attitudes, blame, irritability, verbal eruptions, and violence.

Suppress it. Suppression has both positive and negative results. If we simply bottle up our frustration, the results will be similar to denying it. Breakdown and boil-over are sure to occur. We hold it in as long as we can, but one day the poison will come spewing out.

To suppress anger positively, the first thing we have to do is suppress our expression until we have had time to evaluate the reason for our anger and how it should be properly expressed. Many times this takes an incredible amount of spiritual maturity and inner strength.

In the Old Testament, when Nehemiah was rebuilding the walls of Jerusalem and trying to pull his country back out of 150 years of destruction and poverty, he got wind that the haves were taking serious advantage of the have-nots. He was rightly angry, but notice what he did.

> When I heard their outcry and these charges, I was very angry. I pondered them in my mind and then accused the nobles and officials. I told them, "You are exacting usury from your own countrymen!" So I called together a large meeting to deal with them.
>
> NEHEMIAH 5:6–7

Rather than take immediate action, he took time to ponder the matter. Only after carefully considering it did he hold a meeting and confront the issue publicly. Even then, wisdom dictated an appeal to do right, not a verbal tongue-lashing. I know it would have felt good to rack those greedy hounds up one side and down the other. Not only were they doing something repulsive, they were ruining the county's chances for recovery. Listen to Nehemiah's appeal.

> So I continued, "What you are doing is not right. Shouldn't you walk in the fear of our God to avoid the reproach of our Gentile enemies? I and my brothers and my men are also lending the people money and grain. But let the exacting of usury stop! Give back to them immediately their fields, vineyards, olive groves and houses, and also the usury you

are charging them—the hundredth part of the money, grain, new wine and oil."

NEHEMIAH 5:9–11

Because Nehemiah thought through the proper response to his anger, the nobles responded favorably and did as he asked.

Suppressing angry impulses is important for leaders and anyone who wants to grow spiritually. I need to recognize, not repress, anger, and then consider its proper expression. And I need to teach my children by my example to do the same. When our kids do something selfish to each other that makes us angry, instead of lashing out at them, we can ask them to go to their room, or the car, or someplace where you can talk alone and wait for you. We need to take time to get a grip on our own emotions. This may take a minute, it may take an hour. However long, we need to ask God to give us self-control and wisdom in dealing with the situation. Then we can kindly, but firmly, tell them that what they did made us angry, why it made us angry, and what they need to do to rectify the situation with the person they offended. This unpleasant incident is now twofold teachable moment about selfishness and dealing with anger honestly and in a controlled manner.

Express it. At some point anger must be released. Like a ball in water, you can't keep it down, no matter how hard you struggle. But unrestrained venting is no virtue, no matter if you are just being honest. You may feel better about getting something off your chest, but what value is that if you leave someone bleeding in the hallway after you have brandished your verbal sword? Paul tells us that our words are to be healing, not wounding.

> Do not let any unwholesome talk come out of your mouths, but only what is helpful for building others up according to their needs, that it may benefit those who listen.

EPHESIANS 4:29

Some people control their words very well but let anger out in their behavior. I sat across from Rick in his beautiful office behind the dark glass of the biggest bank in town. He hung up the phone red-faced and frowning. Then he looked at me and said, "I don't get angry. I just get even." I had overheard enough of his conversation to

152

understand that someone on the other end had no intention of keeping his word. Obviously, it was something to be angry about. But verbally abusing the person was not good banking, nor socially acceptable. As we discussed the problem, Rick told me that he had a long memory and would deal with the situation in his own time. He would simply maneuver to ruin the man quietly behind his back. Rick was handling his anger in an equally destructive way to himself and others.

If we're not careful, we can fall into this same behavior pattern as parents. If a child does something wrong, maybe something that has far-reaching ramifications on many people, something that we feel tarnishes our reputation as a parent, we might feel the urge to make her pay for the grief we've suffered. Taking revenge into our own hands, we might withhold our love and forgiveness, we might withdraw from the relationship, we might never let the child forget how she had hurt us.

Revenge is something only God is mature enough to exact. Paul reminds us of the godly response in Romans 12.

> Do not repay anyone evil for evil. Be careful to do what is right in the eyes of everybody. If it is possible, as far as it depends on you, live at peace with everyone. Do not take revenge, my friends, but leave room for God's wrath, for it is written: "It is mine to avenge; I will repay," says the Lord. On the contrary:
>
> > "If your enemy is hungry, feed him;
> > if he is thirsty, give him something to drink.
> > In doing this, you will heap burning coals on his head."
>
> Do not be overcome by evil, but overcome evil with good.
> ROMANS 12:17–21

Yet expressing anger is appropriate in some situations. In fact, righteous indignation in response to injustice and hypocrisy calls for a response.

Confess it.   When appropriate, we should be able to share our feelings without blame. Not, "You make me so angry." That's accusation, not confession. Confession simply states the fact, "I am angry about what has happened." Accusing someone else for making us angry is not only inflammatory, it isn't true. No one makes us angry. Anger is a response of our inner being. We are not victims unless we choose to be.

One thing is sure. It is always appropriate to express our anger to God. Before one word is ever spoken in anger, it should be expressed to God and reviewed in prayer. Sometimes that is the only place to confess it. Even though being able to express anger is an important part of any growing relationship, at times the cost is too high and the results are too destructive.

If we are not willing to acknowledge and limit our anger, Paul tells us that we will give the devil an opportunity. Literally, "give him room." We open the door to our inner being. Make no mistake, he will eat us alive. That's exactly the cause of the first murder. Festering jealousy burned out of control in Cain's heart. Listen to God's warning.

> Then the LORD said to Cain, "Why are you angry? Why is your face downcast? If you do what is right, will you not be accepted? But if you do not do what is right, sin is crouching at your door; it desires to have you, but you must master it."
> Now Cain said to his brother Abel, "Let's go out to the field." And while they were in the field, Cain attacked his brother Abel and killed him.
> GENESIS 4:3–8

As it did for Cain, sin crouches at our door. But in Christ we can master our anger.

Mastering the Monster

Anger has always been a problem to civilized man. Proverbs 16:32 tells us,

> Better a patient man than a warrior,
> a man who controls his temper than one who
> takes a city.

According to Solomon, it's easier to take a city than manage one's own anger. Here are four things we must do.

Recognize the message that your anger is sending. Our angry responses to the frustrations of living in this world are like red lights on a car's dashboard. They warn us that something is wrong under the hood. We need to pull over, stop, and evaluate what is wrong when we respond to our frustrations with anger.

The problem is that deep in our hearts all of us have developed worldly strategies for fulfillment. Even when I do good things, I can do them for the wrong reasons. I can praise a business associate just to get ahead. I can compliment my wife just to get sex tonight. I can serve less-fortunate people because of the affirmation that comes my way. I can seek positions of leadership because it makes me feel significant. I can discipline my children because I want others to know what a good parent I am.

Obviously these are motives that do not please God. But how do we see deep within our being to assess our motivation honestly? Often it is difficult for even us to see why we are doing the things we do. Fortunately, God has engineered the world to frustrate any plans we might have for the world to fulfill us. Our responses to this frustration reveal our true motives. Anger and all its excesses tell us clearly that we're doing it for ourselves.

We must confront and confess our motivation and change our behavior. Paul's command is clear.

> But now you must rid yourselves of all such things as these: anger, rage, malice, slander, and filthy language from your lips.
> . . . Since you have taken off your old self with its practices.
>
> COLOSSIANS 3:8–9

Put them aside. They're old strategies and old frustrations that don't belong to our new self.

Put your eyes on Christ. From our human perspective, life isn't fair. Sometimes, even when we do what's right, we are unappreciated or ignored or even attacked. God never designed this world to satisfy us. At best it can only postpone inevitable emotional starvation. If we continue to demand that the world meet our needs, we are hopelessly bound to a life of frustration. But Christians have the source of life itself: Christ. We have a choice. We can choose to turn to the source of life, who fulfills us and helps us escape from the destructive pattern of anger in our lives.

Refuse to let frustrations and irritations determine your behavior.
Endurance is important for more people than long-distance runners.
It is crucial for men, women, and children to live together. All we
need to do is read the newspaper or watch the evening news to see
that tolerance and patience are in increasingly short supply. When we
practice endurance, we don't let our frustrations and irritations rule
us. Offenses have a way of stacking up until the enlarging machine in
our minds blows things all out of proportion. (Of course, endurance
is not the same as denial. We may admit we're angry, endure the feeling, and patiently reach solutions, but not if we deny we're angry in
the first place.)

Keep short accounts. Keeping our frustration level low demands
that we keep short accounts with others. No one can afford to let
emotional debt build up. The person who pays the highest price for
unforgiveness is me. The longer we allow bitterness to burrow deeper
in our soul, the bigger the price to pay for its removal.

What does it mean to forgive? Forgiveness simply means that I
cover the debt. When someone offends me, in my mind they incur
an emotional debt. Our sense of justice demands restitution.
Forgiveness, on the other hand, demands that I pay the price myself.
It takes responsibility for someone else's offense against you. It says,
I'm willing to pay. I'll absorb the loss. Forgiveness cancels the emotional debt. It bears the pain of restitution and graciously requires no
price from the forgiven.

Of course our concern is the price tag. Like Peter, we want to
know just how high a price we are required to pay. We know how
some people operate and that this forgiveness thing could get entirely
out of hand. Then Peter came to Jesus and asked,

> Lord, how many times shall I forgive my brother when he
> sins against me? Up to seven times?
>
> MATTHEW 18:21

Peter thought he was being very magnanimous since the religious
leaders of the day set the price of magnanimity at three forgivenesses.
But Jesus responded,

> I tell you, not seven times, but seventy-seven times.
>
> MATTHEW 18:22

Forgive from the Heart

I don't know about you, but every time I read those verses, I get uncomfortable, like God is asking more than I can possibly live up to. Actually, He is expressing incredible confidence in just how rich He is willing to make us. It's almost as if Jesus is saying, "I'm the one bankrolling this forgiveness through you, and I'm loaded. So quit counting." To illustrate a point, Jesus told a parable.

Therefore, the kingdom of heaven is like a king who wanted to settle accounts with his servants. As he began the settlement, a man who owed him ten thousand talents was brought to him. Since he was not able to pay, the master ordered that he and his wife and his children and all that he had be sold to repay the debt.

The servant fell on his knees before him. "Be patient with me," he begged, "and I will pay back everything." The servant's master took pity on him, canceled the debt and let him go.

But when that servant went out, he found one of his fellow servants who owed him a hundred denarii. He grabbed him and began to choke him. "Pay back what you owe me!" he demanded.

His fellow servant fell to his knees and begged him, "Be patient with me, and I will pay you back."

But he refused. Instead, he went off and had the man thrown into prison until he could pay the debt. When the other servants saw what had happened, they were greatly distressed and went and told their master everything that had happened.

Then the master called the servant in. "You wicked servant," he said, "I canceled all that debt of yours because you begged me to. Shouldn't you have had mercy on your fellow servant just as I had on you?" In anger his master turned him over to the jailers to be tortured, until he should pay back all he owed.

This is how my heavenly Father will treat each of you unless you forgive your brother from your heart.

MATTHEW 18:23–35

Several things jump out at me from this parable. First, although God is just, it is also His nature to forgive. He is eager to cover the debt personally. The king, of course, is a picture of God, and although God loves to forgive, there is nothing requiring him to do so. Just as the king would have been absolutely just in sending his servant to prison, God would be absolutely just in leaving us to the required penalty of our sin—death. But like the king, He paid the debt Himself. He absorbed the loss. That shouldn't make us less grateful. The debt owed to the king in the parable was an impossible sum, the equivalent of $10,000,000. That kind of hit, of course, was not without personal pain, but not as incredible as the cost of our forgiveness, the death of God's own Son. God is infinitely able to forgive our sin as a result, and eager to do so when we call on Him.

It is our natural disposition to get revenge. Reasoning from our supposed poverty, forgiving someone often looks like more than I can lose. So we make them pay! We do this in two common ways, reprisal or retreat. We lash out verbally or physically in order to hurt them back, or we lock down, withholding love, support, and affection to punish the other person. In reality, the one we punish the most is ourselves.

To refuse to forgive is to invite torment. The price of forgiveness might be high, but the cost of not forgiving is immeasurably higher. If I harbor bitterness, grudges, and resentments, I am nurturing a monster that will eat my soul. Resentment might make a delicious meal, but the main course is me.

To refuse to forgive means poverty of the soul. It cuts me off from riches the enjoyment of the riches that are mine as part of God's household. Not only that, I'll not know the thrill of being used by Him as part of His great agenda on earth. God can't do much with us until we can be merciful to others.

How to Follow Jesus' Advice

How can I set myself free from this prison of my own making? First, I must forgive the people who have offended me. I must be willing to bear the pain of past offenses no matter how large the debt. As an act of my mind and will, I must confront my emotions and declare the debt canceled. The people in my life who have hurt me no longer need to pay. The standoff is over from my side.

> Bear with each other and forgive whatever grievances you
> may have against one another. Forgive as the Lord forgave you.
>
> COLOSSIANS 3:13

Second, I must change my attitude and behavior. Actions that stem from anger toward those who have offended me must change. Since I am a new creature in Christ I can treat people in an entirely new way.

> Therefore, as God's chosen people, holy and dearly loved,
> clothe yourselves with compassion, kindness, humility,
> gentleness and patience.
>
> COLOSSIANS 3:12

Third, once I forgive, I can never bring the debt up again. It's canceled. I must refuse to talk about it. Instead, I need to dwell on God's mercy toward me and His infinite love. And since Christ's love is initiatory and works in creative ways to express itself, I need to seek new ways to express my love for those who have offended me.

Fourth, I must allow God to erase the pain. As we obediently draw on Christ's love to change our mind and will, God promises to silence those haunting memories. God has erased a number of painful hurts and experiences for Kathy and me both. But before He could do that, we had to get to the place where we wanted Him to erase them. Strange as it sounds, sometimes it's comfortable to hang onto past hurts because they provide us with an excuse for not operating optimally in life. We reason that if a particular incident hadn't happened to us, an incident about which we feel justified in feeling the way we do, then we wouldn't be like we are today. This mind-set is not healthy for us or our children.

Fifth, I must seek forgiveness myself. Since conflicts are rarely one-sided, I need to 'fess up to my part, even if I was the minor player. Before I do anything else, I need to stop doing whatever might have been offensive and demonstrate my sorrow. I must then admit where I was specifically wrong without blaming. Unfortunately, the ball is always in our court. We never have the luxury of waiting for the other person to go first. Christ said,

> Therefore, if you are offering your gift at the altar and
> there remember that your brother has something against

you, leave your gift there in front of the altar. First go and
be reconciled to your brother; then come and offer your gift.

MATTHEW 5:23–24

Sixth, be willing to forgive again and return a blessing for a
curse. In fact I may have to forgive someone for not accepting my
plea for forgiveness. Evidently Peter learned his lesson well. He gives
us this encouragement.

Finally, all of you, live in harmony with one another; be
sympathetic, love as brothers, be compassionate and hum-
ble. Do not repay evil with evil or insult with insult, but with
blessing, because to this you were called so that you may
inherit a blessing. For,

> "Whoever would love life
> and see good days
> must keep his tongue from evil
> and his lips from deceitful speech.
> He must turn from evil and do good;
> he must seek peace and pursue it."

1 PETER 3:8–11

For those who love life, this is the way. Rather than lashing back, fos-
tering death, we can stimulate life by offering a blessing. If the person is a Christian, it will help remind her of who she is in Christ. If
the person is not a Christian, my life and speech will be filled with
grace to attract them to the Savior. Not only that, I also remind myself
of who I am. I don't deny the pain, but I actively lay claim to the life
I have in Christ and experience the wealth of His grace in my life. Far
from bringing death, I bring life.

Reconciliation is good, *and* it feels good. When Kathy and I reconciled our differences over those computer glitches, our whole
family breathed easier. I like to think that God breathed a lot easier
as well. And since James overheard our disagreement, our anger, it
was also important for him to hear at least part of our making up.

Reconciling with brothers is a big deal around our house, since
three blood brothers live here part of the time. (John is away at college
for most of the year.) We started early trying to teach them the importance of reconciliation after an argument. When natural teachable

moments arose, like almost hourly it seemed in their younger years, we sat them down and "indoctrinated" them, that is, we told them about our values and what they needed to do to reconcile with each other. It's important for kids to learn this at home so they'll understand the importance of reconciliation with other people.

Aiming High

When I'm stumped in any given situation, not the least of which is what a "good" mom would do, I have made it a habit to stop and ask myself the question, What would Jesus do in this situation? Especially when it comes to dealing with "murderous" anger and the Sixth Commandment, I've found this technique helpful on three levels. If I stop and think, I don't fly off the handle. But, more importantly, stopping to think about what Jesus would do puts me in touch with the Lord who gives an answer I couldn't have thought up on my own. And finally, when I'm tempted to react badly in anger to one of my children, no matter what he's done, stopping to ask the question usually gives me an answer he can learn from as well as I can share it with him.

The ideas here are about taking time to deal with the daily and insidious fact of anger in our lives. We all get angry at our children and our spouses, sometimes for good reason. But teaching our children how to express anger in proper ways, as well as how to deal with their own faults, how to ask for and receive forgiveness from themselves and others, and especially God, is perhaps one of the biggest gifts we can give them for their whole lives.

∞

"Do not let any unwholesome talk come out of your mouths, but only what is helpful for building others up according to their needs, that it may benefit those who listen" (Rom. 15:5–6). Talk about the meaning of this verse as a family. Let your children know that you want to be accountable in obeying this verse. Tell them to remind you when you don't.

∞

All of us lose our temper at times. When this happens, ask forgiveness and move on. Don't wallow in your guilt. Don't abdicate your responsibility just because you make mistakes periodically. It is okay to ask forgiveness from your children.

Identify the consistent conflicts in your home that cause tempers to flair—whose turn it is to feed the dog or do the dishes, how many minutes someone gets to play a video game, how much time can be spent on the telephone, etc. Meet together as a family and map out simple guidelines of fairness. Post them in a conspicuous place.

∞

Coach your child's baseball, soccer, or other sports team. This is a great opportunity to teach that good losers are winners and bad winners are losers.

∞

"There are two sides to every question"—Protagoras. Remember this when you're called upon to referee an argument between your children. Be sure to get all the facts.

∞

Sit down together and make a list of the names and negative phrases you would like to eliminate from your family's vocabulary—dummy, stupid, punk, I don't like you, You make me sick. Sit down together and talk about how each person feels when these things are said to them. Rid them from your conversation. Put each person in charge of him or herself. Have a chart with each person's name. Put a check mark by the name of the person who has a slip of the tongue and uses one of the off-limit words or phrases.

∞

"Be kind and compassionate toward each other, forgiving each other, just as in Christ God forgave you" (Eph. 4:32). Make this your family motto. Are there past offenses family members are still angry about? Sit down and talk about these honestly. Set aside regular times for family meetings to discern ongoing problems so resentments won't build up. Make sure everyone has an opportunity to add to the agenda.

∞

Create simple family rules about how you will and will not express anger. Never go to bed angry at each other. Settle disputes as soon as possible. We do not hit each other, no matter what. Make sure your kids get to help in setting the rules.

∞

Make repaying evil with blessing a family goal. Make a list of blessings you can use. "I love you." "Are you hurting?"

"What can I do?" "Can I do anything to make your day easier?"

∞

Living as a family means learning to put the feelings of others before our own. This means children, as well as mom and dad, exhibit self-control even though they feel like slamming a door, throwing something breakable, or hitting someone. Learn to talk out angry feelings openly and honestly. Physical exercise is also a good way to relieve angry feelings. Send yourself or your angry children to walk around the block a few times.

∞

Create your own set of family rules concerning acceptable behavior. Set them as a goal for every family member to strive to live by them—mom and dad, too. For example, a child's rule might be, "I will try not to leave wet towels on the bathroom floor." One of mom's rules might be, "I will try not to go ballistic when someone leaves a wet towel on the bathroom floor."

∞

Be careful not to provoke your child to anger when asking about questionable situations. For example, if you find a note in your child's room that refers to a friend's drinking, instead of trying to set a trap like, "Do you or your friends drink? No? Then explain this note!" say something like, "I found this note in your room that concerns me. Could we talk about it?" If you come across in a punitive, authoritarian, or mistrusting way, you'll have a defensive child who learns to lie, conceal, and mistrust you.

∞

"No pitching fits" was an early rule with consequences when our boys were small. From an early age children need to know this is not acceptable behavior. Explain the consequences in a way they can understand and follow through. Teach your kids alternative ways to ask for what they want or express with control how they feel.

∞

It is unreasonable to expect your children to heed your advice and ignore your example. Let them see you deal with anger and frustration in a positive way, for example, take them along when you go to the bank to settle a mistake they [the bank] made.

∞

A good test of character is how someone behaves when she is wrong. Talk about how it can make you feel smarter, bigger, better when you admit you are wrong.

∞

Home needs to be a safe place. This does not mean, however, that we should ignore or deny hurt or angry feelings. Instead we should speak the truth tempered with love and kindness, asking forgiveness when we wound each other.

∞

A violent home is the breeding ground for loneliness and depression in children. Seek counsel from a pastor or Christian counselor if you need help.

∞

Be aware that viewing violence on television increases aggressiveness, instills fear of becoming a victim, promotes indifference to victims of violence, and stimulates appetite for more violence. Decide on how much television you will allow your children to watch each week and stick to your decision. Decide what they can watch as well. Make sure they turn on the television to see a specific show, not to just see what's on.

THE SEVENTH COMMANDMENT

YOU SHALL NOT COMMIT ADULTERY.

DEUTERONOMY 5:18

How can a young man keep his way pure?
By living according to your word.
—PSALM 119:9

Chapter 9

Everything You Wanted to Know About Sex, But Didn't Know Who to Ask

OUR OLDEST SON'S FIRST DATE IS A NIGHT I'll never forget, much the same way I'll never forget dropping an iron on my foot. A girl in John's math class invited him to a Sadie Hawkins dance, a leftover from the time when boys did all the asking and girls had this one chance to invite a boy out. John didn't know this girl very well, but she was cute and nice enough, so he accepted.

The night of the event, after a forty-five-minute grooming session, he looked like an ad from *Teen Boffo*. New shirt, new slacks, polished shoes, bulletproof hairdo. He was prepared for everything except the girl.

When she rang the doorbell to pick John up, we all tried to keep our cool. After opening the door, I almost lost mine. The problem was simple. Her dress left a lot to be desired, like more fabric.

Immediately I began to worry, which is the greatest understatement since Noah told his neighbors they might be in for a little rain. This fourteen-year-old girl made Cher look like Mother Teresa.

At that moment I figured I had three options. I could conveniently trip over the dog and spill a two-liter cola down the front of her dress, then insist that she wear my long-sleeve, zip-up-the-back jumpsuit. Or I could pull her aside and whisper that John had a highly contagious skin disease spread by any sort of physical contact. Or I could get on my knees after they left and pray that God would protect them both from raging hormones. In a rare moment of self-control, I chose the third.

That night, Bill and I decided it was time for us to talk to John again and specifically about proper behavior with the opposite sex. Oh sure, we'd explained the birds and the bees and why Charlie, our mild-tempered Border collie, will try to jump a six-foot, electrified barbed-wire fence when the poodle down the street is in heat. But we hadn't talked about how to handle skimpily clad girls with ten arms, and we hadn't talked about why guys can be carrying on a perfectly normal conversation about math, or English, or football and all of a sudden they're undressing the girl they're talking to in their mind. And we hadn't talked seriously about committed relationships, which is really the freedom of the Sixth Commandment. Yes, it's specifically about adultery, but it's also about being true in our relationships without committing to more than we can, which is a good way to hurt others. What remaining true to one person allows us to do is to have the freedom to really learn to love and trust. We wanted John to know that his relationship with God and his future wife depended in large part on how he conducted himself now, something that's not easy to teach kids.

It's in the Air

I shared Kathy's trepidation the night of John's first date. My prayer was that we'd laid the groundwork with John, and that God would give me the wisdom, courage, and persistence I'd need to continue talking with him and to set a good example of a man in a committed relationship. After all, I am just one person, a sort of David against the Goliath of popular culture.

We live in a day when our minds are bombarded with sexual messages. Not only is our society relaxed about what the Bible brands sin, but advertisers have figured out that sex sells. Television, movies, and literature have introduced us all to almost every possible human experience in a context that more often than not treats sin as simply a viable, alternative lifestyle. Everywhere we look a virtual exposition of sexual pathology confronts us. Today we laugh at homosexuality and promiscuity on sitcoms, and we celebrate adultery when it's presented like it is in the moving tale of *The Bridges of Madison County* — all to our harm.

Sex is all around us, and one thing is for sure. If we don't talk to our kids about such things as sexuality, masturbation, and relationships with the opposite sex, they will get the information on their own from the media or from the most prevalent transmitters of sexual information, their peers. The most common sexually transmitted disease is bad information from one's friends.

Personally, Kathy and I don't want another gland-driven teenager in the locker room bringing our boys up to speed on the pleasures of sex. Nor do we want an insecure girl giving them anatomy lessons. But that's how most of today's teens, or even children, get the lowdown. In his book *What I Wish My Parents Knew About My Sexuality*, Josh McDowell reported that only 32% of teenage girls and 18% of teenage boys were informed about sex from their parents. Fifty-three percent of the boys and 42% of the girls found out from their classmates. Even more frightening, 56% acquired their basic knowledge of sex between the sixth and ninth grades and 18% before the fifth grade.[1] Left on their own, kids will get the information—bad information. Unfortunately, bad information almost always produces faulty thinking, and faulty thinking will result in sinful behavior. As always, sinful behavior destroys people's lives. Like all of the greatest God-given pleasures, pursued without restraint, sex can be incredibly destructive.

I just returned from a trip to New Orleans where my room overlooked the Mississippi River. That mighty river looked so peaceful and calm, contained by its banks, ever flowing toward the Gulf of Mexico. It has been the lifeblood of commerce and transportation in mid-America for almost two centuries, bringing progress to the region and bounty to those who took advantage of the fertile soil or harnessed the flowing highway from north to south. Yet very recently, the Mississippi overflowed its banks, destroying farms, homes, and lives, anything in the path of its advancing waters. Some families and towns will never be the same. Others will take years to get things back together after the floods of 1993.

The Benefits of Boundaries

That the Mississippi overflowed its boundaries is a natural phenomenon, inevitable despite man-made dikes and other flood-prevention measures. That human beings should be tempted, because of our sinful nature, to overflow God's boundaries or limitations, to run rampant as a river is also inevitable. But, our flood-prevention measures are not man-made. They are God-given and empowered. With the Sixth Commandment, God teaches us how to stay within the boundaries of commitment and love by placing a levy to contain our sexual appetites. He says simply, You shall not commit adultery.

No discussion, no qualification, no exception. One cannot leave the marital relationship for any form of sexual expression for any reason without violating God's will. Elsewhere the Bible forbids promiscuous sex between the unmarried (Num. 25:1), prostitution (Deut. 22:21), and homosexuality (Judges 19:22; Lev. 8:1–36; Deut. 23:17–18). Clearly God meant the incredibly beautiful gift of sex to be enjoyed by men and women flowing within the banks of a long-term, committed, monogamous marriage relationship. When the levies break, before or after marriage, we can expect devastation.

But there is something even more insidiously destructive about adultery. Adultery implies unfaithfulness and covenant breaking. It was called "the great sin" by the Jews because God uses the husband-wife as a model for the divine-human relationship. It is exceedingly un-God-like to be unfaithful. It not only destroys relationships, it warps the faith of the next generation.

Adultery is one of the most socially destructive forces in any culture because it destroys families. No people can expect to remain free who willingly dissolve the family unit that God designed as the launching pad of life. Adultery is a violation of the most sacred of human relationships, the commitment of one man and one woman to each other. Without this foundation, the family will stumble and society cannot flourish.

There are also personal results. Forget the threat of AIDS, forget the menace of sexually transmitted diseases. Adultery destroys families, and that will effect our personal health. A recent public service announcement from the Christian Medical and Dental Society reported the following:

> Scientific studies show that divorced men are more than twice as likely to die from respiratory cancer—and more than four times as likely to die from other forms of cancer. In fact. medical research shows that divorced men and women are much more likely to die before the age of sixty-five. While some medical experts once discarded God's Word as irrelevant, new scientific research discoveries are

proving that the Scriptures hold some very important secrets for healthful living. If we want to avoid these pit falls ourselves, we need to know both the beauty and the danger of sex.[2]

The Gift of Sex

Focusing on the destructive, self-obsessive potential of the human sexual drive, no small number of individuals have developed a very negative view of sex. But, from God's perspective, sex is without a doubt one of His greatest gifts, intended for our pleasure. Whoever said that our most important sex organ was our brain was right. Faulty thinking about God's view of sex has robbed countless people of the pleasures He has given us to enjoy and produced guilt and heartache from the beginning of time. Yes, there are forms of sexual expression that are forbidden and condemned by God, but that does not change God's mind about His gift. Unfortunately, God's statements about the sinful expressions of sexuality have often been misunderstood as condemning all sexual expression.

The operative word when I was growing up in the 1950s was "nasty." Many of us were raised to think of our own bodies, our sexual organs as "dirty." This view has produced a load of guilt and repugnance in general for even legitimate sexual expression. It has certainly crippled marriages and created an atmosphere that encouraged adultery rather than inhibited it.

Far from biblical, this idea actually comes from pagan philosophy that considers the physical world as unholy and base. They believed that the pleasures of this world were distractions from that which was truly important and should therefore be rejected. They viewed the magnetic effect of these pleasures as things that actually separated us from God. Nothing could be further from the truth.

Unfortunately, this philosophy worked its way into the church. It still leads some to conclude that sexual pleasure is repugnant, and the only reason a Christian should engage in sex is for reproduction. As parents, we need to be careful not to pass on these negative impressions to our children. The way we talk about sex and sexual organs should always be with a great deal of respect for what God has created.

The origin of sex. Let's be very clear about God's view of sex from His own word. First of all, sex is God's idea. It was not thought up by some prehistoric Hugh Hefner. Adam and Eve came fully equipped with sex organs and sexual desires to fulfill the purpose God gave them.

> So God created man in his own image,
>> in the image of God he created him;
>> male and female he created them.

> God blessed them and said to them, "Be fruitful and increase in number; fill the earth and subdue it. Rule over the fish of the sea and the birds of the air and over every living creature that moves on the ground." . . .
> God saw all that he had made, and it was very good. And there was evening, and there was morning—the sixth day.
>> GENESIS 1:27–28, 31

When God commanded Adam and Eve to populate the earth, He didn't have spontaneous regeneration in mind, and I doubt they needed much encouragement to obey.

The purpose of sex.   Christians for the most part have always held that reproduction was a legitimate purpose for sex. But Genesis also tells us something about how God intends for children to raised. Just as a man and woman cooperate together to bring children into the world, they are to cooperate in rearing them. However, there are at least two other divinely ordained reasons for sex given in the Bible.

Sex was given as an expression of spiritual oneness and intimacy. The second chapter of Genesis makes this clear.

> For this reason a man will leave his father and mother and be united to his wife, and they will become one flesh.
>> The man and his wife were both naked, and they felt no shame.
>> GENESIS 2:24–25

When our bodies come together in sexual union, not only is life possible, but an intimate spiritual union takes place—two become one. Sex is meant to be the ultimate expression of oneness. When a man and woman come together sexually in a context of mutual respect, honor, commitment, and delight, they experience not only physical openness, but emotional openness that every one of us craves—the joy of knowing and being known. In fact, the phrase that the Bible often uses to describe sexual intercourse is of a man knowing a woman. Sex is for intimacy. Sex is also for pleasure.

The nature of sexual pleasure. Sex is not sin. Like any gift it can be misused, but by nature it is good. And no amount of misuse or abuse can change that fact. Sexual intercourse is a beautiful gift given to every married couple from God Himself. It is a thrilling physical, emotional, and spiritual experience that no married couple should shun or be ashamed of. There should be no guilt or shame of the desire, the act, or our sexual organs. They are all part of God's gift. Hebrews 13:4 describes the beauty and honor God intended for sexual love.

> Let marriage be held in honor among all, and let the marriage bed be undefiled.

Two equal distortions are corrected in this verse. One is unrestrained sexual passion that overflows the banks of marriage; the marriage bed is to be undefiled. The other is a damming entirely of those passions; the sexual union of a man and woman is to be honored.

We need to remind our children constantly that sex belongs in marriage. One way we can do this is to express disgust toward the countless sexual acts depicted or referred to on television and in movies between unmarried partners. But it's important when we do this that we communicate that our problem is not with sex, but with sex outside of marriage.

Sexual pleasure exists because God created it to feel good. It is not something to be mistrusted but enjoyed. The reason a man or woman's body is attractive to the opposite sex is because God designed our bodies and us to respond to the beauty He created. The reason sex between a man and a woman is so exhilarating, the taste of chocolate is so delightful, or a beautiful sunset is so magnetic is because God made us and these things for us to enjoy. The fact that we can turn each of these things into an object of worship might obscure this, but it does not change the fact that all pleasure is ultimately God's gift. Satan cannot create pleasure, he can only pervert the pleasures God has created. We turn God's gifts into sin when we use them for our own selfish satisfaction rather than to enjoy them as God directs. The gift of taste degenerates into sin when we live for what we eat. The gift of beauty twists into sin when we worship beauty or deify nature. The gift of sex degenerates into sin when we use someone's body as an object for our selfish gratification or seek it unnaturally or outside of marriage.

Sex was also given for pleasure. The Bible is clear on this, and not just emotional pleasure, but physical pleasure. As much as men and women have abused this gift, it is an undeniable fact. God made it to feel goooood! The Song of Solomon is a book of intimacy, romance, and the purity of sexual pleasure in marriage. Listen to these erotic words. No wonder the rabbis made this book off-limits to individuals under thirty.

> Lover
> > I have come into my garden, my sister, my bride;
> > > I have gathered my myrrh with my spice.
> > I have eaten my honeycomb and my honey;
> > > I have drunk my wine and my milk.
>
> Friends
> > Eat, O friends, and drink;
> > > drink your fill, O lovers.
>
> SONG OF SOLOMON 5:1

Even Proverbs, the book of staid wisdom and sensibility speaks of being intoxicated with the graceful beauty of the body of our mate as something we should never outgrow.

> May your fountain be blessed,
> > and may you rejoice in the wife of your youth.
>
> A loving doe, a graceful deer—
> > may her breasts satisfy you always,
> > may you ever be captivated by her love.
>
> PROVERBS 5:18–19

Women who look at such verses and conclude that sexual pleasure is intended only for men forget the fact that a loving man is never satisfied sexually until he has satisfied his wife. But they also overlook an important biblical command in Deuteronomy.

> If a man has recently married, he must not be sent to war or have any other duty laid on him. For one year he is to be free to stay at home and bring happiness to the wife he has married.
>
> DEUTERONOMY 24:5

That's a rather poor translation. His job is to bring "sexual happiness" to his new wife. He is to focus undistracted for one year on developing an intimate sexual oneness with his wife. His own pleasure and his civic duties are all to take a backseat to learning to give her pleasure sexually. Her pleasure is his priority.

Teaching by Example

I am amazed how many kids think they must have been products of immaculate conception. They buy the stuff about growing inside their mother's tummy rather than being delivered by the stork. But they can't imagine that their parents could "do it." Although sex is a private thing between a man and woman, our children need to know that sex is a beautiful act of marriage. They don't need details. They do need to know that their mom and dad enjoy a warm physical relationship that includes sex.

One of the great gifts that my parents gave me was an appreciation of the physical warmth that God intended in marriage. I would often walk into the kitchen and see my dad in an amorous embrace with my mom. Of course, at the time I was totally embarrassed. And yet there was something very satisfying and secure about knowing my parents loved each other deeply and in a way that was exclusive. I never saw my mom or dad hold anyone else like that—even me. Instinctively I knew that the way they held each other was reserved only for that relationship. That made me feel very secure. And it made me look forward to that kind of relationship with a wife of my own.

Take a moment to ponder what you are communicating to your children about sex. Do they see their body as God's creation? Are they developing a deep appreciation for the beauty and rightness of sex between a man and woman in marriage? We also need to be careful that we are not embarrassed by their frank questions about sex or overreact when a child accidentally sees body parts of another member of the family. Nor should we be shocked by anatomically correct language.

Do we laugh at sin on television sitcoms? Does our schedule revolve around getting home to find out who's sleeping with whom on the sleazy evening soaps? If we do, we're teaching them something we may not intend.

The Danger of Sex

As beautiful as sex is, though, there is a tremendous danger that we must recognize and be prepared to deal with, both with ourselves and with our children. Because the gift of sex is so beautiful and so important for emotional prosperity in the family, Satan works overtime to pervert our pleasure. Its not surprising then to find verses in the Bible warning us to be careful about maintaining our sexual purity. Paul clearly outlines God's desire for our sexuality.

> It is God's will that you should be sanctified: that you should avoid sexual immorality; that each of you should learn to control his own body in a way that is holy and honorable, not in passionate lust like the heathen, who do not know God; and that in this matter no one should wrong his brother or take advantage of him. The Lord will punish men for all such sins, as we have already told you and warned you. For God did not call us to be impure, but to live a holy life. Therefore, he who rejects this instruction does not reject man but God, who gives you his Holy Spirit.
>
> 1 THESSALONIANS 4:3–8

Immorality has no place in God's family. But Paul recognizes that there is an incredible pull of sin on our bodies. That's why he says we need to learn to control it.

Control begins with knowledge. Each of us needs accurate, practical information. What is a man's body like? What is a woman's body like? Each of us not only needs to understand our own body, but also the body of the opposite sex. How has God designed the pleasure principle to work for each? Self-centered persons that we are, most of us are very knowledgeable about what pleases us. The question is, Do we know how to please our mates? And how do we avoid defrauding someone whose desire we cannot legitimately fulfill.

Young men and women, for example, need to know that the anatomy of intercourse begins with very innocent touching and kissing and then leads incrementally, step-by-step to intercourse. Once engaged, our physical bodies expect to reach the goal of sexual release. Our mind may know where to stop, intend to stop, but our bodies can easily take control. Before long, young men and women find themselves farther down the track than they intended to travel. Wisdom says not to board the train.

On the other hand, understand that this same information tells married couples that nonsexual touching is extremely important for intimacy. Every warm-blooded creature craves being touched by its own kind. This is especially true of human beings. So if the only time you touch your mate is when you want sex, don't be surprised if you get a cold shoulder. Lack of warm nonsexual touch is a major cause of headaches. It doesn't take a Viennese psychiatrist to figure out that you're treating her as an object of your sexual pleasure, not a person to be respected and honored when you limit your touch to sex.

Obviously practical sexual information is one of the most important jobs of parenting. Not only do we and our children need practical knowledge about sex, we also need a clear understanding of our weaknesses and how to handle them. Every person needs a healthy fear of their potential for moral failure. It is possible for anyone to sin in this way. No one is impervious to temptation and sin. Every person who has confessed a moral failure to me has also uttered these words, "I didn't think I would ever do a thing like that." Each of us has weaknesses, and we better be aware of our vulnerabilities.

Controlling Our Thoughts

Moral failure rarely happens overnight. It almost always begins in our mind. We're usually in bed with a person in our mind before we actually commit adultery. That's why Christ said in the Sermon on the Mount,

> You have heard that it was said, "Do not commit adultery."
> But I tell you that anyone who looks at a woman lustfully
> has already committed adultery with her in his heart.
> MATTHEW 5:27–28

If I am going to control my body, the first thing I need to do is control my thoughts. If I expect my children to win the battle with temptation, they will need to know these basic controls.

Monitor the input. We must control what goes into our minds. You've probably heard the mind compared to a computer—garbage in, garbage out. If we allow sexual images to be implanted by reading suggestive material or watching sexually explicit images on television, we can expect our mind to begin to be patterned toward that kind of sexual gratification. Certain things will be more seductive to us than others, but we cannot afford the luxury of entertaining ourselves with sin if we want to maintain our moral purity.

We need to be careful not only for ourselves, but also for our children, what we allow them to read and what we allow in our home via television and videos. The majority of sexual acts depicted or referred to on television are between unmarried partners. Psychologists tell us that we only need to see something five times before it is indelibly etched in our mind, so we are foolish if we think what our children see on the screen does not affect their values and their decision-making process. We're also foolish if we think it doesn't affect ours.

It is certainly true that we can no longer isolate ourselves or our children totally from sexually oriented material unless we disengage totally from our culture. Although some have tried this, it was never an option even for the early Christians who lived in a much more sexually saturated society than we do. We can take ourselves out of the world, but that is a lot easier than taking the world out of ourselves or our children. How do we deal with these intrusions into our thoughts, and how can we teach our children to do the same?

Control conscious thoughts. Whether abrupt sexual interruptions erupt from our subconscious or from outside stimuli, we can deal with them the same way. Every thought needs to appraised by the truth of God's word.

As our boys have grown older we have practiced a gradual release to freedom, allowing them to make their own decisions. Occasionally one of our older boys has asked to see a movie or watch a television show that we considered potentially questionable. Having released the issue to their freedom, we refrained from telling them no outright, but we made them promise to view the story critically and we would ask for their evaluation afterward. On more than one occasion, they replied, "Dad, that'll ruin it. If I can't just watch it and enjoy it, I'd rather not go." To that I have a standard reply, "If you are not wise enough to evaluate, you're not old enough to go." On other occasions we have watched the program together or gone with them to the movie and then talked about it afterward.

"We can't stop the birds from flying over our head, but we can stop them from building a nest in our hair." We don't know who said this, but it's true when it comes to our thought life. We simply cannot allow unevaluated thoughts to roam freely in our minds. We never know when they will find a home. If a thought is sinful, we need to label it in our mind as sin and focus on something else. We need to filter every image and idea that enters our conscious mind through a critical evaluation process.

Anyone who has done battle with Satan over impure thoughts knows that thoughts are not dismissed willy-nilly. For example, I'm sad to say that my perverted mind loves to run to sexual thoughts when I see a lovely young woman. If I choose to relish that thought, I have crossed the line between sin and temptation. But let's say I recognize the evil of my thoughts and confess this to God. I may even remind myself of the truth of a particular Scripture passage. I try to think about other things and bingo, there she is again in my mind, sometimes over and over again during the day. If I ever stop to dwell on the thought, it has me. How do I get rid of this thought? One of the ways I have found to persuade Satan to leave me alone is to turn temptation into an opportunity to pray. If I find my observation of the beauty of one of God's creations moving from admiration to lust, I stop and ask God, "Father, I pray that this woman will be as beautiful on the inside as she is on the outside." It's hard to continue the sexual thought during that prayer. Then I turn my mind to thanksgiving and thank the Lord for Kathy and the wonderful joy He has given us in sexual love.

It's important that we teach our kids this turn-to-prayer technique early in life. This way they'll understand better when you talk to them about using this technique concerning their thoughts when they hit puberty.

Reprogram the mind. We must take one more step if we want to control sex between our ears. Nature abhors a vacuum. Sinful thoughts need to be replaced with godly thoughts. We must reprogram and renew our minds with Scripture. Paul exhorts us all,

> Do not conform any longer to the pattern of this world, but be transformed by the renewing of your mind. Then you will be able to test and approve what God's will is—his good, pleasing and perfect will.
>
> ROMANS 12:2

Reprogramming occurs with God's word. That's why Paul challenges us

> Let the word of Christ dwell in you richly.
>
> COLOSSIANS 3:16

As this happens, we give our will the ammunition it needs to do battle with sin. And we give our mind the criterion it needs for evaluation.

One of the passages that needs to dwell richly within us is from 1 Corinthians. It provides a great evaluation grid for our thoughts. Paul reminds us first that we shouldn't envy the sexual exploits of others.

> Do you not know that the wicked will not inherit the kingdom of God? Do not be deceived: Neither the sexually immoral nor idolaters nor adulterers nor male prostitutes nor homosexual offenders nor thieves nor the greedy nor drunkards nor slanderers nor swindlers will inherit the kingdom of God. And that is what some of you were. But you were washed, you were sanctified, you were justified in the name of the Lord Jesus Christ and by the Spirit of our God.
>
> 1 CORINTHIANS 6:9–20

In weak moments it's easy to begin to think that we are losing out on a lot of pleasure. Paul reminds us of the whole story. The first question we need to ask ourselves is, Am I considering the pain as well as the pleasure? I may be missing out on a little pleasure, but I need to consider the pain I'm missing as well.

The second questions that he wants us to ask is, Is this really good for me?

> "Everything is permissible for me"—but not everything is beneficial. "Everything is permissible for me"—but I will not be mastered by anything. "Food for the stomach and the stomach for food"—but God will destroy them both. The body is not meant for sexual immorality, but for the Lord, and the Lord for the body. By his power God raised the Lord from the dead, and he will raise us also. Do you not know that your bodies are members of Christ himself? Shall I then take the members of Christ and unite them with a prostitute? Never! Do you not know that he who unites himself with a prostitute is one with her in body? For it is said, "The two will become one flesh." But he who unites himself with the Lord is one with him in spirit.
>
> Flee from sexual immorality. All other sins a man commits are outside his body, but he who sins sexually sins against his own body.
>
> 1 CORINTHIANS 10:12–18

The last question we need to ask ourselves is, Does this activity reflect who I am in Christ or who I was in sin?

> Do you not know that your body is a temple of the Holy Spirit, who is in you, whom you have received from God? You are not your own; you were bought at a price. Therefore honor God with your body.
>
> 1 CORINTHIANS 10:19–20

The fact is that we all belong to God. He made us. He bought us. I simply don't have the prerogative to use my body or someone else's for my own selfish pleasures. I don't belong to me any more.

Last year my friend Clint told me the story of his daughter's first date. Clint said that he asked the boy to come a little early before the date so they could have some time to talk. When the nervous boy arrived, my friend, knowing the boy's interests, took him to the garage to show him a prized restored car. They talked cars for several minutes before Clint turned the conversation to his purpose and said, "I noticed that's a nice car out front you're driving. I bet you're mighty proud of it."

"Yes sir!" the young man answered, "My dad and I have worked on it over a year. It's got fifty coats of lacquer."

Clint responded, "How about letting me drive it down the narrow wooded trail to the storage shed? I don't think I'll scratch her up too bad."

"No sir, that'd ruin the paint job," the young man said in a panicked voice.

"You mean you wouldn't want me to get one little scratch on your car?" Clint inquired.

"No sir," the boy said emphatically.

"You'd be pretty mad if I did, wouldn't you?"

"Yes sir!"

"What would you do if I did?" Clint continued.

"I don't know. I've put so much work into it. I'm not sure what I'd do, but I'd be awfully mad about it."

Then my friend leaned over, put his hand on the young man's shoulder, looked him in the eye and said, "Son, I'm not going to drive your car to the shed, but I want you to know something. How you feel about your car doesn't come close to how I feel about my daughter. I've spent fifteen years working on her, and I don't want her scratched up."

The boy looked down for a moment pondering Clint's words, then looked him back in the eye, grinned, and said, "Yes sir, I understand. I promise I'll bring her back without a scratch."

Aiming High

When it comes to passing on a healthy view of sex to our children, we're fighting a battle with our culture—uphill. We won't win the war by scheduling one night to have a big-deal sex education talk with our child and hope he listens—sort of a Whew-I-got-that-over-with approach. Although it is a good idea to sit and have some serious talks with our children about sex, it's also important to understand that our attitudes and actions speak volumes. Think about these ideas and act upon a few as you feel led.

∞

Set limits on what your children can watch on television as long as they live in your home. Just because older kids may be able to walk into an R-rated movie doesn't mean you have to condone immorality in your family room.

∞

Kids won't buy a do-as-I-say-not-as-I-do philosophy. Parents who want their children to adopt the principle that sex outside of marriage is wrong may send a double message if the family schedule revolves around their favorite nighttime soap opera because they can't wait to see who goes to bed with whom.

∞

Walk out of movies that offend your values and instruct your kids to do the same. Most theaters will either refund your money or give you a pass for another movie if you walk out up to halfway through the show.

∞

Don't allow televisions in your children's bedrooms. It's hard to monitor what they're watching.

∞

One of the greatest things you can do for your kids to teach them this commandment is to make sure your marriage keeps getting better and better. Do something today that tells your spouse and shows your children your love and commitment.

182

Look through a clothing catalog with your young daughter and explain to her what is becoming on a young lady and what is not.

∞

Get to know people very well before you allow your child to spend the night at their home. Talk to your child about what to do if a questionable movie or television show is shown or they're asked to participate in something wrong.

∞

Baby Boomers who grew up in the if-it-feels-good-do-it 1970s and who experimented with sex often have difficulty asking their own children to abstain. Be honest about what you did wrong without going into detail. Teach abstinence, and let your children know you want to spare them the pain.

∞

If you have teenage boys, be careful of the catalogs that come through the mail to your house. Nowadays the lingerie sections of many catalogs could be classified as "soft" pornography.

∞

"When we are not acceptable to ourselves, we have a greater desire to be acceptable to others"—George MacDonald. Let your kids know you are crazy about them, that you accept and love them just the way they are. They won't feel the need to seek acceptance and love from a girlfriend or boyfriend. At our house, we try not to let a day go by without building up each of our boy's self-esteem.

∞

If you are divorced, depending on your children's ages, talk honestly with them about why you and their dad or mom no longer live together as husband and wife. Tell them you are committed to being sexually pure until you marry again.

∞

"What a man thinks of himself, that it is which determines or rather indicates his fate"—Henry David Thoreau. Help your children think pure and positive things about themselves. Don't encourage promiscuity by telling them things like "You look really sexy" or "You look so good you'll have those guys on their knees begging for you." Instead say, "You look very handsome (or beautiful), but you're even more so on the inside." Or "If all kids had a good head on their shoulders like you, we wouldn't have so many problems."

∞

Honestly examine your own life. Are there areas where you are knowingly not setting a good example for your children in the area of sexual purity, like coarse jesting, overt flirting, or condoning ungodly sexual messages on television?

∞

Fathers as well as mothers need to be involved in role modeling and teaching children of both genders to become men and women. Who can teach them loving relationships if both parents aren't involved in their education? If you are a single parent, be sure your children have exposure to a parent figure of the opposite gender from you—an uncle, aunt, grandparent, old family friend, or someone from your church.

∞

Pray with your child about his future mate, even if you have no idea who it will be. Pray that God would protect them both from evil and harm, and that He would help them both remain sexually pure until marriage.

∞

Try to schedule the "True Love Waits" program for the youth department at your church. Call 1–800–LUV-WAIT for information.

∞

When you attend a wedding, talk to your child about what being married means—the rings, the vows, and God's design for a man and a woman.

∞

Tell your son to treat every girl he dates like someone's future wife. Ditto for your daughter.

∞

Provide opportunities to instill God's word into your children's mind and heart. Encourage them to have a daily quiet time using a modern translation of the Bible and a kid-friendly devotional book. Also, do what you can to help your children get involved at church. Volunteer to have the youth group or Bible study meet at your home. Ask if you can chaperone events and trips.

THE EIGHTH COMMANDMENT

YOU SHALL NOT STEAL.

DEUTERONOMY 5:19

Thieves respect property.
They merely wish the property to become their property
that they may more perfectly respect it.
—G. K. CHESTERTON

Chapter 10

ON THE TAKE

I MET BILL IN MY SECOND YEAR OF COLLEGE. Until then I'd been sort of floating along, working toward my degree, partying with my friends, and generally not having much sense of who I was or where I was going. I fell in love with Bill within a month of meeting him, and seventeen months later we decided to follow the injunction, "It is better to marry than to burn." We were "in lust," as they say. Truth to tell we didn't know much about love.

I looked to Bill to make me feel safe, to help me figure out what I was going to do with my life, to guide me, to take care of me, to love me. One night shortly before we were married, I was feeling blue about something, I don't even remember what. I phoned Bill, and he came over and comforted me. He told me he wanted to take all my troubles away. In my insecurity, I believed he could do this. I thought, at last, here is the perfect person. He will meet all my needs, give me everything I need, take care of things.

Basically, we were strangers. People have longer conversations with automated answering systems or "voice jail." Oh, we knew that we both liked Mexican food, enjoyed Paul Newman movies, and wanted to spend our lives in some sort of people-helping ministry.

What we didn't know about each other, nor did we understand about ourselves, was that we were takers. I looked to Bill to give me security. I felt so safe and protected when he held me in his muscular arms. Surely this strong, chivalrous creature would rescue me from my unstable world and gallantly lead me through the storms of life, if not on a white horse, at least in a white BMW. He would be my rock, my spiritual leader, my hero.

The feeling didn't last, as I'm sure you've figured out by now. Early in our marriage when everything should have been new and exciting, Bill and I nearly floundered in a sea of disappointment. It turned out that Bill had insecurities, too. It turned out that we couldn't kiss away all of each other's hurts. It turned out that we'd both gone into marriage—unconsciously, but not unsurprisingly given our culture—with a what-am-I-going-to-get-out-of-it attitude.

Shortly after our honeymoon, I realized the man definitely needed work. Just a few personality adjustments, I thought—me adjusting his personality, that is—and this man will be perfect. First, I'd teach him to pick up his underwear, coordinate his wardrobe, and wash his dishes immediately after eating. And I'd have to do something about his need for reassurance that he was doing a good job, when it was obvious that I needed reassurance more than he did.

Bill didn't have it any easier. He was attracted to me because I made him feel significant. (And because my mother owned dress shops, and I had the largest collection of miniskirts on campus. Ah, those were the days, before children, before thighs.) Here was a girl who told him he was wonderful, strong, and handsome. For the first time in his life he felt needed, like a real somebody. He was ready to take on the world, as long he could take reassurance from me.

Well, he felt like this about a month—two, tops—after the wedding. Then reality set in. We both had needs. And we both wanted our needs met. And we both felt as though we couldn't meet each other's needs until our own needs were met. We were on the take.

A Society of Takers

We live in a society of takers. We might think that this is a perfect description of politicos in Washington or welfare recipients in Detroit or the loan sharks on Wall Street. We all tend to recognize other people's take-stance more easily than we see our own. We all think we have a God-and-George-Washington-given right to get our needs met, now and all of them. And if we don't get our needs met by others, why we'll just take what we need, thank you very much.

It's not as surprising to meet takers in the world of work, whether it is the wage earner who is just there for the paycheck or the young executive who will walk over anyone to climb the ladder. Stealing is a major problem in the workplace. From pilfering to embezzlement, businesses take an estimated $40 billion loss each year. We might expect that theft is predominantly a problem of the unchurched. But studies show that churchgoers are just as likely to walk away with something not theirs as the unchurched.

This taker attitude penetrates parent-child relationships as well. We would do well to ask ourselves the question: Why do we want our children to do so well in school, or athletics, or in social situations? When was the last time they failed at something or disappointed us? Did we feel embarrassed? Did we feel like our kids weren't affirming our role as a good mother or father? Were they supposed to be giving us something they weren't, like the satisfaction of knowing we're raising perfect kids?

Unfortunately the takers have invaded even our most sacred institutions, like the family. Men and women get married every day presumably because they love each other. But we don't need to dig very deep to discover another reason. Whether we say so or not, there is tremendous hope that we have finally found someone who will meet our deepest needs. (And many of us, so sophisticated in the psychobabble of the late twentieth century, would deny we're looking for someone else to fulfill all our needs. But denying it doesn't mean it's not true.)

Not only have Kathy and I experienced this ourselves (the only reason Kathy and I can counsel other families or write books is because we struggle every day with the issues we talk or write about), we've seen countless people in counseling who tell us how their mates are not meeting their needs. Frankly, I can't recall a time when someone has come for help because he felt like he was failing to meet the other's needs.

In Ephesians 4:28 Paul outlines the godliness that is to replace taking:

> He who has been stealing must steal no longer, but must work, doing something useful with his own hands, that he may have something to share with those in need.

This verse takes internal change, not just external conformity. God wants us to do more than take our hand out of the cookie jar. He wants us to bake cookies, not only for ourselves, but to have enough to be able to give some away.

Unfortunately, the idea of servanthood is an idea that most Americans wish went out with the kerosene lamp. But that is exactly what the Eighth Commandment is all about, becoming a giver. Stealing has no place in God's family. Whether it is stealing money, property, affection, or esteem, thievery is wrong. What is right is giving.

Stealing is the disease that makes it difficult to distinguish between mine and thine. It seems the human heart is endlessly unsatisfied with what it has, so the temptation to redistribute wealth personally—so that I will have my fair share—has always been a problem. Interestingly, neither the Ten Commandments nor Paul's directives were written to a pack of thieving outlaws. They were written to those who, in reality, were probably the most honest people in town, especially compared to their neighbors.

I presume that most of the people who read this book are not bank robbers or horse thieves, though some of our ancestors might have been. The real issue is not so much actual theft, which most of us would not only reject, but label as obviously wrong. The issue is a heart attitude behind stealing that plagues most of us more than we would like to admit, having a taker's attitude about life.

Why does this problem plague our hearts? Perhaps it's because we really don't take God at His word. When God called Abraham, He made a special promise to bless him. Over and over again, God promised to provide for the needs of Abraham's children, and He always came through. That's why David could sing in the Twenty-third Psalm,

> Because the Lord is my Shepherd, I have everything I need! (TLB)

They had a provider who gave them everything they needed. Therefore, there was no need to steal. To do so would be to deny God's commitment to them.

The Good News

Christians have even more compelling reasons for confidence. Jesus Christ moves beyond our physical welfare and promises to meet our deepest spiritual needs as well. We, of all people, have no reason to be "on the take." When we do so, we deny the significance of what Christ has done.

God says to us, "Do not steal"—choose a path of honesty. Get off the take. Stop sponging. You have something to contribute to others. Be a giver. Stop demanding that others meet your needs, whether it is a physical need, emotional need, or a spiritual need.

If God is committed to meeting our needs, then we should relax. Christ reminds us of the meticulous way He cares for our needs in the Sermon on the Mount.

> Therefore I tell you, do not worry about your life, what you will eat or drink; or about your body, what you will wear. Is not life more important than food, and the body more important than clothes? Look at the birds of the air; they do not sow or reap or store away in barns, and yet your heavenly Father feeds them. Are you not much more valuable than they? Who of you by worrying can add a single hour to his life?
>
> And why do you worry about clothes? See how the lilies of the field grow. They do not labor or spin. Yet I tell you that not even Solomon in all his splendor was dressed like one of these. If that is how God clothes the grass of the field, which is here today and tomorrow is thrown into the fire, will he not much more clothe you, O you of little faith? So do not worry, saying, "What shall we eat?" or "What shall we drink?" or "What shall we wear?" For the pagans run after all these things, and your heavenly Father knows that you need them. But seek first his kingdom and his right-eousness, and all these things will be given to you as well. Therefore do not worry about tomorrow, for tomorrow will worry about itself. Each day has enough trouble of its own.
>
> MATTHEW 6:25–34

We should think of Christ's words and follow His advice when we're tempted to let the taker inside of us take over, which is exactly what Satan would have us do. Satan has an alternate plan for us. He appeals to our fear and tells us that we better take care of ourselves. He floods our minds with doubts of God's ability or desire to meet our needs. If we listen and believe the lies Satan proposes, we begin to fear for our personal survival. Every time this happens and we grab for the limited resources of the world to meet our needs, we can be sure we'll turn up empty.

Takers Are Losers

Stealing denies the value of God's gifts and interrupts the enjoyment of all of God's provision. When we steal, we say to God, "Sorry, You haven't given me enough. I have to take things into my own hands and get what I need."

Stealing is contrary to grace. The very essence of grace is giving. God gives us His grace, not because we earn it, but because He loves us. He gives us His grace without expecting anything in return. As those who are the recipients of His grace, it is incomprehensible that we should operate by a different principle.

Stealing is contrary to our identity. Can you imagine Mother Teresa being arrested for shoplifting? Probably not, because stealing is contrary to her identity. As men and women who have been made complete in Christ, we of all people should be givers. We are in a position to look at other people, not with a selfish motive of gain, but with genuine concern for their welfare. Christ has made us part of the solution, part of the distribution system of His grace to a needy world.

Since we live in an acquisitive culture, it is easy to see ourselves in terms of what we don't have. When we begin to see what we do have in Christ, we see our call and our ability to be distributors.

Takers Are Users

If we habitually seek our own satisfaction, grabbing what we think we need along the way, we can be sure that we will use others in the process. There are many ways we use our children, spouse, parents, community, employer, employees, and God. Any time we take something that we owe to someone—time, money, belongings, affection, courtesy, appreciation, love—we steal from them.

Any time we withhold something that God requires us to give, we steal from Him. He, of course, has no need for our gifts Himself. But we certainly have a need to give. Giving is a statement of our faith, that we believe that God provides everything we need and have. When we withhold our gifts, we not only steal something God has provided, we steal the credit God deserves as our provider.

Will a man rob God? Yet you rob me.
But you ask, "How do we rob you?"
In tithes and offerings.

MALACHI 3:8

We can steal from an employer not only by pilfering, but by half-hearted work. Paul reminds us that we need to give our employer our best,

working not only when their eye is on you and to win their favor, but with sincerity of heart and reverence for the Lord.

COLOSSIANS 3:22

When we fail to deal honestly in business, we steal the glory God wants us to bring Him at work.

and not to steal from them, but to show that they can be fully trusted, so that in every way they will make the teaching about God our Savior attractive.

TITUS 2:10

Employers can steal from their employees, not only by cheating them out of their wages, but by treating them unfairly.

Do not defraud your neighbor or rob him.
Do not hold back the wages of a hired man overnight.

LEVITICUS 19:13

Masters, provide your slaves with what is right and fair, because you know that you also have a Master in heaven.

COLOSSIANS 4:1

When we use those who work for us, we not only rob them, we also rob ourselves of a blessing that God wants to give us.

We steal from our parents by not honoring them with the respect God says they deserve. And here again, we also cheat ourselves.

Children, obey your parents in the Lord, for this is right. "Honor your father and mother"—which is the First Commandment with a promise—that it may go well with you and that you may enjoy long life on the earth."

EPHESIANS 6:1–3

We steal from our children when we sacrifice them on the altar of our own self-esteem.

> Fathers, do not exasperate your children; instead, bring
> them up in the training and instruction of the Lord.
> EPHESIANS 6:4

Isn't it obvious. The user is always the loser. How in the world can we break loose from this destructive pull on our lives?

How to Become a Giver

John Wesley put it this way, "Make all you can, save all you can, give all you can." We are to spend our energy producing, not acquiring. Or to put it another way, I need to ask myself, "What can I add to the world," not "What can I add to myself?" The later attitude will inevitably lead us to encroach onto someone else's property or person.

Because I have a sovereign provider and have everything that I need, I can think of others. I can work, not only to provide for myself, but also to have enough to share, abound, to overflow for someone else's benefit. Paul describes what happens when we take our eyes off our greed and focus on God and the needs of others.

> Now he who supplies seed to the sowed and bread for food
> will also supply and increase your store of seed and will
> enlarge the harvest of your righteousness. You will be
> made rich in every way so that you can be generous on
> every occasion, and through us your generosity will result
> in thanksgiving to God.
>
> This service that you perform is not only supplying
> the needs of God's people but is also overflowing in many
> expressions of thanks to God. Because of the service by
> which you have proved yourselves, men will praise God for
> the obedience that accompanies your confession of the
> gospel of Christ, and for your generosity in sharing with
> them and with everyone else.
> 2 CORINTHIANS 9:10–13

A taker is convinced that there is only so much to go around and he'd better grab for what he can get. He thinks, "If I don't take care

of myself, no one else will." He believes that happiness and fulfillment are in short supply, so he grabs for all he can get. This attitude
is not only self-centered, it denies the good gifts that God wants to
give. It makes God out to be a miser.

Giving is actually a drain plug for our greed. The only thing we
lose when we open the spigot of generosity is our selfishness. In fact,
God has obligated Himself to continue the flow of resources when we
become the channel rather than the container for His blessings. This
is obviously no token commitment, but a real lifestyle change, from
taking to giving.

One obstacle will get in our way, though, as we become givers.
Fear. Fear of giving is never based on a lack of resources, but on our
own personal insecurity. The question that haunts the heart of every
honest person is simply this: If I let this go, who will take care of me?
(As if we could protect ourselves anyway.) We are afraid that God will
not be able to take care of us, protect us, or at least maintain the
lifestyle that we think we need to make us happy.

Like many of us, the young, materialistic church at Corinth
needed someone else to lead them into the threatening, unfamiliar
territory of giving. Knowing this, Paul related the story of their
neighbors, the Macedonians.

> And now, brothers, we want you to know about the grace
> that God has given the Macedonian churches. Out of the
> most severe trial, their overflowing joy and their extreme
> poverty welled up in rich generosity. For I testify that they
> gave as much as they were able, and even beyond their abil-
> ity. Entirely on their own, they urgently pleaded with us for
> the privilege of sharing in this service to the saints. And
> they did not do as we expected, but they gave themselves
> first to the Lord and then to us in keeping with God's will.
>
> 2 CORINTHIANS 8:1–5

Note several things about their giving.

First, it was generous. Look at the words Paul uses to describe
these people: overflowing, rich generosity, privilege. But this was a
surprise even to Paul. He knew the Macedonians had every reason to
be cautious, to give minimally, or not to give at all. Generosity has no
relationship to the size of one's bank account, which is a lesson our
children need to learn at an early age. They learn it by watching us

and also by our encouragement. We need to help our children get their minds off their greeds and onto meeting others' needs. One way to do this is to teach them to be givers at church, even if it's a small amount of their own money. Or decide as a family to all chip in and support a mission project. Or together buy a gift for a needy family at Christmas. Be alert for your children's generous impulses and encourage their giving spirit.

Second, their generosity was costly. In America, rarely do we see people giving until it hurts. On the contrary, many times the only reason we give is to benefit ourselves. By giving we try to gain influence, power, or even a warm feeling. I met a man several years ago who loved to see his name in bronze displayed on civic buildings. He was willing to write very generous checks to have buildings named after him. The joke was that everyone laughed at his vanity, and he lost the respect he so desperately wanted to gain.

Unlike many, the Macedonians were willing to give to the point of hurting. Scarcity of possessions and lack of abundant financial resources was not a barrier to them. Although their balance sheet listed more debits than credits, they were willing to do without things for themselves in order to give to others. Why did they do this? Why were they willing to sacrifice meeting some of their own needs to meet the needs of Christians in Jerusalem? Paul explained how they saw their balance sheet:

Debit:	severe trial (physical hardship)
	extreme poverty (cash-flow crisis)
Credit:	God and His grace
Action:	rich generosity
Result:	overflowing joy

Their giving made no sense to the accountants. They had mouths to feed and children to clothe and educate. These people were struggling financially, and along came Paul with the story of a people who were worse off. Rather than change the channel, they listened. They pondered, they prayed, and they responded. In fact, their response almost seems as if giving were no big deal to them. Why? Because they had a deep sense of their spiritual wealth. They knew exactly where their resources came from and were eager—they even begged—to be a part. They had such a sense of well-being in Christ, they didn't think it was important to insulate themselves by accumulation. Even in poverty, they saw themselves as rich. So naturally, they asked, "What can we do?"

Their giving was apart from any pressure or cajoling so evident in today's fund-raising drives. It almost seems as if Paul could have said to them, "No. You need to keep this money for yourselves." But they would have none of that. They "urgently pleaded with us for the privilege." How contrary to so many of today's appeals that feel they have to produce guilt or artificial pity to manipulate people to give.

What we see here is also a gracious work of God. These people were just like you and me. They had no extra dose of the Spirit. It took a work of God in their hearts. It is completely natural for men and women to be self-absorbed. But as God revealed the richness of their relationship with Him—His care, His provision, His faithfulness, His generosity, His ability to protect them, His commitment to their welfare—they overflowed.

How do we become generous people? How do we teach our children to be generous? The same way the Macedonians did. It begins when we place our welfare in God's hands. In Luke 9:24 Jesus tells us that those who grabbed for satisfaction in this world end up empty-handed. If we want to be rich, we can read the *Wall Street Journal.* If we want to feel rich, we'll have to read the Bible and come to know the God who is able to make all grace abound to us in abundance. As we feel rich, we'll exude a confidence in God and His provision that is contagious to our children. Let's hope we all catch the Macedonian disease.

Aiming High

It's important when we think about teaching our children this commandment that we ask ourselves if we're living out the message we want them to receive. Am I a giver or a taker? Are there any unhealthy habits or attitudes about stealing—even small, unnoticed things—that I either condone in my children or practice myself? Sometimes small changes can have big results. Perhaps the following list will give you some ideas of some small changes you and your family could make that you know would be pleasing to God.

∞

"We make a living by what we get, but we make a life by what we give"—Winston Churchill. Become a family of givers. At the beginning of the year, or any time, sit down and plan one family giving session per month. You might help an elderly neighbor, volunteer at a soup kitchen, invite a lonely person to dinner. Make sure even the youngest child gets involved.

∞

One of the main reasons kids get involved in activities such as shoplifting is to be accepted. Applaud and show unqualified love to your kids at home, and they will be less likely to turn to the world in a never-ending search for acceptance.

∞

If possible, take an older child with you on a business trip. Let her see you in action, living out honesty in business deals.

∞

Talk with your kids about what nonmaterial things can be stolen: time from an employer, credit for something someone else accomplished, someone's talent or services you use but don't pay for.

∞

Teach your children the importance of valuing the personal property of others. Have a house rule that family members —mom and dad included—are to ask before borrowing something that belongs to someone else.

∞

If you return something for credit at a department store, and the clerk makes an error and gives you more money back than you paid for the item, let your children see you point out the error and give back the extra money.

∞

Begin early teaching your children to respect the property of others. When they are toddlers, although you don't want your house to be like a museum, it's okay to have specific no-no's—television knobs, knickknacks, cabinets. You are really teaching them to respect the property of others, when they are told, "No, don't touch the glass pitcher," or, "No, don't pull the dog's tail."

∞

When you find something that is not yours, let your kids help you make every effort to return the item to the rightful owner.

"Try not to become a man of success but rather try to become a man of value"—Albert Einstein. Our culture tells our children that success is all-important, and no matter what you have to do to get success, do it. This may mean being a little dishonest in culturally acceptable ways. We need to tell them otherwise.

∞

Older children need to be aware that if they are with a friend who decides to shoplift something and gets caught, the culprit as well as those with him can be charged.

∞

Is there anything in your home that you have that you should be paying for, but you're not? Extra cable channels that you get by mistake? A neighbor's magazine subscription that comes to your address? Turn this into a teaching opportunity by telling your children it's wrong to continue accepting something without paying for it. Talk about the right thing to do.

∞

Talk at the dinner table about specific ways you have been treated generously. Brainstorm about how you can live generously. Become givers instead of getters.

∞

Honestly ask yourself why you want your children to do well in school, or athletics, or in a social situation. Did you feel embarrassed the last time they failed at something or disappointed you? Have you been looking to them to give you the satisfaction of knowing you are raising perfect kids? If you've had a taker attitude in any way toward your children, confess it and ask for their forgiveness.

∞

When your older children, especially teenagers, are feeling disappointed in their friends' inability to meet their needs, specifically discuss with them how no other person can ever fulfill all our needs. You might share some of your own learning process as a young adult or teenager with them.

∞

Make sure that the consequences for taking something that belongs to someone else is clear. Taking means borrowing something without asking permission. It also means reading a sibling's private diary. (This does not necessarily apply to parents.) It means going in mom's purse or dad's wallet to get money for a movie without permission. List the things it means in your family.

༄

Even the youngest children can be taught to share. Although child-rearing manuals tend to say that children can't be taught this concept until age three, we think otherwise. Make sure your toddler has the opportunity to play with others. Gently separate them when they disagree over a toy. Make sure each has an equal number to play with at a given time. And if they're interacting nicely with each other, leave them alone.

༄

"A greedy father has thieves for children"—Serbian saying. We should honestly ask ourselves if there are areas in our life where we are greedy—maybe taking things like hotel towels, charging more than we have to for a service, not paying Uncle Sam what we're supposed to.

༄

People who don't have a good sense of self-esteem or strong inner resources tend to become takers. Make sure you tell your children early and often how important they are in your eyes and God's.

THE NINTH COMMANDMENT

YOU SHALL NOT GIVE FALSE TESTIMONY
AGAINST YOUR NEIGHBOR.

DEUTERONOMY 5:20

He who permits himself to tell a lie once,
finds it much easier to do it a second time.
—THOMAS JEFFERSON

Chapter 11

SPEAK NO EVIL

TEACHING OUR CHILDREN THAT IT IS WRONG to lie is a difficult task, especially since we're trying to teach them to be tactful, gracious, and thankful at the same time. My children are in a particularly awkward position when it comes to telling the truth about my cooking. How can they honestly be thankful for my meat loaf when they'd rather walk five miles on broken glass than eat it? And how can they truthfully tell me they don't know who put the telephone number for Poison Control on autodial? Actually the boys have figured out how they can honestly thank God for their daily bread. They simply thank Him for a never-ending supply of bricks for their forts.

On occasion I've encountered perfect teachable moments about truth-telling that go something like this. I'm serving a new pasta dish with a lovely cream sauce, or at least that's how it looked in the magazine. James, who takes telling the truth seriously, might take a big forkful, chew, swallow, stick out his tongue, hold his stomach, and blurt out, "Yuck, this stuff tastes awful, just like the paste at school. Face it, Mom, you're a terrible cook." At this point, I have three options.

I could counter sternly, "You've been eating paste? I've told you not to do that. You don't know what they put in that stuff!"

My son then has the option of owning up to doing something he's been told not to do or of lying, telling me, "No, I just think that it tastes like paste." One opportunity down the drain.

Or I could burst into tears, shout that I'm never going to try a new recipe again, and run from the room, ruining what's left of the family's appetite and the evening. Another opportunity down the drain.

Or I could take a deep breath and say, "Thanks for sharing what you think my dinner tastes like. I'm sorry it didn't turn out. And I know I'm not such a great cook, but it makes me feel bad when you call me a terrible cook and make faces. The kind thing would simply be to say you don't care for it." Voilà, a teachable moment!

We have lots of them around food at our house. But holidays are a special challenge for all of us. In my opinion, some of the best fiction today is written by the food editors of women's magazines. If only the editors would write honestly with domestically impaired women like me in mind, holidays could be a lot easier. This is what my foolproof plan for a happy holiday like Thanksgiving looks like.

Start with a list of necessary equipment: roasting pan, mixing bowls, can opener for various side dishes, hard hats, fire extinguisher, mini "jaws of life" machine, and a stomach pump. Some items are self-explanatory. Everybody knows what a roasting pan is for, besides a perfect place to give the dog a bath on Thanksgiving morning.

The hard hats are to protect you and your kitchen helpers (AKA family) from pots, pans, and bowls precariously perched on high shelves since Easter. The fire extinguisher is, of course, for when the pumpkin pie spills over. Please make sure no one mistakes that foam for whipped cream. The "jaws of life" are to extricate your small child from the back of the cupboard where you sent him on an expedition for pie pans. And, if you're the kind of cook I am, you don't have to ask what the stomach pump is for.

Many years ago I decided to accept the truth about myself and gave up trying to make my holiday table look like a spread from a magazine. Besides, I've heard they spray that food with oil to make it shine, and we all know that much fat is not good for us. What the pictures don't tell is that the foods are "easy-to-fix" if you happen to have access to a walk-in deep freeze, a five-gallon mixer, and a commercial range.

So instead of having Superwoman make herself and everyone else within a five-mile radius miserable while she tries to create the perfect holiday (which, in itself, is a kind of lie), and instead of putting our children in a compromising position about truthfully being thankful at Thanksgiving dinner, our family works together to make the occasion a positive experience.

First off, Bill cooks the turkey. He's better at it than I am. (I want to tell the world the truth about that.) This way the boys don't have to worry about Tom turkey turning into turkey jerky by dinnertime. I decorate the table. And the boys are on-call sous chefs and assistant decorators. Each of them makes sure there's something he likes on the buffet table—something that he can honestly be thankful for.

We can orchestrate some things in life, like a holiday dinner, so as to make it easier for our kids to tell the truth. Many situations we have no control over. Sometimes telling the truth, like owning up to who broke the neighbor's window with a baseball, is hard for fear of punishment. Sometimes it's hard because they've seen the results of their lie—a tearful, devastated playmate or friend. When we're not around, which happens more and more as our children get older and are out in the world alone, they have to make their own choices about whether or not they'll tell the truth. And there's nothing we can do, except tell the truth to them, teach them why we follow the commandment, "Thou shalt not lie," and pray for the best. But that's a lot.

The Head of the List

As a small boy I had problems overcoming lying, because in my family we hid its hideousness behind the inane term "storytelling." Lying was always too harsh a word. We might as well tell our kids the truth, that lying is one of the ugliest hickeys on the human face as far as God is concerned. When Paul lists the old ways of life that Christians should put aside in Ephesians, lying heads the list.

> and to put on the new self, created to be like God in true righteousness and holiness.
> Therefore each of you must put off falsehood and speak truthfully to his neighbor, for we are all members of one body.
> EPHESIANS 4:24–25

Although lying is perhaps the most common sin of the human race, it is incongruous with life in God's family. It's not surprising to find that lying makes the top ten in the Ten Commandments.

Why Do We Lie?

If deceit is so destructive, why do we do it? The story begins not in some den of sin but in the most ideal of environments. Adam and

Eve lived in total harmony with God, the creation, and themselves. Their incredible relationship is described in the last verse of Genesis 2.

> The man and his wife were both naked, and they felt no shame.
>
> GENESIS 2:25

This is not a picture of two streakers, but of human relationship as God intended. It was a relationship of absolute openness, honesty, and acceptance. There was absolutely nothing to fear in God's care and nothing to hide from each other.

The first lie was conceived by Satan and is recorded in Genesis 3:1–7. Satan questioned God's goodness, denied God's justice, and promised real significance if they would take life into their own hands. Adam and Eve believed the lies and took the bait.

Immediately they felt the sting of emptiness as God withdrew from their being, leaving them separated from the source of life. Immediately the cover-up began. Lying always follows disobedience it seems. They covered themselves from each other. Then they covered their guilt by shifting the blame as quickly as they could to hide from God. Why? Because they were afraid. Down through the generations the lie has been perpetuated: If I can hide, then I'm safe.

As a result of sin, men and women have everything to hide. So we cover it. Why? For fear of rejection. We build a facade so good at times that we fool ourselves into believing we are all right.

One way we protect ourselves is to erect a mesh, stucco it with an image of what the world tells us we should be like. Since the culture changes its mind, we are constantly faced with changing our identity. We regularly redecorate if we can. And someone is always better at it than I am, which aggravates my sense of insecurity. Who I am is a function of who I am with. I am a slave to what everyone expects, but deep inside I would love to just be me. If it was only safe!

Another way men and women handle their fear of rejection is to build a brick wall around themselves and declare from their fortress of fear, "This is who I am. If you don't like it, tough!" They isolate themselves from others' evaluation and say it doesn't matter. But deep down inside they crave to come out from behind the wall. If it was only safe!

Whether facade or fortress, insecurity reigns within. Insecurity not only drives the lies we live, but the lies we perpetrate about others. Somehow I feel safer if someone else is weakened or taken down a notch or two. But deep inside, we know there is no safety.

How We Lie

You shall not give false testimony against your neighbor.
DEUTERONOMY 5:20

The particular form of deceit forbidden is the slander of another person, an empty accusation without substance or fact. It is communicating by words or actions something that has no relationship to reality, with the intent to deceive. Lying about someone else is not only destructive to the falsely accused person, it is destructive to the soul of the liar.

In theory, no one is so despised as a liar. God would agree. From whoppers to white lies, He hates falsehood. Solomon minces no words when he talks about how God feels about deception.

> There are six things the LORD hates,
>   seven that are detestable to him:
>   haughty eyes,
>   a lying tongue,
>   hands that shed innocent blood,
>   a heart that devises wicked schemes,
>   feet that are quick to rush into evil,
>   a false witness who pours out lies
>   and a man who stirs up dissension among
>   brothers.
PROVERBS 6:16–19

Of the seven things Solomon says that God hates, four have to do with lying. He hates a lying tongue and a false witness who pours out lies. No mincing of words there. He also hates a heart that devises wicked schemes, which is usually a lying heart, and ditto a man who stirs up dissension among brothers—like telling them two different things, a common family occurrence. There's no getting around the fact that God detests lying.

Today, however, our culture seems quite content to distort the truth. Advertising, politics, business, personal relationships, lying has almost become a way of life in many circles. As we write, Tennessee is in the midst of one of the most bitterly fought elections in the country. Campaign ads on all sides contain accusations and half-truths, designed by professionals to put their candidate in a better light at the expense of the opponent's character. The importance of truth is not the issue; winning is the issue. The result is, of course, that many are misled, and trust for our nation's leaders continues to decline.

But politics certainly has no exclusive patent on lying. Though we hate it, despise it, and denounce it, we all do it. Everyone of us distorts the truth at some point. I started at a very early age. As a matter of fact, I think that lying is the first thing I remember getting into trouble over. I lied to cover my tracks. I lied to shift the blame. I lied to inflate my status with my friends. Lying is about as native to the human condition as breathing.

With a lying tongue. We certainly lie with our words. We speak untruths or half-truths. But falsehood is about more than words. It is about deception in all its forms. A "lying tongue" means just that. If a wife tells her husband that a dress cost seventy-five dollars when it really cost twice that, even if they have the money in the bank and he doesn't care how much it cost, that's speaking with a lying tongue. A "lying tongue" is a straightforward lie, like, "Yes, Mom, I've got my homework done." It doesn't make any difference if the child has her homework done by the time mom gets home or not. The lie is that she does not have it done now. Well-intentioned children and adults often lie with words in an attempt to protect themselves or others. But little lies that are tolerated lead to bigger ones. They are the opposite of truth and reality. The result is that others are deceived and are led to embrace a nonreality.

With a heart that devises wicked schemes. We also lie by our behavior when we deliberately, and sometimes even unconsciously, seek to manipulate people by our actions. We lead them away from the truth toward the error we want them to accept. Most of us want people to think highly of us, but when we act in a way that covers our real motives and draws attention to our behavior, that's wrong. Christ called this behavior hypocrisy. He challenged the Pharisees to take off their religious masks and show the people how wicked they really were on the inside.

> Woe to you, teachers of the law and Pharisees, you hypocrites! You are like whitewashed tombs, which look beautiful on the outside but on the inside are full of dead men's bones and everything unclean.
>
> MATTHEW 23:27

Hypocrisy is the most subtle form of deception because it parades death all dressed up as if it were truly alive. It leads people away from the truth. It is also the most destructive form of deception. When we practice hypocrisy, we not only cripple relationships, we also kill something of ourselves. It is a lie about what God has done in our hearts that we have come to believe. Ananias and Saphira are certainly an example of this destructive force. In the first days of the church in the Book of Acts, they tried to deceive their fellow Christians as to their generosity.

> Now a man named Ananias, together with his wife Sapphira, also sold a piece of property. With his wife's full knowledge he kept back part of the money for himself, but brought the rest and put it at the apostles' feet.
> Then Peter said, "Ananias, how is it that Satan has so filled your heart that you have lied to the Holy Spirit and have kept for yourself some of the money you received for the land? Didn't it belong to you before it was sold? And after it was sold, wasn't the money at your disposal? What made you think of doing such a thing? You have not lied to men but to God."
>
> ACTS 5:1–4

The shocking judgment that fell upon Ananias and his wife not only tells us something about how God values honesty, it reveals how destructive falsehood can truly be. Ananias really fits into the description of a "heart that devises wicked schemes." Now very few of us, if asked, would say that we set out to devise wicked schemes. But any time we try to manipulate people, that's what we do. Even if it's to manipulate people for a good cause, like teaching Sunday school or serving on our pet committee. Trying to manipulate a child into playing a particular sport that would be good for him, but it would also make us look good as a parent. Trying to shame our mate into spending more time with the kids because our own time is limited. We probably won't drop dead when we do something like this, but the damage is there nonetheless. The relationship we really damage is our relationship with God. It's really Him we're lying to when we act hypocritically.

As a false witness who pours out lies. This means more than testifying against someone in court. It is a young child telling a tale to get a sibling in trouble. It is a teenager saying something untrue about a classmate, either to make himself look better or his classmate look worse. It is a mother telling other mothers that because of her child's report card, the teacher is obviously unfit for the job. Surely when we try to make ourselves look better by making someone else look worse, this has the opposite affect in God's eyes.

And who stirs up dissension. More than likely, dissension among brothers means more than a pillow fight over who gets to sleep in the top bunk. I think we can pretty safely say that it's lying to tell two people—brothers, sisters, or friends—things that are patently untrue simply to stir up unrest. But what about the "friend" who says I just thought you should know what your husband, sister, mother, friend is doing for your own good. These busybody liars often operate with less than the full truth, what we euphemistically call half-truths, and cause a lot of trouble.

Another way we lie is by our silence. When we refuse to correct someone's false assumption, whether we are trying to manipulate their response or not, we are lying. In the Book of Acts, Ananias and Sapphira both had the opportunity to correct the misconception that they were giving all the proceeds of their land sale, but they remained silent. Peter made it clear. The land was theirs and the money was theirs. They had the freedom to do as they wished. They chose to delude others both by their actions and by their silence that they were giving all the proceeds to the Lord.

What's Wrong with a Little Fib?

Why is it that God makes such a big deal out of lying? Doesn't all of this seem to be a little overreactive?

Our very security depends on the veracity of God. The fact that we can count on some form of existence and security in the next moment is that God is absolutely reliable. He is not going to change His mind, much less deceive us.

> God is not a man, that he should lie,
>   nor a son of man, that he should change his mind.
> Does he speak and then not act?
>   Does he promise and not fulfill?
>
> NUMBERS 23:19

In one sense, lying not only distorts reality, it denies the existence of God. To lie is to embrace falsehood and cut ourselves off from truth. When we permit this impostor into our homes, we are asking for trouble.

Lying is Satan's native language. Lying is wrong because its source is wrong. The source of falsehood is Satan himself. He is the father of lies.

> Jesus said to them, "If God were your Father, you would love me, for I came from God and now am here. I have not come on my own; but he sent me. Why is my language not clear to you? Because you are unable to hear what I say. You belong to your father, the devil, and you want to carry out your father's desire. He was a murderer from the beginning, not holding to the truth, for there is no truth in him. When he lies, he speaks his native language, for he is a liar and the father of lies. Yet because I tell the truth, you do not believe me!"
>
> JOHN 8:42–45

Satan promised Adam and Eve a world that didn't exist, where men and women could be their own gods and meet their own needs apart from God. Satan continues to lie to us, to weaken our grip on reality and strengthen his grip on our lives. When we lie in any form, we indicate that we have an affinity with evil. To speak his native language is to suggest that we are part of his kingdom. When Christians lie, we deny what God has done for us. He has not left us in the dark of Satan's deception, his empty promises of nonreality, but,

> has qualified you to share in the inheritance of the saints in the kingdom of light. For he has rescued us from the dominion of darkness and brought us into the kingdom of the Son he loves, in whom we have redemption, the forgiveness of sins.
>
> COLOSSIANS 1:12–14

Lying is foreign to the new nature of Christians. That's why Paul tells us to put it aside. It doesn't fit the new us.

> Do not lie to each other, since you have taken off your old self with its practices and have put on the new self, which is being renewed in knowledge in the image of its Creator.
>
> COLOSSIANS 3:9–10

For those caught in the darkness of Satan's kingdom, lying makes sense. When you're lost in the dark, in a way you have to attempt to create a reality in your mind. But it makes no sense for Christians. It is as foreign to our new nature as it is to God. To continue to embrace deceit short-circuits our development.

Lying destroys people's lives.   Lying not only hurts me, it hurts others as well. James describes the devastation that the tongue can bring in some of the most pointed words in the Bible.

> Likewise the tongue is a small part of the body, but it makes great boasts. Consider what a great forest is set on fire by a small spark. The tongue also is a fire, a world of evil among the parts of the body. It corrupts the whole person, sets the whole course of his life on fire, and is itself set on fire by hell.
>
> All kinds of animals, birds, reptiles and creatures of the sea are being tamed and have been tamed by man, but no man can tame the tongue. It is a restless evil, full of deadly poison.
>
> JAMES 3:5–8

A tongue energized by Satan is one of the most destructive forces on earth. Lives have been ruined by careless words, the passing on of thoughtless rumors, and the spread of malicious slander. Most of us at one time or another have felt the brunt of malicious words. Incredibly, knowing the pain of verbal daggers, we can turn and induce the same pain by attacking others. But a malicious lie is a double-edged sword cutting both ways, and we always inflict the worst wounds on ourselves.

Lying destroys us.   The one hurt most by a lie is the perpetrator. Lies destroy our grip on reality. Fallacies have an incredible power to draw us into the deceit. Before long we begin to believe the lie we have invented. This pattern can start early in children. We knew of a young boy who saw a toy he liked at preschool and secretly took it home in his backpack. When his mother asked where the toy came from, he said it was a gift. Because the child was so enamored with the toy, he wouldn't let it out of his sight and began to see it as his own. He believed the lie he had invented. The mother asked the teacher about the toy and learned the truth. Wisely, the mother didn't treat this lightly saying, "Oh well, boys will be boys," and simply tell her son to give back the toy. She dealt firmly, but lovingly, with the root problem of the situation—lying—for which she disciplined him, made him give back the toy, and made him confess what he did to the teacher and ask her forgiveness.

Removing the Need to Lie

There is only one thing that will draw us out and remove the need to lie. Only in an atmosphere of true security will we lower the mask, tear down the facade, come out from behind the walls, and call off the attack on our fellowman. The only place of safety like that in this world is Jesus Christ. He has reversed the spiritual effects of the fall in you and reconciled you, reconnected you with God, the source of life.

> For God was pleased to have all his fullness dwell in him (Christ), and through him to reconcile to himself all things, whether things on earth or things in heaven, by making peace through his blood, shed on the cross.
> Once you were alienated from God and were enemies in your minds because of your evil behavior. But now he has reconciled you by Christ's physical body through death to present you holy in his sight, without blemish and free from accusation—if you continue in your faith, established and firm, not moved from the hope held out in the gospel.
> COLOSSIANS 1:19–23

God has opened a way to safety and acceptance to all who place their faith in Christ and the way of forgiveness He offers through His death on our behalf. His death has canceled the sin and ugliness that separated us from God. And through this act of love, we are reconciled, made acceptable to God. The very One who knows you best, knows you better than you know yourself, loves you anyway. That is all the security anyone needs to come out from behind the lie. To know that I am accepted by the king of the universe, that's enough. So what are we hiding from?

> What, then, shall we say in response to this? If God is for us, who can be against us? He who did not spare his own Son, but gave him up for us all—how will he not also, along with him, graciously give us all things? Who will bring any

charge against those whom God has chosen? It is God who justifies. Who is he that condemns? Christ Jesus, who died—more than that, who was raised to life—is at the right hand of God and is also interceding for us. Who shall separate us from the love of Christ? Shall trouble or hardship or persecution or famine or nakedness or danger or sword? As it is written:

> "For your sake we face death all day long;
> we are considered as sheep to be slaughtered."

No, in all these things we are more than conquerors through him who loved us. For I am convinced that neither death nor life, neither angels nor demons, neither the present nor the future, nor any powers, neither height nor depth, nor anything else in all creation, will be able to separate us from the love of God that is in Christ Jesus our Lord.

ROMANS 8:31–39

When we open up to God and begin to know His security, we can open up to others. Transparency is a function of security. If I have no need to protect myself, I have no need to lie any more to God or man.

Coming Out from Behind the Walls

Confront a lie for what it is. Ask God to help you recognize deceit in all its forms from outright lies to subtle manipulation. Don't get caught minimizing deception in yourself, others, or your children. As I said, I had problems learning not to lie as a child because lies were called "stories." A lie by any other name is a lie.

When your children lie, even about small things, make it a big deal. Though the issue may be small, the method they are using is the height of sinfulness. If it's not confronted, their view of reality will be slanted.

Grasp acceptance in Christ. Even though you still have problems and unlovely parts to your character, you are accepted in Christ. Don't let Satan tempt you or someone else lure you into searching for security in any other source.

Of course, if you are grasping other things you'll have a hard time focusing on Christ. Reject every other source as the primary source of your acceptance. Turn it loose. If you have been trusting in yourself, admit that you are failing. You can't make yourself acceptable. Only Christ can do that.

Refuse to speak the deceiver's language.   If you know Christ, you are no longer part of Satan's kingdom. Instead, speak the language of truth and love.

> Therefore, as God's chosen people, holy and dearly loved, clothe yourselves with compassion, kindness, humility, gentleness and patience. Bear with each other and forgive whatever grievances you may have against one another. Forgive as the Lord forgave you. And over all these virtues put on love, which binds them all together in perfect unity.
> COLOSSIANS 3:12–14

When we are committed to being truthful, we can accept others as they are. We have no need to lie and manipulate family, friends, and associates to accept us or make us feel adequate.

> These are the things you are to do: Speak the truth to each other, and render true and sound judgment in your courts; do not plot evil against your neighbor, and do not love to swear falsely. I hate all this," declares the LORD.
> ZECHARIAH 8:16–17

I can reveal my weaknesses without fear. Being accepted does not mean that I have no problems. It does mean that I can face my frailties and deal with them honestly rather than covering them.

I can listen with openness and face the truth about myself. I can honestly go to God, who accepts me as I am, and ask Him to help me change.

I can refrain from counterattacks. When others point out my character flaws, I have no need to strike back whatever their motive. When I discover someone else is ahead of me, I have no need to belittle them in hopes of making my own stock rise.

I can speak the truth in love. I have no pressing self-need to tell someone else their shortcomings. I have no need to take someone else down a notch to make myself feel more righteous. I can approach someone with genuine concern for their welfare.

I do not write to you because you do not know the truth, but because you do know it and because no lie comes from the truth.

1 JOHN 2:21

Honesty and openness in interpersonal relationships is essential for men and women to live in freedom.

Aiming High

I can't think of a better time to remember why God gave us the Ten Commandments than when we're talking about telling the truth, the whole truth, and nothing but the truth. Is there one among us who can say he's 100 percent truthful 100 percent of the time? I think the best place to begin teaching children about this commandment is probably to acknowledge humbly that we all break it sometimes. Once that's done, you can make it a family priority—and a priority for every individual in the family—to strive to be truthful, to come out from behind the wall of insecurity that makes us all lie. And we can do it on a daily basis.

Lying is sneaky, and it's important to be vigilant. We once heard what we thought was a cute story. Some parents wrote a note to a teacher on the first day of class: "The opinions expressed by this child are not necessarily those of the parents." Unfortunately, this note probably reflects another way of lying, a situation in which there are "two truths," one for school and one for home.

The suggestions here are by no means comprehensive. The publisher didn't want this book to be ten thousand pages long. And we'd be lying if we said we had all the solutions for this pervasive behavior.

Make sure you call a lie a lie. It's okay to encourage your children's ability to tell imaginative stories. Just make sure you also reinforce the difference between lying and writing or telling a story.

Half-truths aren't whole. You can make a family "game" of discovering half-truths. Have each person think of an imaginary situation in which she might be tempted to tell only half the truth. For example, I finished my homework, but only after I talked on the phone for an hour with my friend.

216

Don't make promises to your child that you are not willing or able to keep; don't make threats you are not willing to enforce. Your children need to know that telling the truth applies to parents, too.

∞

If your child tells a lie, don't take this lightly. Lying is one of the automatic discipline behaviors at our house.

∞

When playing board games or card games with your children, talk about the importance of playing fairly and telling the truth, even when playing a game.

∞

"I hold the maxim no less applicable to public than to private affairs, that honesty is always the best policy"— George Washington. Read a book about George Washington with your children. Talk about the decisions he made to tell the truth.

∞

Praise your children for being courageous when they tell the truth, even though they know they'll get in trouble.

∞

When you buy a house or borrow money to buy a car, let your children go with you to the bank. Explain to them the importance of signing a contract, that you are promising, or "telling the truth," that you will fulfill certain obligations.

∞

When you catch your child in a lie, make sure she knows that you don't approve of what she did but you still approve of her.

∞

If your child catches you in a lie, acknowledge it, explain that you realize this is wrong in God's sight. No excuses.

∞

"Character calls forth character"—Wolfgang von Goethe. If you are a truthful person, your children will be more likely to be truthful.

∞

Do not allow your children to tell white lies. There isn't such a thing.

Never instruct your child to lie for you. If someone you do not want to talk to calls you at home, and your child answers the phone, don't ask him to say, "Dad isn't here." If you don't want to accept the call, simply have the child take the caller's number and explain that you will call back later.

∞

Evaluate how much of your family's table talk is about other people. Are the comments positive or negative? Can you verify the truthfulness? A good way to stop a habit of gossiping is to stop and pray for the person you're gossiping about.

∞

Never let an opportunity go by for you to tell the truth by not maintaining silence. If a friend compliments you on your lovely dessert (whether your children are there to hear it or not), own up to who really made the dessert.

∞

Do your own truth-in-advertising review. Have every member of your family bring an advertisement clipped from a magazine or newspaper to a family group time. Look at each ad to discover how the truth is being stretched or manipulated. What's the real message of the ad? That we'll be happy, healthy, wise, loved, pretty if we buy Product X?

∞

Search out books, videos, and tapes for your child regarding telling the truth. One sure classic is any version of "The Boy Who Cried Wolf."

∞

As a family, pray together for the grace to feel God's gracious love so that the need to lie is removed from your everyday lives.

The Tenth Commandment

You shall not covet your neighbor's wife. You shall not set your desire on your neighbor's house or land, his manservant or maidservant, his ox or donkey, or anything that belongs to your neighbor.

Deuteronomy 5:21

You never know what is enough
unless you know what is more than enough.
—William Blake

Chapter 12

THE GRASS IS
ALWAYS GREENER

I MISSED BEING NAMED MOTHER OF THE YEAR by four votes—all cast by my family. I deluded myself into thinking I had a pretty fair shot at the title. When Cynthia Got-It-All-Together entered the race, I knew I was in trouble.

Gracious person that I am, I tried to befriend Cynthia. I've never liked anyone who wears a size five, so I prayed for God's help. I broached a number of topics with her, but frankly I found it impossible to carry on a conversation with a woman who coaches her daughter's hockey team, is known as Our Lady of Perpetual Adventure to the seventeen boys in her son's scouting group, delivers home-baked goodies to all four of her children's classrooms every month, and always knows where her car keys are. Besides that, when she mends her children's clothing, she doesn't have to slide her bare feet through the carpet looking for a needle. She goes straight to her sewing box. But what could I expect from a woman whose checkbook balances every month?

How do women like Cynthia do it? They bake, volunteer, and keep their baseboards clean. They run businesses, households, and marathons. Their children are gifted, their husbands devoted, their thighs are toned. They never seem to break a sweat or a fingernail.

I don't know, maybe I'm jealous. Maybe I'm doing exactly what I'm trying to teach my kids not to do by not following the Tenth

Commandment: "You must not burn with desire for another man's wife, nor envy him for his home, land, servants, oxen, donkeys, nor anything else he owns."

Now I don't have a problem with oxen or donkeys, but if I were honest I'd admit that I do have a problem with another man's wife or another child's mother. I am insecure about who I am, and I want to be like her. Maybe I've let myself follow Eve's example and concentrated on what's wrong with my life instead of what's right with it. Maybe I should rechannel the time and energy I spend comparing myself to someone I'm not and find my security in who God says I am. After all, when it comes to naming the mother of the year, God's got the inside track. In His eyes, we all get to be mother (or father) of the year, every day and every year that we use the skills and abilities that He has given us in the great adventure of parenting. In other words, I can stop coveting (and still enjoy) worldly awards when I realize in my mind and in my heart that God loves me just the way I am.

The Heart of the Matter

From the time I first seriously studied the Ten Commandments in seminary, I've thought this one to be the hardest to follow as a man, a husband, a father, a professional—in all my roles in life. The subject of coveting nails all of us where it counts: in the heart. This commandment reminds us that sin is not just a problem of our actions, but also our attitude. God is interested in what our heart is gawking at as well as what our hands are grabbing for. As a matter of fact, we usually violate this commandment before we violate any of the other commandments. It's as if God has given us a way to identify sin while it's in the attitude stage, before it erupts into behavior that damages others.

People who describe themselves as content are few and far between. It seems we're all grabbing for something to satisfy the deep longings within our heart. When we look at what someone else has that we don't, tangible or intangible, and desire it to the point that we think we can't be satisfied without it, we're doing what the Bible calls coveting. To covet is to desire someone else's blessings. It's to look at what someone has been given and say, If only I had that, then I would be happy, or content, or successful, or satisfied, or safe.

We can covet just about anything: property, money, relationships, physical features, status, spiritual gifts, toys, athletic prowess, or intellect. Coveting is a passion to acquire something from the world that will satisfy our deepest longings, or so we think. In a real sense, coveting drives almost every sin we commit and brings excessive disharmony among humankind. James was rather blunt about our lust for more when he wrote,

> You want something but don't get it. You kill and covet, but you cannot have what you want. You quarrel and fight.
>
> JAMES 4:2

The Origin of Desire

It might be natural for us to focus on our passions as the problem and wish they would just go away, but God points us in a different direction. God's goal is not for us to be passionless, but instead for us to focus our passions on Him. God gave us these passions, and like all of God's gifts, they can be turned toward sin. The words used to describe the sin of coveting, both in the Old and New Testament, are morally neutral. They simply mean to have a strong desire, to delight in, to long for, to be passionate about acquiring something. I can desire or be passionate for something that honors God. For example, David uses this word to describe his hunger for God's Word, here translated "precious."

> They are more precious than gold,
>   than much pure gold;
> they are sweeter than honey,
>   than honey from the comb.
>
> PSALM 19:10

More often, however, these words for coveting have a sinful goal and are translated as "lust" or "desire" and are used to describe our greed to acquire more. For instance, Solomon warns us to avoid fixing our passions on an adulteress,

> Do not lust in your heart after her beauty
>   or let her captivate you with her eyes.
>
> PROVERBS 6:25

What makes our passionate desires sinful is what we focus on and why we want it. It's not wrong to think how much fun it would be to have a boat like our neighbor's so we can take our kids and their friends water-skiing on Saturdays. It is wrong to think that we deserve a boat more than he does, and we resent the fact that we can't have one. It's not wrong for our daughter to desire that a particular girl in her class be her friend. It is wrong if she feels she can't be happy without that friendship. Don't misunderstand, the problem is not enjoying or even looking forward to certain good things in life. Paul told us that God

> richly provides us with everything for our enjoyment.
>
> 1 TIMOTHY 6:17

The problem arises when our heart fixates on something we think we must have to be happy. We say, "I am miserable because I don't have that house or that car." Or our child says, "I won't be happy if I don't get that toy." Or our teen says, "I'll just die if I'm not elected cheerleader or class president."

Driven by Emptiness

We covet what others have because we want to feel satisfied and content. It's as if I have a hole in my soul that I am constantly trying to fill. Like an empty stomach that craves to be filled, this soul hole craves to be satisfied and aches when it is empty. When it is filled, I feel content. And just like the stomach wants something specific to be filled with—nourishing food—so our soul hungers after specific things. Every soul hungers for two things to be content: feelings of significance and assurance of security. God created us with these desires. Each of us hungers to know that we are important, that we have value, and that there is some meaning for our lives, a vital part for us to play. Each of us also craves to be assured that we are safe, accepted as we are, protected from harm, and that we will have what we need to survive.

We have each developed specific foods we seek to satisfy our stomachs. I love Mexican food. Offer me a bowl of chili, and I'll take it every time. But put a bowl of clam chowder in front of me, and I'll gag. I'm never tempted to use chowder to satisfy my hunger. In fact, I'll go hungry before I'll eat the stuff. This probably has something to do with being raised in Texas, and the fact that the first dish of clam chowder put in front of me had been in a can for months. I might feel very differently had I been brought up in New England and introduced to fresh chowder at an early age. Whatever, I have never connected the smell of chowder with feelings of contentment. Not so a big, thick, steaming bowl of chili. On a cold day, I can almost smell a television commercial.

In a similar way, I have learned that certain things seem to satisfy my soul's hunger for significance and security. God made this world with an endless variety of delightful creations and experiences for me to enjoy. As I grew up, I've developed a taste for certain ones. Something in me says, Bill, when you have this, then you'll be satisfied. The problem is that no matter what I obtain, what I experience, how successful I am, I seem to need a new meal for my soul as often as I need a meal for my body. The hunger of my soul is as insatiable as my physical hunger. No matter how significant or secure I feel at any one given moment, there is always something around the corner that undermines my momentary contentment.

As parents, every Christmas we get a first-hand demonstration of how this principle operates. Our children make their list of can't-live-without toys, then they remind us twice a day, every day in December that these things will make them immensely happy. So happy, in fact, that they say they'll never ask for anything else as long as they live. Then when Christmas morning rolls around, and they do indeed receive at least some of the items on their list, they are thrilled, at least for an hour or two. Then boredom sets in, and they want to know why the stores aren't open on Christmas day so they can spend the money Aunt Jean sent to buy something else.

The fact is, in this day of unprecedented wealth and opportunity, when modern technologies have boosted everything the world has to offer, we are experiencing a famine of fulfillment. We have achieved and obtained things that we thought would make us happy, only to find they're not enough. Most of us are living at a higher standard of living than our grandparents did, and yet we are not fundamentally happier. For all our prosperity, it seems we are still at a subsistence level when it comes to the feeding the hunger of our soul.

There is a reason that we never seem to be satisfied, and it's simple. The world was never designed to satisfy us. Just like a car can't run on water, we simply can't run on what the world has to offer. As wonderful and marvelous as God's creation is, He created it only for our enjoyment, not for our satisfaction. God created us for a relationship with Him, and as much as we try to satisfy ourselves with other things, we can only find satisfaction and contentment in a relationship with Him, period.

What Happened to Us?

We were created for fellowship with God.   Adam and Eve enjoyed a perfect relationship of unbroken fellowship with God. They knew an absolute acceptance before God and each other that we can only dream of. They knew His approval and affirmation in everything they did. The fears and insecurities that plague relationships in our world did not exist.

They also recognized in each other God's perfect provision to complete each other in the world. What a contrast to our world, where most of us wish our mates were something more than they are, and we covet, if not another person's spouse, at least some of that spouse's attributes.

Deep inside we know that we were created for that kind of security and acceptance. Our soul longs for that kind of intimacy with God.

We were created for use by God.   Adam and Eve were here on Earth to work for God. They were not only to cultivate the garden, they were given the job of growing a civilization.

> God blessed them and said to them, "Be fruitful and increase in number; fill the earth and subdue it. Rule over the fish of the sea and the birds of the air and over every living creature that moves on the ground."
>
> GENESIS 1:28

Their lives had significance because they were commissioned by the author of meaning and purpose. And, incredibly, everything they did worked. There were no failed crops, no fruitless endeavors, no wasted efforts. Hard work was always rewarded with abundance. There were no fears of inadequacy, only endless opportunities unfettered by questions of competency or doubts about success. And knowing their place in God's plan, they didn't need to scramble for power or prove themselves better than someone else.

The contrast with our world is obvious. Here I long for these same feelings of significance, that I am adequate, that I am important, and that what I do is not just a study in futility. Every success I have is dogged by the knowledge that my satisfaction will be short-lived. Then I must venture out again, wondering whether I am really capable and facing the real possibility of failure.

No wonder we're all looking for Eden, whether it's a perfect wife, perfect children, or a perfect job. We were meant for more than this world has to offer. Our souls' hungers can only be met in a relationship with God. But when Adam and Eve chose to meet their own needs in the world apart from God and in violation of His one command to them, they discovered a new attribute of God: His justice.

Since God's justice is never capricious and allows us to experience the logical consequences of our behavior, He withdrew, leaving us, their descendants, with the task of meeting our own needs in the world apart from His direct provision. Separated from God, the human race experienced an immediate internal emptiness. Without God's love, we became insecure and hungered for acceptance. Without God's power and purpose, we came to feel insignificant, to crave meaning and competence.

All our conflicts, wars, divorces, abuses, corruptions, failures, and frustrations are a result of the choice of choosing to seek our satisfaction in the world. That's why we lie, steal, cheat, commit adultery, and crave what someone else has. We are betting on a long shot, that just around the corner, in some new experience, some new success, some new relationship, some new acquisition, some new something, or some new someone will bring more than a momentary easing of this insatiably painful hunger inside and fill our soul.

The Possibility of Contentment

Is there hope to curb our appetite? Is it possible to stop craving, coveting, lusting, and grabbing for more? Can I help my children avoid some of the painful experiences I have had because I tried to demand that the world meet needs only God can meet?

The answer is yes and no. Because God created me with this hunger, I can never change my need to feel significant and secure. I will never become passionless without first ceasing to be a person. As long as I continue to demand a diet of satisfaction from people, things, and experiences, I am doomed to gnawing emptiness, a nagging sense of insecurity, a haunting fear of insignificance, and seeking hostile or distant relationships. But I can satisfy that hunger by choosing another meal, a different meal, at God's dinner table, so to speak. If I return to the only real source of satisfaction, there is hope. Paul holds out the possibility in his own experience,

227

I have learned to be content whatever the circumstances. I know what it is to be in need, and I know what it is to have plenty. I have learned the secret of being content in any and every situation, whether well fed or hungry, whether living in plenty or in want. I can do everything through him who gives me strength.

PHILIPPIANS 4:11–13

Strategy for Satisfaction

Now that's the picture of a satisfied man. How did he get there? How did he overcome the tremendous tendency we all have to focus on the world rather than on Christ? He offers us some help for us in our struggle in his letter to the Colossians.

Because contentment is a matter of the heart, our whole inner being must be renewed—mind, will, and emotions. In a sense, the battle must be fought on three levels. Though they are logical in sequence, our whole inner being must be engaged at the same time. We must, however, begin with the gate to our heart or our mind, then move to our choices or our will, and then to our feelings or emotions.

We must refocus our mind. The fact is I can't define myself. Even though some of us are more independent than others, all of us are incredibly dependent on others to tell us who we are. The first place we look is to those around us, our family. Parents have the most staggering power to shape the identity of their children. To the extent that our parents had healthy identities themselves, they helped or hindered us. But since no one is perfect, distortions are communicated. If we are going to know the satisfaction that our souls hunger for, we must look beyond ourselves and others and focus our minds on who we are in Christ. I am not what I think others think I am; I am what Christ thinks I am. That's why Paul tells us,

Since, then, you have been raised with Christ, set your hearts on things above, where Christ is seated at the right hand of God. Set your minds on things above, not on earthly things. For you died, and your life is now hidden with Christ in God. When Christ, who is your life, appears, then you also will appear with him in glory.

COLOSSIANS 3:1–4

Even though I may feel empty, insecure, and insignificant, I am not. If I trust Christ as my Savior, I am no longer dead, separated from the source of life, I have been raised up with Christ. I must listen to Christ and decide if I am going to believe Him or the other insecure people around me who might give me erroneous information. If I listen to Christ, I will move toward knowing and experiencing the satisfaction my soul has only dreamed of. I will begin to see exactly where my soul must feed if I am to know contentment.

Paul is not suggesting I focus on "apple pie in the sky by and by." He wants me to know my true identity, my significance and security in Christ. My life is not some frail, anemic existence on earth. There is a heavenly reality today—my life is in Christ. No place is more secure. What is there on earth to fear if my life is secure with Christ? If I am with Christ, seated at the right hand of the Father, is there any place more significant? Can any achievement or success move me beyond that position? Is it possible that I can wield any more power than the authority I have in Christ?

Through the death and resurrection of Jesus Christ, my whole life has changed. The death of Christ removed the penalty of sin and restored me to fellowship with God my Father. His resurrection broke the power of sin in my life, restoring our spiritual power. I have been raised up with Christ.

Whatever the world is telling me, I need to refocus my mind and listen to what Christ is saying. And as I do, I also need to communicate these truths to my children.

Who am I? I am a forgiven sinner. I have been reconciled, made acceptable to God. I am part of God's own family. I have the power to be who I was created to be and impact the world according to God's plan. I am free from the bonds of sin. I can choose to do the right thing. I am a son of God, with all the privileges of that rank. I am rich. All the blessings of heaven are mine.

In order to begin to experience all of these blessings, I must turn away from any thought that tells me I am anything other than who Christ tells me to be, no matter how dear the source. If my children rebel and I feel like a worthless parent, if my wife criticizes me and I feel like a failure, if my banker turns me down and I feel unsuccessful, I must refocus my thoughts on what God says is true about me.

We have found that it is really important to have God's opinions stored away in our memory to face successfully the lies that Satan constantly sends us. That's why we've committed Scripture, including many of the verses above, to memory. This way, when a false message presents itself in our minds, the truth is easily accessible, and we can remind ourselves that we are full.

As parents, we need to be so careful with the messages we give our children. Conditional love and acceptance teaches them that they are unworthy and becomes a barrier to their accepting their security in Christ. We need to set our goal to look at them as God sees them and treat them accordingly.

We need also to be careful of the examples we set. Even though we may not tell them, they recognize instinctively where we are looking for our contentment. If they see us overly anxious about our bank account, they will quickly conclude that money is an important source of security. On the other hand, if they see our faith in God's goodness grow as things get hard, they will learn where their true security lays.

If I don't take this first step to focus on who Christ says I am, I will never be able to deal with my will, the second level of battle.

We must change our behavior.   A new identity means a new strategy for fulfillment and a new way of living. If I come to the table knowing that I am significant and secure with nothing to lose, it stands to reason that I should play the game differently. In fact, if my behavior isn't changing, I can be sure that my mind is not changing either. That's why Paul goes on to address our behavior.

> Put to death, therefore, whatever belongs to your earthly nature: sexual immorality, impurity, lust, evil desires and greed, which is idolatry. Because of these, the wrath of God is coming. You used to walk in these ways, in the life you once lived.
>
> COLOSSIANS 3:5–7

As we've already learned, actions can be wrong outright—lying, impurity, lust, evil desires, and greed—or they can be wrong because of their motive—telling the truth to hurt someone else, selfish sexuality in marriage, using our anger to extract revenge. As Christians we need to look not only at our actions, but also behind our behavior and examine the strategy. Am I doing something for what it will do for me, or am I doing it because of who I am in Christ? Behind every action is a goal. If that goal is my personal satisfaction, I am operating from emptiness, not satisfaction.

I must take what God says I am and make choices of the will to act in accordance with my true identity—who Christ says that I am. For example, if one of my boys behaves in a way that embarrasses me in public and questions my significance as a father, I have a choice. I can either do what comes naturally, reasoning from a deep-seated fear that I am really inadequate, and make sure that the boy and everyone else within shouting distance knows that I'm the in-charge, Big Dog Dad. Or I can reason from my significance in Christ and refuse my natural instinct and seek to understand why he is behaving the way he is. In this case I may learn that he is behaving out of insecurity (possibly because I haven't spent enough time with him lately) and try to minister to him in a way that reminds him of his security in Christ, without condoning misbehavior or overlooking rebellious attitudes.

It's important that we make a clear distinction between our demands and our desires. When I reason from feelings of emptiness, I usually end up setting goals, trying to manipulate or obtain things that I can't control, for example, how my children behave when they are in public. If my sense of insignificance demands that they always behave a certain way, even if it is something God would want them to do, then I am operating from a base of emptiness and not looking to Christ as the source of my significance. This does not mean that I can't desire that my children be well-behaved. It does not mean that I do not teach them proper behavior and discipline them when they don't obey. But the moment that I place my identity in their hands, I have moved from desire to demand, which guarantees my disappointment. If that isn't bad enough, this shift in my thinking will always issue forth in manipulative behavior to move my kids into the place where they will gratify my desire for worldly significance.

Christian psychologist Larry Crabb, who taught Kathy and me many of these principles, gave us a good rule of thumb. We pray for our desires and leave them in God's hands to extend to us or to withhold from us as He sees fit. I need to limit my demands to the only thing that I can control: my own behavior. In other words, I can demand that I be a godly father, but I transgress proper motives when my lack of self-worth demands that my boys be godly children.

We can help our children move toward contentment not only by helping them understand their identity in Christ, but by helping them identify behavior that simply does not fit with a Christian's new nature. One of the most important ways we do this is to make sure they know right from wrong. But we must also let them feel the natural consequences of sinful behavior—seeking satisfaction apart from God. The more we protect them from feeling the pain of these consequences, the harder it is for them to learn that sin doesn't really bring us what we ultimately want. It simply doesn't work.

Another thing we can do is help our children evaluate their motives. The most natural time to do this is at a time of disappointment, when something doesn't turn out the way they wanted. This is a wonderful opportunity to affirm our love for them and remind them that God thinks they are great, regardless of what else happened. By doing this we model for them how Christ really sees them.

As children get older, more significant and impressive opportunities arise. This past year our oldest son experienced a major disappointment. Since we live more than six hundred miles from his college, all we could do was talk to him by phone and pray. While Kathy and I felt much of his pain, I sensed that God was doing something much deeper in his life than we could have possibly engineered. It was not only a perfect time for a motive check, but also an opportunity to learn just how God could meet his needs in this time of pain. We experienced great joy with our pain as we saw him continue to pursue his relationship with God when the external motive was removed. There was no longer anyone to impress, just a deep inner need and a new awareness of how much he needed God.

We must confront our emotions. Through John's experience he began to learn to trust God to meet his deepest needs as a man, and hopefully this will one day help him be a godly husband and father. One of the things he discovered through this situation was that knowing who he was and acting on this fact was easier than dealing with his runaway emotions. If our heart ever knows fullness, it will be because we have dealt decisively with the last and most difficult part of the heart—our emotions.

Without a doubt, our emotions are the slowest part of us to change and the hardest to deal with. After years of disappointment and attempts to manipulate the world to satisfy us, our emotions become tangled and even damaged. Unlike our mind and will, emotions refuse to be controlled. Any time we feel threatened, either emotionally or physically, our emotions move into action as a self-preservation device. Deep within our subconscious, an evaluation of threat is made and strong feelings move into our consciousness. The purpose is to move us to action. However, as Christians, we need to look before we leap. That's way Paul tells us,

> Let the peace of Christ rule in your hearts, since as members of one body you were called to peace. And be thankful. Let the word of Christ dwell in you richly.
> COLOSSIANS 3:15–16

The word "rule" means to act as an umpire. In other words, before we allow an emotion to move us into action, we need to stop and evaluate that emotion. There are things every day that make me feel insecure and inadequate. Emotions such as fear, displeasure, and anger often result in pain that drives me to accept wrong behaviors or veil impure motives behind strategies to make me feel better. Paul tells us clearly that our umpire is "the peace of Christ." Peace is more than lack of fighting. It actually means wholeness and prosperity. The umpire is the truth of who I am in Christ—my fullness, my wholeness, my spiritual prosperity in Him. And if a particular emotional response doesn't jive with who I am in Christ, I have to call it "Out!"

Several years ago I began a practice of reminding myself and my family of this truth. Every time we give thanks at a meal, I always say, "Thank you Lord for meeting all our needs." There have been more than a few times when my emotions told me this wasn't true. But by this simple affirmation, I remind myself and my family of the facts. Whether I happen to feel like it or not, I want to rest in the truth of this statement, and I want my kids to learn to do the same. I have found that offering a prayer of thanks in faith is one of the most effective ways to confront my panicking emotions and seize the truth.

Obviously, in order to teach our children to deal with emotions, we have to accept the presence of these emotions in our own lives. If either we as parents or our children have a problem accepting emotions, we are both in trouble. Emotions are God-given components of our personhood and cannot be repressed or denied without significant personal damage. Not only do we deny part of our being, but we eliminate our ability to deal with emotions that deny our identity in Christ. Actually our feelings will dominate us if we deny their existence. Therefore it is imperative for our homes to be a safe place to express our emotions. There are certainly ways of expressing our anger that are off-limits, but while we limit these behaviors we need to be careful to help our children discover appropriate ways to acknowledge how they feel.

It is only when we as parents operate from a place of personal contentment in Christ that we can help our children learn to express and evaluate their emotions in a godly way, without being pulled into the vacuum of emotional outbursts.

The Great Choice

As Christians, God has given us an incredible opportunity to escape the tyranny of nagging emptiness. But the choice is still ours. Impossible as it seems, people who have all the wealth of heaven still chose to live as spiritual paupers. God reports the shocking truth in Jeremiah 2:11–13.

> Has a nation ever changed its gods?
>> (Yet they are not gods at all.)
> But my people have exchanged their Glory
>> for worthless idols.
> Be appalled at this, O heavens,
>> and shudder with great horror,"
>>> declares the LORD.
> "My people have committed two sins:
> They have forsaken me,
>> the spring of living water,
> and have dug their own cisterns,
>> broken cisterns that cannot hold water.

What an incredible picture. God is the only source that will satisfy our hunger for acceptance and our thirst for significance. Looking anywhere else invites only frustration and pain. It's like trying to collect water in a leaky bucket. The more we put in, the emptier we are and the more we need.

Two clear paradigms for living emerge: one that seeks satisfaction in the world and one that finds contentment in God. We only have these two options. Either God and what He provides is all we need, or we must have the things of this world to make us happy and fulfilled.

When we trade the riches of our relationship with God for temporal fulfillment, a predictable scenario results.

The more I put in, the more I want.
That's GREED.

The more I want, the more I need.
That's EMPTINESS.

The more I need,
the more I become obsessed.
That's SLAVERY.

This is the fate of anyone who forsakes the Tenth Commandment. On the other hand, God offers real freedom for those who put Him first.

The more I focus on my spiritual wealth,
the more content and fulfilled I am.

The more content I am,
the less I require from this world
to make me happy.

The less I require,
the more freedom I have
to enjoy God and the wealth of His creation.
That's FREEDOM[1]

The choice is ours.

Aiming High

Coveting will always lead us to sin. Contentment in Christ will always lead us to obedience. That's why the Tenth Commandment is so important. Don't forget, however, that change from coveting to contentment happens incrementally, thought by thought, behavior by behavior, and emotion by emotion. The day will come when our emotions will change and reinforce godly strategies and actions, if we keep our focus clear. Contentment in God, after all, breeds contentment. As parents and as children of God, we need to work on two fronts: to bring the *whats* of our contentment into line with what God wants for us and to discover that the *hows* of our contentment rest in trusting God. None of us is going to cease coveting overnight. But we can begin with the first step and then the next. Let the ideas here spur you to take a first step.

If a child has a problem with wanting to be like her friend, or maybe even belonging to that friend's family instead of her own, take the time to listen to what it is she wants that's missing in her life. Perhaps you need to spend more time with her. Perhaps she needs to feel more loved. Perhaps she just needs to hear that every family faces problems and challenges and usually we can't see those from outside.

∞

Instant gratification—without the need to save or sacrifice—has become a common way of life in America. Buying the latest clothes, electronic games, and sports equipment as soon as they hit the market is unhealthy. If your kids badly want something like this, let them earn the money to pay for half of it.

∞

Make a family "Contentment Scrapbook." Fill it with memories of times when your family has had fun together, when you've worked together on a project. Also add nice things family members did for each other that made them feel good. Thank God for these good gifts.

∞

Talk about your own desires with your children and the reasons you have them. Be honest. Maybe you want to lose weight so you'll look like a friend. And you could point out to your children that with this kind of motivation, you probably won't be successful. Maybe you want to lose weight so you'll feel better. Then you can model achieving a worthwhile desire *and* enlist your children in helping you achieve a behavior change.

∞

When anyone in your family wins an award, is chosen for an honor, or accomplishes a task, make sure you celebrate together. We all need some attitude adjustment when it comes to counting our blessings and celebrating them is one way to adjust.

∞

Talk with your children about the origin of desire. One of the things we risk when we concentrate on the "not" in this commandment is that our children will feel perpetually guilty for wanting anything. If we know that God desires for us to be fulfilled and to experience joy in Him, we can begin to make choices about what we want that are in line with His desires for us.

∞

Make sure your kids see you model an attitude of contentment when you are content. Mention the details often. We can be content with a good meal, a shared family time, pleased that our day went according to plan, or even content that God sent problems to sidetrack a goal we shouldn't have been trying to achieve in the first place.

∞

As your children get older, talk with them about specific values regarding worldly goods. Share with them times you coveted what other people had and the consequences.

∞

"The covetous person is always in want"—Irish saying. Talk with your children about how contentment is more a matter of attitude than accumulation. Sometimes younger children understand numbers best. Ask questions like, Would you rather have ten toys you didn't want or one toy you really wanted? Why?

∞

Don't get caught in the trap of spending money on your children to ease your guilt of not spending enough time with them. In doing this, you teach them that possessions are more important than they are.

∞

"When I fed them, they were satisfied; when they were satisfied, they became proud; then they forgot me" (Hosea 13:6). Acknowledge your blessings regularly as a family so that you may never forget God is the source of your blessings.

∞

Make sure your children feel good about themselves on the inside—then they won't depend on money or possessions for their self-esteem.

∞

Poverty in its truest sense is a child who gets everything she wants, has a closet full of clothes but still doesn't have a thing to wear, has a closet full of games of toys—and still has nothing to do, has so many things on his want list, spends money on perfume, makeup, jewelry, and designer clothes—and still worries about her image, she doesn't have any money to help others. Work with your children to make realistic lists of their needs and wants. Encourage them to feel "rich" in helping others.

∞

"I have learned the secret of being content in any and every situation, whether well fed or hungry, whether living in plenty or in want. I can do all things through him (Christ) who strengthens me" (Phil. 4:12–13). If my children witness this attitude in me, chances are good it will rub off on them. Unfortunately, the converse is also true. We all need to examine our own attitude.

∞

Teach your children that even though the grass may be greener on the other side, it still needs mowing.

∞

"Reflect upon your present blessings, of which every man has many; not on your past misfortunes, of which all men have some"—Charles Dickens. Talk about the meaning of this statement one night at dinner.

∞

Teach your kids that we all have a choice about what we will concentrate on—the positive things in our life or the negatives, what we have or what we don't have. What do your children see you concentrating on?

∞

Do something today that will model an attitude of contentment for your children. Write a list of your blessings and have your children to do the same.

∞

When your child has gotten into trouble as a result of trying to find satisfaction in the world, lovingly walk with him through the consequences, but make sure he faces them.

∞

Pray prayers of gratitude, thanking God for how much you already have, both in material possessions and in feeling content in your relationship with Him.

If you would win a man to your cause,
first become his friend.
—ABRAHAM LINCOLN

Chapter 13

HOW TO GO
AGAINST THE GRAIN

IN CASE YOU HAVEN'T NOTICED, TEACHING spiritual values to children is hard. Really hard. Not only is it difficult to practice what we preach consistently, but if we're teaching God's principles, hoping our children will live lives of integrity with strong values, we're going against the grain. Every night when the television goes on, our children watch the glorification of dishonesty, immorality, murder, and a blatant disrespect for any kind of authority—not the principles from the Ten Commandments we hope will be manifest in their lives. And what they see and hear cannot help but affect the lifestyle they choose and the decisions they make. A commitment to instill God's principles and values in our children is an important and worthy battle. It is a battle for their very lives.

Although we don't know what specific challenges our own children will encounter, what temptations they'll face, what decisions they'll be forced to make today or tomorrow, one thing's for sure: the spiritual lessons—good or bad—they learn in the family will make a big difference in what values they embrace and whether or not they will live by these values. Dr. Armand Nicholi of Harvard Medical School concurs:

> Our family experience is the most significant experi-
> ence of our lives. Regardless of differences in cultural,

241

social, educational and religious backgrounds, we all share the experience of being a child and for good or evil, spending our days of childhood in the context of the family. Here the seed is sown for what we become as adults. Early family experience determines our adult character structure, the inner picture we harbor of ourselves, how we feel about ourselves, how we perceive and feel about others, our concept of right and wrong—that is, the fundamental rules of human conduct that we call morality.[1]

William Coleridge once spoke with a man who did not believe in teaching values to children. His theory was that a child's mind should not be prejudiced so he could choose his opinions for himself. The great poet said nothing in response but asked if his visitor would like to see his garden. The man accepted the invitation, and Coleridge took him to the garden where only weeds were growing. The man looked at him in surprise and said, "Why this is not a garden! There is nothing but weeds here!"

"Well, you see," answered Coleridge, "I didn't want to infringe upon the liberty of the garden in any way. I was giving the garden a chance to express itself and choose its own production."

If we want the garden of our children's minds to grow more than weeds, we must tend it well by teaching them values. But teaching spiritual values to our children is more than pouring the Ten Commandments into their heads. It is penetrating their *hearts* with spiritual truth. It's practicing the four I's we talked about in chapter 1: Incarnation—consistently living out the values we want our children to embrace. Indoctrination—formally teaching our children the tenets of our faith. Initiation—marking the passages of new privileges and responsibilities as they grow in faith. Immersion—plunging them into a spiritual value system where they can see, experience, and practice spiritual truth in the midst of everyday living.

If we want our children to own spiritual values, rather than superficially possessing hand-me-down values, three A's must characterize our teaching.

Our teaching must be affirmative. It is sometimes easy, as Christian parents, to be much better at defining what we are against than what we are for. It's critical that our children understand that we are *for* life, not just against aborting unborn babies. We are *for* mutual respect between men and women, not just against pornography. We are *for* healthy, productive families, not just against the myriad of anti-family-value forces attempting to tear families down. We are *for* healthy sexual expression in marriage, not just against homosexuality, adultery, and promiscuity.

Whenever we say no to something a child asks to do, like go to a party at a friend's house where we are not sure what will go on, it's important that we try to fill the vacuum we've created and offer a positive alternative. Maybe we can host a party at our house the next weekend and provide plenty of kid-friendly food and music and videos that we approve of. The kids will have a warm, welcoming, and wholesome atmosphere where they can have fun and we know what's going on. The same is true of the issues of right and wrong. Every time we label something as wrong, we should describe or ask what would be right.

Our kids need to know that the Christian faith is, by and large, a positive faith leading to an abundant life. Christians do not run from the pleasures of life, but embrace them on the high ground of God's will, the only place they can be truly enjoyed. Christianity's real power, both for the individual and society, comes much more from the positive proclamation of the truth, not the negative confrontation of sin. Of course, we need to be crystal clear about sin, but also make a point to affirm what is pure and right.

> Finally, brothers, whatever is true, whatever is noble, whatever is right, whatever is pure, whatever is lovely, whatever is admirable—if anything is excellent or praiseworthy—think about such things.
>
> PHILIPPIANS 4:8

We need to spend much more time talking about what is noble and true than what is wrong. We need to pursue that which is excellent rather than spend all of our time fighting that which is substandard.

It must be attractive. Do our children really know that we love them? That we are on their team? That God is on their team? More often than not, it seems we have a greater concern for getting our point across than we do for the child. Our kids are the same as anyone else. They won't care how much we know until they know how much we care. If they feel like they are constantly having to audition to be on our team, we will drive them away from God and the truth. Children don't care about our values unless they know we value them and love them unconditionally.

One of the worst things any of us can do is to use the Ten Commandments as the yardstick to measure our kids' success. We can't hold them over our kids' heads as a condition for our approval. While they need to know that we might disapprove of their behavior, they need to be secure in the fact that their value to us never changes. They need to know that they are already on our team and nothing they do will cause us to "put them on waivers."

When we consistently give our children the message that our love for them is conditional and based on their behavior, we exasperate them. We exasperate them with messages like, "I love you if you make straight A's," "I love you if you make the team," or, "I love you if you weight 115." Even "if you don't lie or steal" are messages we can't afford to send. Paul warns us,

> Fathers, do not exasperate your children; instead, bring them up in the training and instruction of the Lord.
>
> EPHESIANS 6:4

As parents, we must try to understand and care about the emotional makeup of our children. When our children sense that we love them, try to understand their feelings, and value them, they are motivated to learn what we want them to learn and to do what we want them to do. They have an internal pull to please us because we've already let them know that they are pleasing. On the other hand, they will not accept our values if they don't value their relationship with us.

If John gets hurt by a friend, Kathy and I need to understand and be sensitive to his pain. This might mean dropping our work to take a walk and talk things over. Or if Joel is down because he didn't play well in a golf tournament, it might mean taking time out to plan a special spur-of-the-moment family outing to get his mind off the situation and encourage him in some special ways. If James and a friend get into a fight, it means expressing our firm disapproval without belittling him. It means rejecting his behavior without making him think that we are rejecting him. It means correcting him without crushing him. He needs to know clearly that while I disapprove of his behavior, I do not disapprove of him. If I stop touching him, refuse to make eye contact, fail to reaffirm my love, refuse him my attention or time, then he may well get the picture that his behavior has caused me to stop loving him. When I do this, I am speaking his language and saying, whether I realize it or not, "I don't love you."

The most compelling idea we have to impart to our children is that Jesus Christ, the sovereign ruler of the universe, loves each of us and wants to deliver us to a new plane of existence. If we want our kids to believe this higher life really exists, we must live there ourselves and demonstrate the same unconditional love toward them that Christ demonstrates toward us. When He walked the earth, people knew He cared and were attracted to Him. Are we modeling this kind of magnetism?

It must be authentic. If we want our children to understand that the Ten Commandments are not just suggestions, then we must strive to obey them as well. Our values must change us before we can expect them to change our children. If we want our kids to take God seriously in their relationships, we must take God seriously in our relationships. If we want them to learn honesty, they must observe our integrity. If we want them to love and respect others, they must see how we love and respect others—starting with the members of our own family. We're not talking perfection here, but if we want our kids to listen to us, they must see in us an authentic desire to please God.

Yes, the values we want our children to embrace must be evident in us first. The Luke recorded these pointed words of Jesus:

> A pupil is not above His teacher; but everyone when he is fully trained, will be like his teacher.
>
> LUKE 6:40

As parents, we see this as the bottom line of teaching spiritual truth to our children. We must do more than proclaim the truth; we must live out the truth ourselves.

Parting Words

If you're like us, living out the truth on a daily basis is, well, impossible. Every day we fail, every day we let ourselves down as well as our kids and our God. But every day we're thankful that we can confess our sins, our shortcomings, and our failures to God, and He graciously forgives us. And not only does He forgive us, He empowers us to change.

The fact is that the only person who ever lived up to the standards of the Ten Commandments perfectly was Jesus Christ. Every one of us falls short. We sin. That's a given for us, but the question is what do we do with that sin. We have two options. We can hold it and attempt the impossible; namely, to reform ourselves. Or we can give our sin to God and allow Him to remove it. Quite frankly, it's almost too tempting to believe that we can really be better. The deadly lie we all want to believe is that we have the resources within us to turn from selfishness and make ourselves acceptable to God, to be a perfect parent, always patient, always wise, never selfish, always giving. But after thousands of years of trying, even after remarkable social advances, we are still chained hopelessly to our own selfishness. Perhaps sin's most hideous expression is in the home where we are still prone to use our children to build our own self-esteem. It's not surprising to anyone who has come face to face with his or her own wretchedness to discover that the wages of sin is still death in God's economy.

God's remarkable plan of redemption could have only been born in the heart of a perfect parent. Unwilling to bend His standards and yet unwilling to let us perish, God's remarkable commitment to offer His own Son to die in our place combined His extravagant love with absolute justice. Through Christ's sacrifice, God offers us forgiveness in exchange for the only thing we have to trade, our faith. Jesus Christ offers to exchange His perfect righteousness for our sin the moment I move my confidence to gain forgiveness in what I do to Christ and what He has accomplished for me on the cross.

But far more than forgiveness happened at the cross. The penalty of sin and the power of sin no longer have a claim on me. I was given a new life, Christ's life dwelling in me, which gives me the power to be all that I was created to be. He desires to live His life through me in every area of my existence, including parenting. If you have turned to Christ as your Savior, He has given you a new life capable of living and loving as only God can do. And He—

> is able to do immeasurably more than all we ask or imagine, according to his power that is at work within us.
>
> EPHESIANS 3:20

Our prayer is that if you have been trusting in yourself and failing, you will come to know Christ's power in your life as you place your confidence in Him.

The Peels would love to hear from you. If you have comments, or if you would like to be on their mailing list, please write to them at:

Bill and Kathy Peel
P.O. Box 50577
Nashville, Tennessee 37205–2244

To inquire about their speaking schedules, please call Ambassadors Artist Agency (615–370–4700).

Notes

Chapter 4

1. J. I. Packer, *Knowing God* (Downers Grove, Ill.: InterVarsity Press, 1973), 45.
2. Jeff Gordinier, "On a Ka-ching! and a Prayer," *Entertainment Weekly*, 7 October 1994, 36.
3. A. W. Tozer, *The Knowledge of the Holy* (New York: Harper & Row, 1961), 16.

Chapter 6

1. Westminster Confession of Faith, quoted by Stuart Briscoe, *The Ten Commandments* (Wheaton, Ill.: Harold Shaw Publishers, 1993), 62–63.
2. William C. Peel, *The Leadership Connection* (Tyler, Tex. Foundations for Living, 1991), 28.
3. Os Guinness, *Winning Back the Soul of American Business* (Washington, D.C.: Hourglass Publications, 1990), 4.

Chapter 7

1. Edith Schaeffer, *What Is a Family?* (Old Tappan, N.J.: Fleming H. Revell Company, 1975), 121.
2. Joy Davidman, *Smoke on the Mountain* (Philadelphia: Westminster Press, 1954), 60–61.

Chapter 9

1. Josh McDowell, *What I Wish My Parents Knew about My Sexuality* (San Bernardino, Calif.: Here's Life, 1987), 54–55.
2. David Stephens, M.D., The Christian Medical and Dental Society, P.O. Box 830689, Richardson, Texas 75083.

Chapter 12

1. William C. Peel, "A New Identity," *New Life in Christ* (Tyler, Tex.: Foundations for Living, 1991), n.p.

Chapter 13

Dr. Armand Nicholi, Jr., *What Do We Know About Successful Families?* (n.p., n.d.).

Where is Moses when we need